Archibald R. Adamson

Rambles Through the Land of Burns

Archibald R. Adamson

Rambles Through the Land of Burns

ISBN/EAN: 9783744753616

Printed in Europe, USA, Canada, Australia, Japan

Cover: Foto ©Andreas Hilbeck / pixelio.de

More available books at **www.hansebooks.com**

RAMBLES

THROUGH THE

LAND OF BURNS.

BY

ARCHIBALD R. ADAMSON,

AUTHOR OF "RAMBLES ROUND KILMARNOCK," &c.

"Thrice hallow'd the land of our Minstrel's birth,
  The fields that once gladden'd his eye,
The echoes that rang to his woe and his mirth,
  And the mountains that bounded his sky!
Lo! *there* is the scene of his own Vision-dream—
  The mantle his Coila then wore,
Still flower'd with the forest, enstriped with the stream,
  And fringed with the fret of the shore!"

HEW AINSLIE.

KILMARNOCK:
PRINTED AND PUBLISHED BY DUNLOP & DRENNAN,
"STANDARD" OFFICE.

MDCCCLXXIX.

THIS WORK,

ILLUSTRATIVE OF PLACES AND SCENERY

RENDERED FAMOUS

BY THE MUSE AND RESIDENCE OF SCOTLAND'S MINSTREL,

ROBERT BURNS,

IS RESPECTFULLY DEDICATED TO THE ADMIRERS

OF HIS GENIUS.

PREFACE.

To ramble through the land of Burns is an easy matter; but to describe it, so as to make the reader enjoy it in a description, is a somewhat difficult task. Notwithstanding, after considerable misgiving, the writer has essayed it, and in following the footsteps of his illustrious countryman, ROBERT BURNS, from the cottage of his birth to the scene of his death and burial, he has called attention not only to the rich natural beauty of the various districts celebrated by the residence and muse of the Poet, but also to their historical and traditional associations, and to passages in his life and writings inseparably connected with them. Having done this, and pointed out numerous interesting objects, he lays no claim to originality, and aspires to no higher merit than that of having gathered a posy of other men's flowers and bound it together with a string of his own, in a manner, he fondly hopes, that will interest the reader and make it a not unworthy contribution to the thought-gemmed literary cairn already raised to the memory of the Peasant Poet.

A. R. A.

7 GLENCAIRN SQUARE,
KILMARNOCK, AUGUST, 1879.

CONTENTS.

CHAPTER I., ... 1

On the Road to Ayr—The Daisy—Scenery in the Vicinity of Kilmarnock—Craigie Castle—Barnweil Hill—Symington—The Cradle-Land of Burns—The Bramble—A Peculiarly Situated Monument—A Ludicrous Adventure—Monkton.

CHAPTER II., ... 9

Monkton—Its Ruined Church—A Nephew of Robert Burns—The Graveyard and its Memorials—Governor Macrae's Grave—The Story of his Life—A Fortunate Family—"Captain Macrae"—Musings—The Manse—"Lang, Lang Syne."

CHAPTER III., ... 19

From Monkton to Ayr—Scenery—Orangefield—James Dalrymple—A Worthy—"The Pow Brig"—Prestwick Kirk and Burying-Ground—Interesting Memorials—Prestwick—Historical Notes—Kingcase Well and Lazarhouse—A Tradition of King Robert The Bruce.

CHAPTER IV., ... 27

Ayr, its Appearance, Trade, and Antiquity—Its Charters, Privileges, Wall, and Castle—The Barns of Ayr—The Burning of the Barns and Massacre of the English—"The Friar's Blessing"—The Castle Destroyed by Bruce and Rebuilt by the English—Taken by the Townspeople—The Religious Houses of Ayr—The State of Society in Ayr at the Reformation—The Pest—The Fort—Cromwell's Troops—Martyrs.

CHAPTER V., ... 36

    Newton-upon-Ayr—The Constitution of the Burgh—The Church and its Pastors—The Auld and New Brigs of Ayr—Was Burns a Prophet?—The High Street of Ayr—The Site of the Tolbooth—The Old Church and Graveyard—Provost Ballantyne — Robert Aiken — Heroes of "The Kirk's Alarm"—The Martyrs' Stone—A Curious Epitaph—Daft Rab Hamilton.

CHAPTER VI., ... 52

    The Wallace Tower—The Tam o' Shanter Inn—Drouthie Cronies—Scenery in the Vicinity of Ayr—The Chapman's Ford—"The Meikle Stane"—The Cot in which Burns was Born—Its Appearance and Desecration—Its Erection-When and How it was turned into a Public-House—Miller Goudie—Curran's Visit—What Keats had to say about "The Flummary of a Birthplace"—The First Burns Club.

CHAPTER VII., ... 67

    From "The Cottage" to Mount Oliphant—The Appearance of the Steading—Gossip, etc.—Privations Endured by the Parents of Burns when Residing at Mount Oliphant—The Poet's First Sweetheart—The Flitting—"The Festival" on the Banks of the Doon—Alloway Kirk—A Legend—The Grave of the Poet's Father—Old Stones.

CHAPTER VIII., ... 83

    The Monument on the Banks of Doon—Its External and Internal Appearance—Relics of the Poet—Highland Mary's Bible—Scenery—The Statues of Tam o' Shanter and Souter Johnny—The Scheme for Erecting the Monument and how it Originated—Laying the Foundation Stone—Mr. Boswell's Address, etc.

CHAPTER IX., ... 91

    The Hotel and Shell Palace—The Auld Brig o' Doon—The New Brig and its Petition—View from the Heights in its Vicinity—Newark Castle—Greenan Castle—The Return Journey.

CONTENTS. ix.

Page.

CHAPTER X., - . . . . - 99

From Kilmarnock to Coilsfield—Riccarton Graveyard—An Eccentric Miser—A Burns Worthy—Craigie Road—Scargie—Howcommon—A Good Joke—Scenery—The Farm of Lochlea and Crannog—The Old Dwelling-House and New Barn—The Death of the Poet's Father—Wild Flowers—The River Ayr—Failford, etc.

CHAPTER XI., ... - 111

The Entrance to the Domain of Coilsfield—Coilsfield Mains—King Coil's Grave and what was found in and near it—The Castle o' Montgomery—"Highland Mary"—"Highland Mary's Thorn" and Associations—From Coilsfield to Tarbolton—The Village—Burns—An Old Inn—The Debating Club and Dancing School—The Old Hall, etc.

CHAPTER XII., ... - 125

Hoodshill—An Ancient Custom—The Scene of "Death and Dr. Hornbook"—"Willie's Mill"—Grannie Hay's Recollections of Burns and the Miller's Wife—A Souvenir of their Friendship—Tarbolton Church and Churchyard—The Village Smithy—A Walk to Tollcross and its Object—"Brother Burns"—Fail Castle—The Friar—The Warlock Laird and his Cantrips—Adam Hill—Home Again.

CHAPTER XIII., ... - 138

Kilmarnock—A Glance at its History, Progress, and Appearance—Kilmarnock House—The Lady's Walk—Burns in Kilmarnock—Friends, and Places Associated with his Name—The Town of his Day—The Laigh Kirk—The Churchyard—The High Church—"Black Jock Russell" and Burns—The Soulis Monument—"Wee Johnie"—The Kay Park—The Burns Monument.

CHAPTER XIV., ... - 158

From Kilmarnock to Mossgiel—Notes by the Way—Mossgiel—A Noisy Reception—The Dwelling-House—The Spence—An Interesting Relic—The "Mouse" and "Daisy"—John Blane's Recollections—The Old Dwelling-House—The Poet's Study—The Scene of "The Vision"—The Poet's Personal Appearance and Misfortunes when in the Farm.

CHAPTER XV., - - - - - - - - 168

Mauchline—The Rise and Progress of the Box-making Trade—Nanse Tannock's House—The House in which Burns lived after his Marriage—Gavin Hamilton's House—The Parish Church—The Kirk-Yard—The Holy Fair—John Doo and Poosie Nansie—The Public Green and Martyrs' Stone: A Word about them—An Anecdote of Burns and Jean Armour—The Auld Manse and who was seen in its Haunted Room—The Haggis.

CHAPTER XVI., - - - - - - - - 185

Ballochmyle—The Braes—The Lass o' Ballochmyle—Her Account of Meeting the Poet—Burns' Seat—The Poet's Letter to Miss Alexander—Apologies for her Silence—The Bower—Caught by the Gamekeeper—Catrine—An Excursion Party—The River Ayr—Ballochmyle Bridge—Haugh—Barskimming Brig—"Man was made to Mourn"—The Railway Station—Back to Kilmarnock.

CHAPTER XVII., - - - - - - - - 194

From Kilmarnock to Newmilns—The Ayrshire Hermit—Loudoun Kirkyard and Ruined Church—The Queir—Lady Flora Hastings — The Scottish Milkmaid — Galston—Loudoun Castle—The Old Castle—Loudoun Manse—Dr. Lawrie and Burns—Loudoun Hill—Newmilns—The Old Tower—The Parish Church and Churchyard.

CHAPTER XVIII., - - - - - - - - 216

From Kilmarnock to Dumfriesshire—Notes by the Way—Auldgirth and its Scenery—The Hotel—On the Road to Dumfries—Gossip—The Banks of the Nith—Friar's Carse—Friendships of Burns—"The Whistle"—The Hermitage and its Associations.

CHAPTER XIX., - - - - - - - - 233

Ellisland, its Situation, Appearance, and Associations—Burns as an Exciseman—His Antipathy to the Office—His Humanity, Hospitality, and Industry—The Poet's Favourite Walk—The Composition of "Tam o' Shanter"—The Wounded Hare—The Isle—Holywood Past and Present—Lincluden Abbey.

CHAPTER XX., - - - - - - - - - 249

    Dumfries—The Old Bridge—Greyfriars' Monastery—The Castle—A House in which Burns Lived—High Street—The Globe Inn and its Associations—The House in which Burns Died.

CHAPTER XXI., - - - - - - - - 257

    The House in which Burns Died—His Circumstances and Last Illness—Goes to Brow—His Anxiety for the Welfare of his Family—An Affecting Anecdote—The Poet's Return to Dumfries—The Anxiety of the Inhabitants—Jessie Lewars—His Death and Funeral—The Family of Burns—The Exemplary Life of the Poet's Widow—Sale of Household Effects.

CHAPTER XXII., - - - - - - - - 267

    St. Michael's Churchyard—The Erection of the Mausoleum—The Disinterment of the Poet's Remains—Phrenological Description of his Cranium—The External and Internal Appearance of the Mausoleum—Inscriptions—A Grandson of the Poet—Burns' Connection with the Dumfries Library—Concluding Remarks.

Rambles through the Land of Burns.

CHAPTER I.

ON THE ROAD TO AYR—THE DAISY—SCENERY IN THE VICINITY OF KILMARNOCK—CRAIGIE CASTLE—BARNWEIL HILL—SYMINGTON—THE CRADLE-LAND OF BURNS—THE BRAMBLE—A PECULIARLY SITUATED MONUMENT—A LUDICROUS ADVENTURE—MONKTON.

INTENT upon a pilgrimage to the cottage wherein the immortal poet, Robert Burns, first saw the light, and the interesting places in its immediate vicinity, I left Kilmarnock one beautiful summer morning before its inhabitants were stirring, and having crossed the Irvine by the new bridge at Riccarton, held onward, regardless of "the lang Scots miles" which lay between me and the goal of the journey. Nature was newly waken from the slumber of night—the sun poured its exhilarating rays from the radiant east, and in its strength was quickly dispelling the vapoury mist which hung over the river and floated lazily across the fields, as if reluctant to depart and allow the god to quaff the pearly drops of dew which decked the grass and hedges. A solemn stillness—which was occasionally broken by the distant lowing of cattle and the chirrup of a lightsome bird—pervaded the scene, for the village was wrapt in slumber, a slumber fated soon to be broken by the deep-toned bell in the church spire calling the labouring poor to renew the turmoil of life. As the gate of the domain which surrounds Caprington Castle was neared the scene became more romantic and grand, for the estate of Treesbank, with its manor-house peering from the bosom of its woods, came in view, as also Craigie Hill and the rugged chain of eminences running east. At Peace-and-Plenty the miners were preparing for toil, and several smoked their pipes with a gusto which showed how they enjoyed the beauty of the flowers which decked the little plots in front of their dwellings, and the glorious sunlight which the burrowing nature of their employment would shut from their gaze. One sturdy fellow gifted me a "posey," but its radiant gems were not so dear to my heart as the simple daisies and buttercups which grew by the dusty wayside and spangled the fields in its vicinity—for, as I trudged along, they were scattered here and there in little clusters, and nodded in the breeze as if courting attention. The daisy has ever been a favourite with poets and children. Chaucer in his quaint way tells that he loved it, and Wordsworth does the same, but Montgomery sings of it so sweetly that a stave or two from his address deserves quoting :—

> "This small flower to nature dear,
>   While moon and stars their courses run,
> Wreathes the whole circle of the year,
>   Companion of the sun.
>
> "It smiles upon the lap of May,
>   To sultry August spreads its charms,
> Lights pale November on its way,
>   And twines December's arms.
>
> "The purple heath, the golden broom,
>   On moory mountains catch the gale,
> O'er lawns the lily sheds perfume,
>   The violet in the vale :
>
> "But this bold flow'ret climbs the hill,
>   Hides in the forest, haunts the glen,
> Plays on the margin of the rill,
>   Peeps round the fox's den.
>
> "Within the garden's cultured round
>   It shares the sweet carnation bed,
> And blooms on consecrated ground
>   In honour of the dead.
>
> "The lambkin crops its crimson gem,
>   The wild bee murmurs on its breast,
> The blue fly bends its pensile stem
>   That decks the skylark's nest.

> "'Tis Flora's page in every place,
> In every season fresh and fair,
> It opens with perennial grace,
>   And blossoms everywhere.
>
> "On waste and woodland, rock and plain,
> Its humble buds unheeded rise;
> The rose has but a summer's reign,
>   The daisy never dies."

Like other wild flowers, the daisy was a favourite with Burns. In the one that "died to prove a poet's love" on the farm of Mossgiel he saw his own fate portrayed.

> "Even thou who mourn'st the daisy's fate,
> That fate is thine—no distant date;
> Stern Ruin's ploughshare drives, elate,
>   Full on thy bloom,
> Till crushed beneath the furrow's weight
>   Shall be thy doom."

It may be added that botanists class the "bonnie gem" in the order of *compositæ*, or composite-flowered plants, because each head or gowan is composed of a cluster of distinct but minute flowerets, each of which consists of a single petal—a fact doubtless which will astonish many young readers; but let them, when next out for a ramble, pluck one, and it will be found that none

> "But He that arched the skies,
>   And pours the dayspring's living flood,
> Wond'rous alike in all He tries,
>   Could raise the daisy's purple bud,
>
> "Mould its green cup, its wiry stem,
>   Its fringéd border nicely spin,
> And cut the gold embossèd gem,
>   That set in silver gleams within.
>
> "Then fling it unrestrained and free,
>   O'er hill, and dale, and desert sod,
> That man, where'er he walks, may see
>   At every step the stamp of God."

About a mile beyond the miners' dwellings referred to the road rises over an eminence named Spittalhill, and as the pedestrian nears the summit he has a capital view of Kilmarnock and its surroundings, and also of a vast track of country along the coast—indeed, I was so much charmed with the prospect that I leaned on a fence and earnestly gazed on the tranquil landscape unmindful alike of the fleeting moments and the melody of a skylark which rendered the air musical with its morning lay. Beyond the height a long vista of road came in view, but before entering it I paused beneath the shade of a gigantic willow which casts its broad arms over the roadway, and admired the rhododendrons and laurels, and their more majestic companions—the larch and spruce firs, which line the pleasant drive to Coodham House, the residence of W. H. Houldsworth, Esq. The fragrance was delightful, but the trees bending over the monotonous stone wall by the side of the footpath seemed to beckon me to their shade, and I hastened onward. Beyond Bogend Toll the country opens up, and on the summit of an eminence called Barnweil Hill the Wallace Monument stands boldly out from a belt of wood; while to the north, in a hollow near some rising ground, the ruin of Craigie Castle raises its shattered form on the plain. It was long the residence of a branch of the Wallace family, but on their removal to the castle of Newton-upon-Ayr it gradually got out of repair, and its sculpture-decked halls ultimately succumbed to the ravages of time and decay, and now, with the exception of two gables and some portion of side walls, vaults, and ramparts, it is one mass of weed-covered *debris*. A stone, bearing a curious heraldic device, was found amongst the ruins some years ago, and may be seen in the wall of an out-house on the adjacent farm. It is well worth the attention of the curious, and the necessary deviation from the highway will be amply repaid.

The Wallaces of Riccarton and Craigie were a family of considerable note in Ayrshire, and being a branch of that which gave birth to "The Knight of Ellerslee," Burns makes mention of it in a stanza of "The Vision," when referring to Sir John Wallace, a memorable lord of the domain, who was second in command at the battle of Sark:—

> "His country's saviour, mark him well:
> Bold Richardton's heroic swell.
> *The Chief on Sark,* who glorious fell
>   In high command;
> And he whom ruthless Fates expel
>   His native land."

This hero, although borne from the field severely wounded,

died of his wounds in the Castle in the 59th year of his age, and his body is interred in the now almost forgotten family vault in Craigie churchyard.

The hill on which the monument stands is said to derive the name of Barnweil, or Burnweel, from the circumstance of Sir William Wallace laconically remarking—"The barns o' Ayr burn weel," as he paused in his flight on its summit to view the flames he so dexterously raised. An excellent view of Ayr is obtained from the site of the monument, but unfortunately for the tradition the district bore the descriptive Celtic term Barnwiel, or Barnwield, long before the days of Wallace—therefore, as the author of *The History of the County of Ayr* pertinently remarks, the statement is nothing more than "an unsupported vulgar tradition."

Beyond "the half-way"—as a roadside public-house and favourite halting place between Kilmarnock and Ayr is termed—I passed the road leading to Symington, a sequestered commercially-forgotten village which nestles beneath the shade of some old trees a short distance from the highway. The little place possesses a curious old church and burying-ground of considerable historic interest, but otherwise calls for little notice.

A mile beyond Symington the road makes a sudden descent, and the pedestrian unexpectedly encounters an excellent view of the cradle-land of Burns—indeed, I stood enraptured and mutely gazed on the scene. Away in the distance lay the hills of Carrick—hills on whose brown bosom it may be safely inferred the boy-poet sported, and " pu'd the gowans fine," for it was under their shade he first saw the light. More near, and " in a sandy valley spread," Ayr nestled among green fields and patches of woodland, interspersed with gentlemen's residences, near the broad-bosomed Frith, at a point where it bends into a fine bay. As my eye wandered over the delightful scene, it rested on the Castles of Newark and Greenan, and ultimately on the ruggedly grand heights of Arran, behind which, there is little doubt, the bard of Coila often watched the red sun go down, and that too after having industriously plied the flail on the threshing floor, or followed the plough on the braeside of Mount Oliphant.

After enjoying this imperfectly-described scene, I renewed

the journey, and having passed the plantation which encircles the mansion-house of Rosemount, reached a wood-fringed pasture field in which a herd of Kyle cows were contentedly browsing. There was nothing remarkable in the scene, so far as the cattle were concerned, but a monument of an ancient weather-beaten appearance, partly concealed among trees on a neighbouring height, excited my curiosity to such a degree that I determined to examine it, and for that purpose entered a traffic-worn path in proximity to the wood in which it was embowered. The wild roses with which the hedge was decked, and the bramble bushes trailing their long prickly stems on the grass, looked luxuriant, and called to mind the joyous days of boyhood and the well-known lines of Ebenezer Elliott, which I give out of genial sympathy with their spirit:—

THE BRAMBLE.

"Thy fruit full well the school-boy knows,
   Wild bramble of the brake !
So, put thou forth thy small white rose ;
   I love thee for his sake.
Though woodbines flaunt and roses glow
   O'er all the fragrant bowers,
Thou need'st not be ashamed to show
   Thy satin-threaded flowers ;
For dull the eye, the heart is dull,
   That cannot feel how fair,
Amid all beauty beautiful,
   Thy tender blossoms are !
How delicate thy gaudy frill !
   How rich thy branchy stem !
How soft thy voice, when woods are still,
   And thou sing'st hymns to them.
While silent showers are falling slow,
   And 'mid the general hush,
A sweet air lifts the little bough
   Lone whispering through the bush !
The primrose to the grave is gone,
   The hawthorn flower is dead,
The violet by the moss'd grey stone
   Hath laid her weary head ;
But thou, wild bramble ! back dost bring,
   In all thy beauteous power,
The fresh green days of life's fair spring,
   And boyhood's blossomy hour.
Scorn'd bramble of the brake ! once more
   Thou bidst me be a boy,
To gad with thee the woodlands o'er
   In freedom and in joy."

When near the plantation I opened a field gate, held along the side of a tall hedge, and entered a beaten track running zig-zag among the trees. It was an "eerie" place, for the solitude was only broken by the rustling leaves and dry grass under my feet, and the occasional flutter of a startled bird; but I held on, and soon reached the object of my search, which proved to be a massive pyramidal block of masonry surmounted by an urn, and embellished with Corinthian pillars and emblematic devices. Being void of an inscription, there is nothing to tell its purport, but I afterwards learned that it covers the burying place of the Dalrymples of Orangefield—a now extinct family—and was erected in 1748 to commemorate ex-Governor Macrae, a gentleman whose curious history forms the subject of another chapter.

After examining the pile, I found my way to the verge of the plantation, vaulted a fence, and traversed a field, as it appeared to be the most convenient mode of reaching the highway. Near its centre, I paused to examine a ruined pigeon-house, which serves in its wrecked state as a shelter for cattle—a circumstance of which I had ample proof, for a cow rushed out as I was about to enter, and nearly upset me in its hurry. I am not altogether certain as to whether the animal or myself was most frightened, but, if anything, the balance of terror was in my favour—for, in the excitement of the moment, it was mistaken for a sulphurous individual with whom it is not safe to have dealings. However, I soon recovered, and without further adventure reached Monkton—a humble agricultural village, containing no object of interest beyond its ruined ivy-mantled church and grass-covered burying ground; but if its commercial prosperity had equalled its antiquity, then it would have been a busy place indeed. So early as 1163 the church and village were in existence. In that year the church and lands were, along with the church of Prestwick, gifted to the monastery of Paisley by Walter, the son of Allan, first High Steward of Scotland, and lord of the northern portion of Kyle. Monkton then bore the name of Prestwick, but shortly after coming in the hands of the friars it was termed *Prestwick Monachorum.* In course of time, however, the name again changed, and it began to be called "Monktoun," from the circumstance, as many suppose, that a religious house existed in the village. But it is not altogether certain that such was the case, for no reference is made to it in any work on the monastic institutions of Scotland, nor does the oldest inhabitant remember of seeing or hearing of the ruins of any building which tradition averred the monks occupied. However, it is nevertheless probable that the Abbot of Paisley would have a bevy of the brotherhood stationed in the district to superintend the possessions of the institution and to look after the interests of mother church; for it is a well-known fact that they were well acquainted with agriculrure and the construction and management of corn-mills. There is nothing of interest connected with the village, and the parochial registers (which only date back to the beginning of last century) throw no light upon its history; but it is evident that hard drinking and moral lapses were the besetting sins of the inhabitants somewhat less than a century ago. This is not at all surprising, however, when it is known that along the whole Ayrshire coast smuggling was extensively carried on, and that Monkton was a noted seat of the contraband trade. The suppression of a traffic fraught as it was with such immoral tendencies, was as great a blessing to the people of Monkton as it was to the inhabitants of every town and village engaged in it. In course of time its pernicious influences were entirely removed, and the villagers of to-day, as a rule, are both sober and industrious. The population last census amounted to 467, but from the appearance of the hamlet one would scarcely think it so large. The parishes of Monkton and Prestwick have been united since the beginning of the seventeenth century, but the object of the union cannot at this date be ascertained with any degree of certainty.

CHAPTER II.

Monkton—its ruined church—a nephew of Robert Burns—the graveyard and its memorials—Governor Macrae's grave—the story of his life—a fortunate family—"Captain Macrae"—musings—the manse—"Lang, lang syne."

Monkton is eight miles from Kilmarnock and four from Ayr, and the weather-beaten thatch-covered buildings which constitute the village line both sides of the highway. Upon entering its street, I was struck by its quaint appearance, and more so by the picturesque, ivy-clad, ruined church which stands in a grass-covered burying place by the wayside. After availing myself of the hospitality which a village inn affords, I turned my attention to it; but although I rugged and tugged at the rusty iron gate guarding the entrance, it refused to yield, and in a quandary I began to look round. The next best apparent means of entering the sacred enclosure was by scaling the wall, and this I was in the act of doing when a villager drew my attention to an avenue a little farther down the road in which she stated a wicket would be found which would open to the touch. Following her directions it was soon discovered, and also the fact that the residence of the parish minister nestled in a secluded nook at the end of the shady path. Passing through the wicket, I reverently trod on the resting places of "the rude forefathers of the hamlet," and approached the ruined sanctuary adorning the centre of the little Golgotha. The polished ivy clung to the tottering walls, and clasped the stones with its sinewy-like tendrils, as if desirous of binding them together and warding off the assaults of time and decay.

The modest building appears to have been dedicated to Saint Cuthbert, but when or by whom it was erected is unknown. Blind Harry mentions it in his metrical biography of Wallace as the building in which the hero had a wonderful vision, which he narrates with considerable minuteness.

In making mention of Monkton church, Chalmers, the celebrated antiquary, says :—" In 1227 Walter, the Bishop of Glasgow, made an ordinance respecting all the churches belonging to the monks of Paisley, within his diocese, whereby it was settled that the vicar of *the Church of Saint Cuthbert* should have, in the name of vicarage, six chalders of meal yearly, with the alterages. . . . . In Bagimont's roll, as it stood in the reign of James V., the vicarage of Monkton was taxed £4, being a tenth of the estimated value." At the Reformation, when church property was very liberally sliced up and divided, Lord Claud Hamilton, the commendator of Paisley, obtained a grant of the patronage of Monkton Church and its tithes, along with other property which belonged to the monks. The old bell hanging in the western gable of the ruin is not only a curiosity, but evidences the Romish origin of the structure. It bears the following in raised letters:—"SANCTE CUTHBERTI ORA PRO NOBIS" (Saint Cuthbert pray for us), but no date. Although this relic has done duty for many centuries, it has not rested from its labours, but may be heard any Lord's day summoning the villagers to the house of prayer.

After the parishes of Monkton and Prestwick were united, Monkton church was looked upon as the parish church proper, but the clergyman of the united parishes preached every third Sabbath in that of Prestwick. In 1834 both churches were suppressed by the Court of Tiends, and authority granted for the erection of a new church equally distant from both places. When this was done the structures were gutted and unroofed, and left to the mercy of the elements.

The Rev. Thomas Burns, son of Gilbert, the poet's brother, was the last clergyman who officiated in the old church of Monkton. He was tutor to Sir Hew Dalrymple of North Berwick, and afterwards minister of Ballantrae. For a series of years he so ably discharged the ministerial duties of Monkton that the parishioners still remember and speak of him with the utmost respect. He came out at the Disruption, and was for some time minister of Portobello Free Church. In conjunction with Captain Cargill and others, he projected a Free Church settlement in Otago, New Zealand, and sailed from Greenock in the end of 1847 as minister of the first body of settlers. He afterwards became minister of the Scottish Church in Dunedin, and died there in the 75th year of his age, on the 23rd January, 1871, leaving a widow with one son and six daughters.

From the ruin I turned my attention to the heaving turf around it, and while wandering among the long grass here and there

> " Read auld names on auld grave stanes
> Grown grey in the auld kirkyard."

The majority of the unassuming memorials are comparatively modern, and merely record the fact that the sleeper lived and died—but what of that?

> " Can storied urn or animated bust
> Back to its mansion call the fleeting breath?
> Can honour's voice provoke the silent dust,
> Or flattery soothe the dull cold ear of death?"

Two stones with semi-obliterated inscriptions bear date 1608, but the most ancient has the following in yet legible characters :—"HERE LYS YIN VARY HONRIBLE MON, DAVIT BLAIR OF ADMONTOUN, SPOUS TO MARGET HAMILTOUN, QUO DECESIT, SEP., 1577." This relic was discovered buried several feet beneath the sward. It is now reared against the back gable of the old church, and forms not the least of the many curious objects to be met with in its vicinity.

When strolling through the tangled grass I stood on the hard turf which covers the dust of the once affluent and somewhat famous James Macrae, a favourite of fortune, who, from a state of the most abject poverty, rose to the high position of Governor of the Presidency of Madras. No stone marks his resting place, nor was there at any time anything to protect his grave from desecration. It is situated close to a tombstone to the memory of an individual named Bryden and within a dozen paces of the manse offices, and about the same distance from the wicket which serves as a back entrance to this obscure place of sepulture. Some years ago a sexton met with the defunct Governor's coffin when scooping out a grave, and plundered it of its leaden casing, but in justice to the callous individual it may be stated that the silver plate on the lid was delivered up and handed to the Sheriff of Ayr, who, in his turn, handed it to the representatives of the deceased.

In the previous chapter a monument to the memory of this remarkable personage is referred to ; but now that mention of his grave is being made, a brief sketch of his life may be appropriately introduced, for its incidents are not only singular, but go a great way to prove that truth in many instances is stranger than fiction. The date of his birth is unknown, but it is generally supposed that he was born about the close of the reign of merry King Charles, and that he was the son of a poor widow who resided in a thatched cottage in the vicinity of Ayr, and earned for herself and boy a miserable subsistence by washing and doing other odd work for her well-to-do neighbours. The pittance thus earned was occasionally increased by odd coppers which her son picked up by looking after cattle, running errands, and such like. While thus employed, and while knocking about in an Arab-like condition, he became acquainted with a Hugh M'Quire,* a jobbing carpenter, and an accomplished player on the fiddle, whose musical talent was highly appreciated by the " honest men and bonnie lasses" of the district, for to the strains of his instrument they delighted to whirl on the light fantastic toe. This man took a fancy to the boy, and, although poor, put him to school and acted the part of a father towards him for some considerable time. This guardianship would have continued had the protegé not been caught in the pardonable offence of pilfering apples from an orchard and severely punished by the authorities. The disgrace being more than his proud spirit could bear, he no sooner obtained liberty than he stowed himself away on board an outward bound ship, and for forty years never set foot in "the auld toon," nor, it is believed, held any communication with his friends. The events of his seafaring life must for ever remain unknown, for nothing can be ascertained about him until thirty years

---

* Next to nothing is known of this individual. Mr. John Shaw, attorney of the High Court of Justiciary, Madras, considers him to have been the husband of Isabella Gairdner, a daughter of Macrae's mother's brother ; while Mr J. Talboys Wheeler, Professor of Moral Philosophy in the College of Madras, distinctly states, in his "Annals of James Macrae," that he was the husband of Macrae's sister. Another writer—the late Dr. Norman M'Leod—states that he was his stepfather ; but the popular opinion is that he was no relation whatever. However, it is a matter of little importance

after he had so suddenly and mysteriously disappeared from his native place. Then he is referred to in the records of the Madras Government as Captain Macrae, and from this it is surmised that he had risen to be master of a vessel engaged in the trade of that country and had sailed between China, Sumatra, and Pegu. However, by some means he got into the good graces of the government of his adopted country and was sent to the West Coast of Sumatra to reform abuses which prevailed in an English settlement. This he did to such good purpose that he effected a saving of £25,000 a year, and rendered services by executing reforms which promised to greatly increase the amount. For this display of business tact he was appointed Governor of Port St David, and shortly afterwards (1724) second member of Council at Fort George. On the 18th January, 1725, the washerwoman's fatherless boy took his seat as Governor of the Madras Presidency, which was at that time, and for half a century afterwards, the chief British settlement in India. The proceeding is thus recorded :—

"Monday, 18th January, 1725.—The President, James Macrae, Esq., opened this consultation by telling the Board that as this was the first time of their meeting since his taking the chair, he thought it would not be improper to acquaint them with his resolutions, of which the principal was that he would prosecute the Company's interest to the utmost, and endeavour to remove the abuses that had crept into the management of their affairs. He added that he was determined not to interrupt in any manner the commerce of the place ; but that all the inhabitants, both whites and blacks, the free merchants as well as the Company's servants, should have free liberty of trade, and that he should expect the same freedom from interruption in whatever he should undertake ; that he would endeavour to be as agreeable to the gentlemen as any of his predecessors, but that he was determined to maintain the privileges and immunities belonging to the President ; and he concluded by saying that he expected a ready assistance from them in the pursuit of the above resolutions, which was accordingly promised."

During his tenure of office the trade of the place prospered beyond all precedence, nothing being too insignificant or too arduous for his attention. In 1731, having amassed a vast fortune, Governor Macrae sailed for England, and upon his arrival in Ayr sought out his benefactor, "Fiddler M'Quire," and from him learned that his mother had been dead for a considerable time.* The fiddler and his family were in very poor circumstances, and to relieve his immediate necessities his old protegé gave him £100. The joy of the musician and his better half was unbounded, and to celebrate the event she purchased many delicacies, amongst which was a loaf of sugar and a bottle of brandy. When the banquet was spread, the solid mass of sugar was scooped out and the hollow filled with the generous liquor, which they supped with spoons until they became "owre a' the ills o' life victorious," and soothingly sank on the floor into the arms of Morpheus.

Having no heirs, and being grateful for the kindness bestowed upon him when a boy, Macrae resolved to elevate the fiddler and his family. With this object in view he purchased Drumdow, a small estate in the parish of Stair, and presented it to his early benefactor, and afterwards sent his family—a son and three daughters—to the best boarding school he could find. In 1733 he was admitted a burgess of Ayr, and is styled in the records—"James Macrae, late Governor of Madras." In 1734 he presented the city of Glasgow with the handsome equestrian statue of King William which still adorns its Cross. It is well worth the attention of the visitor, for on its pedestal a long Latin inscription will be found which concludes thus—"POSUIT CIVIS STENNUUS ET FIDUS JACOBUS MACRAE, COLLONIÆ MADARASSIANAE EXPRAEFECTUS. M.D.CCXXXV." This statue cost £3000, which says much for the Governor's admiration of "William of Immortal Memory." It may be also stated that the two old guns which protrude their rusty muzzles out of the causeway at its base blazed at the Battle of the Boyne, and were handled with deadly effect by the "Protestant Boys." In 1736 the old veteran purchased the estate of Orangefield, and in 1739 that of Ochiltree. The latter cost £25,000. The same year he purchased and conveyed to James M'Quire, the fiddler's son, the barony of Houlston, on the condition

---

* I am inclined to think, from the time Macrae had been away, that the individual on whom he showered his wealth was a son of the violinist, for it is probable that his old friend had paid the debt of nature before his return, or he must have married a young woman very late in life.

that he ever afterwards assumed the name Macrae. The fiddler's three daughters were considered handsome. Elizabeth, the eldest, was married to William, thirteenth Earl of Glencairn, and received from the Governor as dowry the estate of Ochiltree and £45,000. The old gentleman took a deep interest in this match, but being seized with a severe illness before its consummation he sent for his medical adviser and inquired if he could keep him alive until the nuptials were performed. The doctor replying that he could not promise, Macrae raised himself in bed and exclaimed passionately—" Then d—— you and all your drugs!" He did live, however, for the marriage took place in 1744, and he did not die until 1750.

This marriage did not prove happy, for it turned out that the Earl admired his wife's wealth more than her person, and it is supposed that the twittings he received from his equals about her humble birth heightened the dislike. Upon one occasion Lord Cassillis made some taunting allusions to his wife's origin, and concluded by remarking that he wondered that he so far forgot himself and his rank as to marry a fiddler's daughter. Without the least show of anger at the insult, the Earl coolly said—" Yes, my lord ; and one of my father-in-law's favourite tunes was ' The Gipsies cam' to Lord Cassillis' yett.' " The repartee was pointed, for it will be observed that it referred to a frail but famous Countess of Cassillis who eloped with a gipsy named Johnny Faa. It is said that the Earl purchased the estate of Kilmarnock with his wife's dowry, and formed the fine street bearing his name.

James, the second son of the above marriage, became fourteenth Earl of Glencairn in 1775, and died unmarried in 1791. It was he who befriended the poet Burns, and it was on his death that the bard wrote the celebrated lament which concludes with the pathetic lines:—

> " Thou found'st me, like the morning sun,
> That melts the fogs in limpid air ;
> The friendless bard and rustic song
> Became alike thy fostering care.
>
> " Oh ! why has worth so short a date ?
> While villains ripen grey with time ;

Must thou, the noble, generous, great,
  Fall in bold manhood's hardy prime !
Why did I live to see that day ?
  A day to me so full of woe ;
Oh ! had I met the mortal shaft
  Which laid my benefactor low !

"The bridegroom may forget the bride
  Was made his wedded wife yestreen ;
The monarch may forget the crown
  That on his head an hour has been ;
The mother may forget the child
  That smiles sae sweetly on her knee ;
But I'll remember thee, Glencairn,
  And a' that thou hast done for me !"

Margaret, the second daughter of "Fiddler M'Quire," married in 1749 James Erskine of Barjarg, advocate. He was elevated to the bench as one of the Lords of Session in 1761, and took the title of Lord Tinwald. His wife's dowry was expended in the purchase of the estate of Alva. Macrae M'Quire, the third daughter, was married to Charles Dalrymple, Sheriff-Clerk of Ayrshire, and received from the Governor as dowry the estate of Orangefield and a handsome sum of money.

At the death of the fiddler's son, the estate of Houlston devolved upon his son, "Captain" John Macrae. He walked not in the footsteps of his father, for he was known in fashionable circles as a libertine, bully, and professional duellist; and had ultimately to fly the country for the killing of Sir George Ramsay of Edinburgh in the settlement of an affair of honour. A story is told which aptly illustrates the character of the man. A servant having committed a mistake, in an outburst of passion he struck him a violent blow in the face. "Were you my equal," said the menial indignantly, "I'd make you smart for that." "Would you?" replied Macrae with a scornful sneer. "I would," answered the man. "Oh, very well, if it's boxing you mean I'll give it to you to your heart's content ; but remember, you mustn't hit me on the face." This was agreed to, and both retired to a secluded part of the garden, where they fought with much bitterness ; but the bully, finding that he had for once met his match, and was likely to get himself severely punished, cried "Hold!" and declared himself satisfied with what he had received. "There," said Macrae, as he handed the servant five guineas, "take that; you are a piece of capital stuff." "Thank you," replied the man, quite astonished at the result of the combat, "and if it please your honour I'll take a thrashing every day for the same amount."

As I closed the wicket of Monkton Churchyard, and stepped into the avenue, I felt sad, sad—for beneath the turf which my feet had pressed innumerable beings moulder and silently fulfil the immutable decree which pronounces man to be dust, and declares that to dust he must return. What wisdom, valuable experience, misery, injustice, wrong, and misfortune lie buried in the bosom of mother earth! But we are comforted by the ennobling faith in immortality — the knowledge that the thinking something in man survives the silence of the grave—and this ray of hope illumes the dark hours of terrestrial existence.

Thoughts like these occupied my mind as I strolled towards the manse—a plain two-storied building, delightfully situated in a tastefully laid out plot of ground. At present (1878) it is the residence of the Rev. W. F. Lorraine, minister of the united parishes of Monkton and Prestwick, but was for thirty-four years that of his predecessor, the Rev. George James Lawrie, D.D., a grandson of the worthy minister of Loudoun, who was the means of introducing Burns to the literati of Edinburgh, and whose intercourse with the bard is noticed at length in another chapter. Being long in delicate health, he resigned his charge and removed to Elm House, Hythe, Kent, the residence of a very near and dear relative, and there "fell asleep" on the morning of the 14th February, 1878, in the 82nd year of his age. Like Goldsmith's preacher,

> " To relieve the wretched was his pride,
> And e'en his failings leaned to virtue's side;
> But in his duty, prompt at every call,
> He watched and wept, he prayed and felt for all;
> And, as a bird each fond endearment tries
> To tempt its new-fledged offspring to the skies,
> He tried each art, reproved each dull delay,
> Allured to brighter worlds, and led the way."

He was not only sensible, upright, and kind-hearted, but possessed a highly-cultured mind, as his *Songs and Miscellaneous Pieces* (which, undoubtedly, will perpetuate his name) amply testify. The following popular lines by the worthy Doctor will awaken an echo in every heart :—

LANG, LANG SYNE.
Tune—"John Peel."

Hae ye mind o' lang, lang syne,
When the simmer days were fine,
And the sun shone brighter far
Than he's ever dune syn syne?
Do you mind the Hag Brig turn,
Whaur we guddled in the burn,
And were late for the schule in the mornin'?

Do ye mind the sunny braes,
Whaur we gathered hips and slaes,
And fell amang the bramble busses,
Tearin' a' our claes;
And for fear they would be seen
We gaed slippin' hame at e'en,
But were licket for our pains in the mornin'

Do ye mind the miller's dam,
When the frosty Winter cam',
How we slade upon the curlers' rink
And made their game a sham;
When they chased us through the snaw
We took leg-bail ane and a',
But we did it o'er again in the mornin'?

What famous fun was there,
Wi' our games at houn' and hare,
When we played the truant frae the schule
Because it was the fair;
And we ran frae Patie's mill
Through the woods on Winny Hill,
And were feart for the tawse in the mornin'.

Where are those bright hearts noo
That were then so leal and true?
Oh! some hae left life's troubled scene,
Some still are struggling thro',
And some hae risen high
In life's changeful destiny,
For they rose wi' the lark in the mornin'.

Now life's sweet Spring is past,
And our Autumn's come at last,
Our Simmer day has passed,
And Life's Winter's coming fast;
But though lang its nights may seem
We shall sleep without a dream
Till we wauken on yon bright Sabbath mornin'.

CHAPTER III.

FROM MONKTON TO AYR—SCENERY—ORANGEFIELD—JAMES DALRYMPLE—A WORTHY—"THE POW BRIG"—PRESTWICK KIRK AND BURYING-GROUND—INTERESTING MEMORIALS—PRESTWICK—HISTORICAL NOTES—KINGCASE WELL AND LAZARHOUSE—A TRADITION OF KING ROBERT THE BRUCE.

Upon re-entering the highway, I turned my face towards Ayr. In the distance lay the somewhat scattered village of Prestwick, with its roofless barn-like church topping a mound in its vicinity, while westward the heights of Arran towered from the glistening Frith in all their rugged grandeur. The coast here is studded with barren sand-hills, and were it not for a few scattered villas along the shore the scene would be monotonous and dreary in the extreme. Notwithstanding this, the landscape to the east of the road is verdant and the soil productive, but there is nothing to engage the attention of the pedestrian, save the mansion house of Orangefield—a residence already referred to—which stands a short distance off the road. It was long the residence of James Dalrymple, the friend and correspondent of Burns, who, it will be remembered, introduced the bard to his cousin James, fourteenth Earl of Glencairn, and subscribed for ten copies of the first edition of his works. Robert Chambers describes him as having been "a warm-hearted, high-pulsed man, enthusiastically given to masonry and an occasional scribbler of verses," and adds that it was he who furnished Burns with the pony on which he rode to Edinburgh. From a letter to Gavin Hamilton, we learn that he stood high in the estimation of the poet, and that he interested himself in his affairs in the same enthusiastic manner as Mr Aitken and the few patrons who took notice of his early poetic days. This stay of struggling genius was the last of the Dalrymples of Orangefield, for being a fast liver, his requirements swamped his fortune, and the estate was sold. Since then it has passed through several hands.

A short distance beyond Orangefield, I paused on a substantial stone bridge which crosses the Pow Burn, and leaning over the parapet watched the minnows sporting in the clear shallow stream. By its side stands the very handsome church of the united parishes of Prestwick and Monkton, which forms a conspicuous object on the landscape. Near to the same structure stood the humble residence of Thomas King, a well-known village character who held the office of sexton in Monkton churchyard for the long period of thirty years. Thomas is now over eighty, and from the infirmities of age is no longer able to wield the mattock and spade. When young, however, he was a great pedestrian, and made long journeys, but the chief event of his life was a visit to London. The journey being performed under peculiar circumstances, it continued the subject of gossip in the district for the proverbial nine days, and afterwards became a theme for the muse of Robert Fisher, a Prestwick bard. As the verses flow smoothly, and have a homely ring, they are subjoined:—

The Pow Brig.

I mind when a boy o' an auld-fashioned house,
Whaur twa bodies leev'd that were wonderfu' douse,
Beside a wee burnie sae cleanly an' trig,
That wimpled its way 'neath the Auld Pow Brig.

It was built in a kind o' semi-circular form,
An' had lang stood the beating o' mony a storm ;
Wi' a bonny wee garden, a coo and a pig,
They leev'd happy as kings at the Auld Pow Brig.

Tam was blythe as a king, tho' a king just by name,
Was prood o' his weans an' tidy wee dame ;
He ance started for London, drove through't in a gig,
Wi' the rent o' the house at the Auld Pow Brig.

His wife was neither to bin nor to haud ;
She really imagined that Tam had gane mad ;
She vow'd when she got him she'd kame his auld wig,
And learn him to leeve at the Auld Pow Brig.

I mind o' these scenes, though I then was but wee,
Aye rinnin' for grozets wi' ilka bawbee ;
And the lads and the lasses danced mony a jig,
In the lang simmer nichts, at the Auld Pow Brig.

But the house is awa', and the wifie is gane,
And puir auld Tam noo is sad and alane ;
An' nocht marks the spot, but the bonnie lea rig,
Whaur stood the wee house at the Auld Pow Brig.

Crossing the road, I entered the unenclosed common, and directed my steps to the old church of Prestwick and soon arrived at the burying-ground by which it is surrounded. Seeing a group of children playing at "hide and seek" among the grave stones, I vaulted the low wall and began to explore this rugged unkept place of burial, for it is sterile and bleak in appearance, being unadorned with shrubbery and totally exposed to the chill sea breeze.

The roofless sanctuary in its centre has no feature of interest, but notwithstanding this great antiquity is ascribed to it. It was dedicated to Saint Nicholas, and granted along with Monkton Church to the Monastery of Paisley by Walter, the son of Allan, the first High Steward of Scotland. After the Parishes of Prestwick and Monkton were united it fell into disrepute, for the minister of the latter place of worship only preached in it every third Sabbath. This arrangement the Court of Teinds brought to a close by erecting the commodious church noticed above. Upon its completion, Prestwick Church, like its sister fabric in Monkton, was gutted and unroofed, and left like a gaunt skeleton to battle with the elements, and as such its bare walls remain a prominent object on the landscape, and are seen to advantage from road, rail, and sea.

When wandering among the graves I deciphered many a stony page, read many a holy text and disjointed couplet containing sage advices and moral lessons, but cannot say that any curious or remarkable inscription came under my notice. One stone, announcing that it is "IN MEMORY OF CAPTAIN JOHN BOGG OF THE BRIG MERCURY OF GREENOCK, WHO WAS LOST OFF AYR THE 3RD OF NOVEMBER, 1807," tells a woeful tale of the sea—a tale whose incidents are by far too often repeated in this era of rotten ships. Many stones to the memory of Prestwick freemen stud the sandy soil, but the most interesting to be met with are those which are said to cover the graves of Knights Templar. They are weather-worn and decayed, but bear no inscription, save a rude tracing of something resembling a cross. In the records of the Burgh of Prestwick repeated mention is made of Templar lands, and of sums of money derived from them which were paid yearly to a person named "Sanct John of Irvine." From this it is probable not only that knights of the order were at one time located in the district, but also that the tradition has some foundation in fact.

From the Churchyard I passed up a respectable, closely-built street, and soon arrived in Prestwick Cross, which is situated on the highway between Kilmarnock and Ayr.

Prestwick, or the Priests' Village, as the name signifies, is a pleasant little place, with a Council House, and very many substantial houses and neat villas of recent erection. Although situated on the highway within two and a half miles of the county town, and close to a line of railway, it has little to boast of in the way of trade, and in the meantime is only famous for the excellent quality of its kail plants. Its future, however, is promising, for it is gradually growing in importance as a fashionable watering place. Like Monkton it owes its origin to its church or other religious house erected in its vicinity, but at what time it sprang into existence is unknown.

The charter erecting it into a burgh or barony—which was renewed by James VI. at Holyrood, 19th June, 1600—expressly states that it was known as a free burgh or barony 617 years previous to that date. Now this borders on the fabulous, for it brings its erection back to the year 983, a period "far beyond the epoch of record," as Chalmers shrewdly remarks. "The lands of the burgh," says the same writer, "extend to about 1000 Scots acres, and are divided among thirty-six freemen or barons,* as they are called, each of whom possesses a lot of arable land, and a right of pasturing a certain number of sheep and cattle upon the common. None of these can sell their freeholds but to the community, who have a right to sell them again to whom they please. The magistrates have power to regulate the police of the burgh, and a jurisdiction over the freemen for enforcing the recovery of small debts. Though they have the power of committing a freeman to prison, they cannot lock the doors upon him; but if he comes out of the prison without proper liberation by the magistrates, he loses his freedom or baronship in the burgh." By the renewed charter the freemen

---

* In the olden time a freeman was a vassal in earnest. By a statute dated October, 1561, it was enacted that "ylk freman of this burgh (Prestwick) at has hors, at thai haf ryden geyr wyth ane sadyl, brydyll, gak, steyl bannet, and ane slot staf, or ane pow ax, suerd, and buckler."

were privileged to elect annually a provost, two bailies, a treasurer, and several councillors, to grant franchises to several trades, and to hold a weekly market, as also a fair on the 6th of December, the feast of St. Nicholas, the patron of the burgh.

The records extend as far back as 1470, and throw considerable light upon the history of the place, and more especially upon privileges enjoyed by freemen, but lengthy extracts would be out of place here.

The original number of freemen is still kept up, but the freeholds have decreased, and at this date do not exceed 700 acres. It is almost needless to add that the privileges so long enjoyed with immunity are now valuable only on account of their antiquity.

The cottages skirting the highway have a remarkably tidy appearance, and look so snug with their gardens and flower-plots that town folk are almost tempted to break the tenth commandment by coveting their neighbour's house. The good people of Prestwick, however, render the violation unnecessary by offering to let apartments for a given term, as numerous little cards peering from the folds of snow-white window curtains testified. The locality, if not the most picturesque, has at least the advantage of being salubrious, for the children were rompish and rosy, and every countenance beamed with health. Reaching new Prestwick, which is just a continuation of the old village, I was thoughtlessly pushing onward when the words "Kingcase Cottage" caught my eye. Surely, said I, the ruins of the lazarhouse and the well, whose waters were so potent to cure leprosy, must be at hand. Turning into a rugged unkept road on my right, I tapped with my stick at the door of a humble cottage. After some delay a woman made her appearance, and with the frankness of an old acquaintance informed me that the well and the "pickle ruins," as she termed the remains, lay on the brae face behind her dwelling; but lest I should not conveniently find them, she singled out a boy from a group engrossed in a game of marbles to be my guide. He proved a nimble chap, for he darted round the corner of the house and led the way up a steep wire-fenced path until he came to an opening. "There," said he, pointing to an old well and a pile of stones lying in a field to the west. "There, there it's," and before I could either tender thanks or offer a gratuity, darted off at the top of his speed to continue the game of "knuckle down." Finding myself alone I approached the well, which is about a stone-throw from the path referred to, and found it enclosed with rude masonry. Stepping down to its brink I drew a drinking cup from my coat pocket, and lifting a dripping bumper of the pure liquid, heroically drank to the memory of King Robert the Bruce, for tradition tells how that monarch was cured of a leprous disease by imbibing its waters. The draught proved cool and of excellent quality, but the flavour was greatly enhanced by the addition of a little brandy and a snack of bread and cheese.

From the well a dozen paces brought me to the "pickle ruins," or, in other words, the meagre remnant of Kingcase Hospital. As a ruin it is of no interest, and only consists of a portion of a side wall and some loose masonry, amongst which dock-weeds and long grass luxuriantly flourish. Finding nothing worthy of attention I sat down on a portion of the grass-covered foundation and began to gaze from the elevated position upon the village and fertile district beyond. No tree or shrub adorns the site of this ancient institution or relieves the monotony of the scene in its immediate vicinity. The soil all around is composed of dry loose sand, upon which it is difficult to walk; but, notwithstanding its barren appearance, a great portion is under cultivation and excellent crops are raised upon it, as was evident from the fine grain waving in more than one field on the occasion of my visit.

"At Kilcase, which is now called *Kincase* or Kingcase, on the coast of Kyle, in the Parish of Prestwick," says Chalmers, "there was founded an hospital for leprous persons, which was dedicated to St. Ninian. Tradition relates that the founder of this establishment was King Robert Bruce, who was himself afflicted with leprosy, the result of hard fare, hard living, and hard work. This hospital was endowed with the lands of Robertloan, which is now called *Loans*, in Dundonald parish, with the lands of Sheles and Spittal Sheles, in Kyle-Stewart, and with other lands which cannot now be specified. As the foundation charter of this hospital does not exist, it cannot be ascertained what number of persons were originally maintained in it. It appears, however, to have been governed by a guardian or prior, and it had a chaplain. In the reign of James II., Wallace of Newton acquired the lands of Spittal Sheles which belonged to this hospital, as the name implies, and the hereditary keeper or governor of the hospital and lands belonging to it. In 1515-16 all these were resigned by Hugh Wallace of Newton in favour of his brother Adam. After the whole property of this hospital was thus granted away, the only revenue that remained to it was the feu-duties payable from the lands, in this manner granted in fee-farm; and these, amounting to 64 bolls of meal and 8 merks (Scots) of money, with 16 threaves of straw for thatching the hospital, are still paid. For more than two centuries past this diminished revenue has been shared among eight objects of charity in equal shares of eight bolls of meal and one merk (Scotch) to each. The leprosy having long disappeared, the persons who are now admitted to the benefit of this charity are such as labour under diseases which are considered incurable, or such as are in indigent circumstances. The right of appointing these belonged to the family of Wallace of Craigie for a long time, and was purchased about 1790 [in 1787] by the Burgh of Ayr, which still retains this patronage. The old hospital, which existed in the better days of this charity, has long been in ruins. In the description of Kyle by Robert Gordon, in the reign of Charles I., he mentions the chapel of this establishment, and says that the persons admitted to the charity were then lodged in huts or cottages in the vicinity."

Reference is repeatedly made to Kingcase Hospital in the records of the Burgh of Prestwick. From these it is evident that leprosy was much dreaded, every precaution being taken to keep the inmates apart from the general community, and fines and imprisonment were in many cases inflicted upon persons brought before the "burro court" for visiting the institution.

When the building became ruinous is not exactly known. From the following entry in the above-mentioned records it appears to have been tenanted so late as 1740:—"24th May, 1740.—William Alexander, in King's-case, applys for the liberty of a yeard as now inclosed by their allowance formerly, and a piece of ground for the house he presently possesses southward to the Coall road. The freemen allow the same during his life, and allow the same to Elizabeth Shearer, his spouse, in case she survive him, and live in the hospital of Kingcase altenarly; for which they agree to pay two shillings sterline yearly."

There is a popular juvenile tradition connected with Kingcase well, which states that King Robert the Bruce when afflicted with leprosy wandered about the country. When skulking in the neighbourhood of the then very small village, it avers, he thrust the shaft of his spear into the sand and lay down beside it to rest his weary limbs. Having slept some time he rose to resume his wanderings, but when he withdrew his weapon to his surprise a stream of pure water issued from the indentation. Kneeling, he drank copiously, and shortly thereafter became whole. Attributing the cure to virtue in the water, and wishing others to participate in its benefits, he built and endowed the hospital, and also as a mark of royal favour erected the village into a burgh, and endowed it with the track of land lying between the Pow Burn and the river Ayr.

The tradition may be taken for what it is worth, as also the popular idea that the hospital was founded by Bruce; but it is just probable that it existed before his day, for Blind Harry tells how Sir William Wallace and his uncle, Sir Ranald Crawford, made a halt at it when on their way to Ayr to attend "the Black Parliament."

From the ruin, and tradition-hallowed well, I returned to the wire-fenced path and followed its course to the highway. From New Prestwick to Ayr the road runs in an almost straight line, studded here and there with neat cottages and comfortable, capacious mansions. Numerous pedestrians and vehicles passed and re-passed, and several pleasure-seekers from Kilmarnock drove along in holiday glee, and at Tam o' Shanter speed. Holding on the even tenor of my way, I soon reached the outskirts of Ayr, and at "Tam's Brig" stopped to dust my travel-stained boots and apparel before entering Newton. The bridge referred to crosses a line of railway, and from it one commands a fine view of the county town and its environs. But here I will take leave of the reader, and devote next chapter to a descriptive and historical sketch of the town of Ayr.

CHAPTER IV.

Ayr, its appearance, trade, and antiquity—its charters, privileges, wall, and castle—the barns of ayr—the burning of the barns and massacre of the english—"the friar's blessing"—the castle destroyed by bruce and rebuilt by the english—taken by the townspeople—the religious houses of ayr—the state of society in ayr at the reformation—the pest—the fort—cromwell's troops—martyrs.

Ayr nestles in a beautiful valley at the mouth of the river Ayr, and has a harbour which, in early times, ranked amongst the first ports in Scotland. Of late years it has been improved and deepened, and on its north side a spacious dock, capable of accommodating vessels of heavy tonnage, has been constructed. The burgh may be said to include Newton and Wallacetown, for all three are under the same local government, connected by bridges, and included in the same Parliamentary constituency. The streets are clean, well built, and for the most part spacious; but its trade, which consists of engineering, shipbuilding, agricultural implement making, plumbing, iron and brassfounding, tanning, brewing, and other crafts, is not carried on with any degree of spirit, for its business to a considerable extent depends upon the residence of persons in easy circumstances, and it may be added, upon the thousands of visitors who annually flock to view scenes which the memory and genius of Robert Burns have rendered famous. The population last census amounted to 17,954. The town contains twelve places of worship—viz., four Established, three Free, two United Presbyterian, one Evangelical Union, one Episcopal, and one Roman Catholic—and the educational requirements of the community are superintended by an efficient School Board.

That a settlement of some kind occupied the site of the town of Ayr in prehistoric times is more than probable, and that it was a Roman station is evident from the fact that relics of that wonderful people have been discovered embedded in the soil in and around the town, and also that a road of their construction has been traced from Kirkcudbright to its very centre; but those wishing further information on this point had better consult the third volume of Chalmers' *Caledonia.* "There are manifest indications," says the *Statistical Account,* "that the whole of the lower part along the sea coast from river to river (Ayr and Doon) has been the scene of some great struggle in which the Romans and the natives were combatants, and that probably in more than one conflict. Throughout the whole of this space Roman and British places of sepulchre are found, with Roman armour, swords, lances, daggers, and pieces of mail and brazen camp vessels intermixed with British urns of rude baked clay, hatchet and arrow heads, and other implements of warfare used by the Caledonians." In what form the town existed at that period cannot now be ascertained, but one thing is certain, that although often remodelled, it has witnessed in some shape or other three great eras in the history of our country—viz., the Roman invasion, the war of independence, and the struggle for civil and religious liberty.

The charter erecting Ayr into a royal burgh was granted by William the Lion on the occasion of his having built what he terms his new castle of Ayr. The deed conferred extensive property and many important privileges upon the burgh, but when it is considered that the district was an almost impregnable forest at the period, the gift appears the reverse of munificent. Alexander II. confirmed this charter, and in addition to his father's grant, bestowed the lands of Alloway on the burgh, and conferred on the burgesses the right of acquiring such portions of land as they might clear of timber, at the rate of twelve pennies yearly for every six acres. Alexander III. frequently held court at Ayr, and from this it may be inferred that it was at that period an important town. To guard against freebooters and the assaults of more deadly foes, it was protected by its castle, and by a strong wall on the east and south, and the sea and river on the north and west. Lord Hailes supposes the castle to have been erected to check the incursions of the men of Galloway, and probably the wall was built for the same purpose. But both had to withstand the assaults of more determined foes—more so the castle, for it was the main point of attack in time of war. It is said to have been stormed by the Norwegians under Haco, but it is more certain that it and the town were occupied by the English during that critical period of Scottish history, when the usurper, Edward I., held every town and fortress in the kingdom. According to Blind Harry, Wallace performed some daring and almost improbable exploits in Ayr, but the most noteworthy was the burning of the Barns, a retributive act that the English merited for the treacherous murder of his uncle (Sir Ranald Crawford) and other Scottish nobles. Although Lord Hailes has questioned the truth of this event, yet the veracity of the blind minstrel regarding it has been sufficiently attested by other writers of a less prejudiced disposition, and on that account a brief notice of the transaction is appended.

The Barns of Ayr are supposed to have been granaries for the storage of the produce of farms cultivated by the burgh tenantry. That such buildings existed in Ayr is sufficiently attested by the burgh records and by the fact that stacking was but little resorted to by our forefathers and that it was customary to store the harvest in buildings for the purpose. From the text of Blind Harry, however, the Barns in question appear to have been a kind of temporary barrack of one apartment for the accommodation of that portion of the English garrison to whom the limits of the castle could not afford quarters. A kind of parliament, or "justice aire," to which Sir William Wallace and the leading Scottish nobles were invited, was ordered to be held in the Barns on the 18th June, 1297. They flocked to the place of meeting on the day appointed, but the treacherous English had matters arranged so that every visitor was seized and strangled the moment he entered. In the language of the minstrel—

> "No Scot escaped that time who enter'd in,
> Unto the baulk they hang'd up many a pair;
> Then in some by-nook cast them there.
> Since the first time that men did war invent
> To so unjust a death none ever went.
> Thus to the gods of their cruel wrath
> They sacrificed the Scots and broke their faith;
> Such wickedness, each Christian soul must own,
> Was ne'er before in all the world known.

> Thus eighteen score to death they put outright,
> Of barons bold and many a gallant knight;
> Then last of all, with great contempt and scorn,
> Cast out the corpse, naked as they were born."

By a fortunate mishap Wallace did not arrive in Ayr until late in the day, but he had no sooner done so than he was hailed by a woman and informed of the foul butcheries at the Barns. He was overwhelmed with indignation at the tidings, and wept when he learned that his uncle and other relatives and friends had been ignominiously slain. Burning with revenge, he bade her farewell, and rode to Langlane Wood in the hope of meeting with a band of followers in its recess. In this he was not disappointed, but his joy knew no bounds when at dusk he again descried the female who accosted him in Ayr at the head of a band of trusty burgesses, and heard that the English soldiery were rioting and drinking in the Barns in all the recklessness of fancied security. A council of war being held, it was decided that the town should be entered at midnight, and that the Barns and every house in which any portion of the enemy resided should be given to the flames. As a preliminary arrangement, the woman and a burgess were sent to chalk the door of every house in which Englishmen dwelt. Twenty men afterwards fastened them with ropes; but while they were so engaged Robert Boyd of Kilmarnock, at the head of fifty men, passed stealthily into the town and lay in ambush near the castle gate to prevent the garrison issuing forth. The arrangements being complete, Wallace, at a given signal, appeared on the scene, and with a reserved force of two hundred and fifty men surrounded the Barns, and in a twinkling had them and every marked house in the town in a mass of flame. The scene was appalling, but the minstrel's description is so graphic that it deserves quoting—

> "The buildings great were all burn'd down that night;
> None there escaped, squire, or lord, or knight,
> When the great roof-trees fell down them among—
> O such a sad and melancholy song!
> Some naked burnt to ashes all away,
> Some never rose, but smother'd where they lay;
> Others attempting to get to the air,
> With fire and smoke were burnt and chocked there.
> Their nauseous smell none present could abide;
> A just reward; for murder will not hide.

> With sorrow thus, and many a grievous groan,
> They languish'd till their sinful days were gone.
> Some sought the door, endeavouring out to get,
> But Scotchmen them so wisely did beset,
> Out of the burning flames who ever got
> Immediately were cut down on the spot,
> Or driven back with fury in the fire :
> Such wages got these hangmen for their hire."

As the flames shot up and illumined the district, the inmates of the castle threw open the gate with the idea of assisting their fellows and the townspeople to subdue the fire, but they had no sooner done so than Boyd

> "Won the port and entered with all his men,"

and put every southerner to the sword before their consternation and confusion were allayed. Among the religious houses that existed in Ayr at the period was that of the Black Friars. In it "seven score Southron loons" had taken up their quarters, but the instant the prior learned what was being transacted at the Barns and throughout the town, he armed himself and brethren and slew his unwelcome guests as they slept. The affair was ever after referred to as "the friars' blessing."

According to Blind Harry, 5000 Englishmen perished by fire and sword that night. The awful revenge taken by Wallace did not go unpunished, however, for Edward sent down 4000 men to chastise him and recapture the castle. After a desperate struggle this was accomplished ; but the triumph was brief, for shortly after the event the English were compelled to evacuate this stronghold, being as unable to hold it as they were every other place of strength in the country.

In 1299 this castle was held by Bruce, but when forced to retreat before the overwhelming force marching westward to attack him, he burnt it, as that was the only available means of preventing it falling into the hands of the foe. The English, however, deeming it an important stronghold, had it speedily rebuilt, and in spite of all opposition occupied it until the decisive battle of Bannockburn, when it was, along with other fortresses, surrendered to the victorious Scotch. After the battle of Halidon Hill, it again fell into the hands of the English, but the lads of Ayr, led on by their Sheriff, surprised the garrison, and put every Southron to the sword. At this date no vestige of the building remains, and its exact site is somewhat uncertain, but it is generally agreed that it stood behind the present academy, and was swept away by the revolutionizing Cromwell.

Besides its castle, Ayr possessed in early times a church and two religious institutions. The first was dedicated to St. John. It had four altars, eight chaplains, and a bevy of monks. In it the Parliament was held which fixed the succession to the Scottish throne on the family of Robert the Bruce; but despite this and its consecration, Cromwell in after years turned it into an armoury, and ultimately pulled it down to make room for a fort. Its tower still stands, but is so incorporated with other buildings that it is not easily distinguished.

The institutions referred to have completely worn out of the traditional mind, but their positions have been pretty accurately ascertained. One was the Monastery of Dominicans or Black Friars, and was founded in 1230 by Alexander II. It was possessed of considerable wealth, and frequently received gifts from royalty, especially from James IV. and V., who often visited Ayr; but its coffers were oftener replenished by individuals of less note. For instance, it is stated in the *History of the County of Ayr* that the lands of Dankeith, in the parish of Symington, belonged to the Dominican friars. This appears from a curious document among the records of the burgh bearing date 4th May, 1411. It is termed—"Ane testificat, witnessing that a noble and worshipful man, Allan Lander, gave in perpetual almonds the lands of Dalnkeith to the friars preachers of Ayr, for the soul of umql. Allice Campbell, his wife, and for the souls of his posteritie, for continued prays of the friars, and for the anniversary of the said Allice, and that the same was honestlie and reverentlie done." When suppressed, nearly the whole property of this house was inherited by the burgh. The other institution was the Monastery of the Franciscan order of Grey Friars, founded by the inhabitants of Ayr in 1472. It also received royal patronage, and was celebrated for a statue of the Virgin Mary—at whose shrine the halt, the blind, the maimed, and the diseased were miraculously cured.

When vast wealth, and consequent sensuality, rendered

the clergy and the laity of the Romish church intolerable, the social revolution which ensued convulsed Ayr as much as it did every other town in the kingdom. The people, however, although sufficiently daring to break away from the thraldom of the Mother Church, were at first rather unwilling to submit with any degree of meekness to the rigour of the new faith, and the charge of "wicked" which Burns brings against the town was more than merited at the period. Howie, in his life of John Welch, its first Protestant minister, states that that "worthy" found it in a very wicked state when he first came to it—"so wicked that no one would let him a house to dwell in." "The place," he goes on to say, "was so divided into factions, and filled with bloody conflicts, that a man could hardly walk the streets with safety; wherefore Mr. Welch made it his first undertaking to remove the bloody quarrellings, but he found it a very difficult work; yet such was his earnestness to pursue his design, that many times he would rush betwixt two parties of men fighting, even in the midst of blood and wounds. He used to cover his head with a head-piece before he went to separate these bloody enemies, but would never use a sword, that they might see he came for peace and not for war, and so, little by little, he made the town a peaceable habitation. His manner was, after he had ended a skirmish amongst his neighbours, and reconciled these bitter enemies, to cause a covered table to be put upon the street, and there brought the enemies together, and beginning with prayer he persuaded them to profess themselves friends, then to eat and drink together, then last of all he ended the work with singing a psalm. And after the rude people began to observe his example, and listen to his heavenly doctrine, he came quickly to such respect amongst them, that he became not only a necessary counsellor, without whose counsel they would do nothing, but also an example to imitate." That society in Ayr was in a very disturbed state long after that period is fully borne out by the session books and town records. Street brawls, wife-beating, and drunkenness were of frequent occurrence, and the Sabbath was looked upon as a day of recreation, and people were continually lapsing into the habit of working, buying, selling, and playing at games on that day, but the session stamped out the practices by

c

summary and severe punishments. During the ministry of the Rev. Mr. Welch, the plague or pest, as it was termed, visited the county, and, the better to guard the town against infection, the Magistrates ordered the gates to be closed and closely watched, so that infected persons might be kept out. One day a brace of packmen presented themselves and demanded admittance. The Magistrates being called, sent for Mr. Welch to obtain the benefit of his counsel, but he promptly told them to send the men away for they had the plague in their packs. This was afterwards verified, says the account, for in Cumnock where they disposed of their goods "such an infection was kindled that the living were hardly able to bury the dead." Notwithstanding precautions adopted, the pest entered the town, but its ravages were more severely felt in after years. In 1610 it is estimated that 2000 persons died of it, and upon another occasion the population was so far reduced by it and famine together that the town was in a measure depopulated.

After the battle of Dunbar the troops of the Commonwealth occupied Ayr, and upon its churchyard and some sixteen acres of adjacent ground built a regular fortification (the fort alluded to), with a fosse and an esplanade, which was considered one of the most complete works of the kind in the kingdom. At the Restoration the whole was dismantled and gifted in 1663 to Hugh, seventh Earl of Eglinton, in consideration of *his father's services* (!) during the usurpation. In 1681 it was purchased from that noble family by the magistrates of Ayr for the town, but was re-purchased by the same house and a distillery erected within it in 1734. It afterwards came into the hands of the Culzean family. It is now the property of John Miller, Esq., an enterprising gentleman, who has feued out the grounds and transformed the castle into a handsome residence. A considerable portion is now traversed by streets and terraces of elegant villas, and when the whole is built upon the locality will be a fashionable and populous suburb of the old and much-respected town. Although these changes have taken place, a considerable portion of the citadel remains, and fragments of its massive walls are still to be seen.

There is a current tradition that Cromwell demolished Ardrossan Castle and shipped the stones to Ayr to aid in the construction of the fort. This is probable, and partly borne out by the fact that a considerable portion of that castle has been removed by some means and for some purpose.

"During the Cromwellian period, and while the troops of the Commonwealth garrisoned the fort," says James Paterson in his history of the county, "the session records bear ample evidence that, in morals at least, the soldiers were by no means puritanical. They appear to have arrived in Ayr in 1651. . . . . There are innumerable instances of Sabbath breaking and uncleanness on the part of Cromwell's troops. One entry records the fact of an English soldier having been scourged through the streets for adultery."

During the attempt to force Episcopacy upon the people of Scotland the lads of Ayr stood nobly to the front, and boldly maintained the tenets of civil and religious freedom, and that with their lives, for many suffered martyrdom; but the sentences of eight were considered so unjust that the hangman fled in dismay, so utterly horrified was he at the idea of having to execute guiltless men. To fill his place the Irvine executioner was applied to, but he stedfastly refused to put the men to death, and although dragged to Ayr and placed in the stocks, and threatened with death, he would not be prevailed upon to perform the odious task. One of the condemned, however, was tempted by the offer of a free pardon to execute his companions; "but he," says Woodrow, "would have refused at the last had he not been kept partly intoxicated."

Beyond the stirring events of early times there is little connected with Ayr calling for particular notice. The advance of the rebel army in 1745 created considerable excitement amongst the inhabitants, and proved their loyalty to the house of Hanover. The Radical movement also made some stir, but the troops held in readiness to preserve law and order in the event of a rising awed the malcontents, and they never engaged in anything save a war of words. Since then Ayr has been in a measure remodelled, and prosperity has been its constant attendant.

CHAPTER V.

Newton-upon-Ayr — the constitution of the burgh — the church and its pastors — the auld and new brigs of Ayr — was Burns a prophet? — the high street of Ayr — the site of the Tolbooth — the old church and graveyard — Provost Ballantyne — Robert Aiken — heroes of "the Kirk's Alarm" — the Martyrs' Stone — a curious epitaph — Daft Rab Hamilton.

The situation of Newton-upon-Ayr is not striking, nor is its neighbourhood remarkable for beauty. Although containing a population of 4686 souls, and forming part of the Parliamentary burgh of Ayr, it has few manufactures and little traffic, and as to its buildings, they are of such a common-place description that a rambler might stray through its streets without harbouring a wish to linger on his way. The constitution of the burgh, however, is of some interest on account of it being only paralleled by Prestwick, but when it was created cannot, at this date, be ascertained with certainty, its original charter being lost. Notwithstanding this, tradition states, and the freemen affirm, that the lands were conferred by Robert the Bruce upon forty-eight individuals who distinguished themselves at the battle of Bannockburn. This may, or may not have been, but it is certain that the privileges enjoyed by the burghers in early times were renewed by a charter from James VI., which empowered the *community*—as the forty-eight participators are termed—to grant feus and divide amongst themselves the lands acquired by their ancestors, and also to elect two bailies, one treasurer, and six councillors.

Each *lot* or *freedom* extends to about six acres of arable land, and the right of succession is limited to direct descent. For instance, a son succeeds to his father; and a widow, not having a son, enjoys the property of her husband as long as she lives, but daughters are excluded from benefit, and the consequence is that freedoms frequently revert to the community. These, however, are not retained, but disposed of to the most respectable and industrious inhabitants of the burgh, and in this manner the commune has been kept in existence. At this date many of the freedoms have been disposed of, and the privileges which the charter conferred are of no practical utility, but notwithstanding, the freemen are still the superiors, and meet frequently to transact business.

Wallacetown adjoins Newton, and is also part of the Parliamentary burgh of Ayr. It originated towards the end of the last century, and is entirely built on ground feued from the Wallaces of Craigie.

The church, and ancient churchyard of Newton, are hid from view by the Council Chambers—an odd-like building which stands near the centre of Main Street—but they afford no inducement to the rambler to linger by them. The church, however, although obscurely situated, has gained a kind of celebrity on account of the number of ordinations which have taken place in it since the Disruption, and the fact that many of its clergymen have risen to eminence. For instance, the Rev. Dr. Caird, Principal of Glasgow University, was its minister for some time; as also, the Rev. John Stuart of St. Andrew's, Edinburgh; the Rev. Dr. Boyd (long connected with *Fraser's Magazine*); the Rev. Dr. George Burns of Glasgow Cathedral; the Rev. Dr. Wallace, formerly of Greyfriars, Edinburgh, and now editor of the *Scotsman*; the Rev. John M'Leod (cousin of the lamented Dr Norman); and others equally deserving of notice.

From Newton I passed through Wallacetown and sought the Auld Brig o' Ayr—a ponderous old-fashioned structure of four lofty arches, whose weed-covered buttresses and solid architecture have, according to general belief, witnessed the passage of six hundred years and the many changes which have followed in their train. A pretty little legend has it that the old pile was erected by two maiden ladies named Lowe to prevent the annual loss of life which ensued from the crossing of a ford near the spot it occupies, and that the chief incitement to the praiseworthy act was the melancholy circumstance of a young man to whom one of them was betrothed having perished while attempting to cross the stream during a flood. Be this as it may, two faded effigies which tradition points to as theirs may still be seen on the inside of the eastern parapet, and also the time-worn figures "1, 2, 5, 2," which possibly denote the year in which the edifice was constructed. This legend may be an historical fact, but the annals of the venerable structure are few and fail to record it.

Although early occurrences associated with the venerable pile are unchronicled, many a regal, many a warlike, and many a devotional cavalcade has doubtless defiled across its narrow path in times passed away, when it formed the principal if not the only means of communication between the northern and southern banks of the Ayr in the district; but a truce to speculation.

About 1785 the ancient bridge began to display such symptoms of decay that the magistrates of Ayr had it examined, and the result was, that it was pronounced no longer capable of withstanding the strain of heavy traffic. At first they thought of taking it down, but after considerable deliberation and negotiation, an Act of Parliament was obtained which empowered them to build a new bridge, and place a toll upon it, to refund the money expended on its construction. In May, 1786, the first stone of this structure was laid, but it was not until November, 1788, that the last was imbedded and the whole work finished.

Mr. John Ballantyne, banker, Ayr, a very warm friend, and a sincere admirer of the poetical and personal merits of Robert Burns, was Provost during the time of its erection, and took a deep interest in its progress. He generously offered to advance the necessary funds to print a second edition of the poet's works. This, and many another kindness, seem to have been fully appreciated by Burns, for in a letter to his earliest Ayr patron—Robert Aiken—he says:— "I would detest myself as a wretch if I thought I were capable in a very long life of forgetting the honest, warm, and tender delicacy with which he (Mr Ballantyne) enters into my interests." Poets have seldom more to give than a song, and at this most unfortunate and vexatious period of his existence Burns had little else. However, as a mark of his esteem and gratitude, he inscribed to him the clever dialogue in which he makes the old and new bridges hurl all the opprobrious epithets at each other a poet's fancy could command, and thereby rescued his name from oblivion.

"The Brigs of Ayr" is one of our poet's happiest efforts, but little did he think when he penned it that he had put a prophesy into the mouth of the presiding genii of the old bridge which would be fulfilled to the letter before a century rolled into the vortex of eternity. Mark the language. The hour is midnight, and

> "The Goth is stalking round with anxious search,
> Spying the time-worn flaws in every arch,"

when his "new-come neebor"—in course of erection some hundred and fifty yards farther down the stream—catches his eye.

> "Wi' thieveless sneer to see his modish mien,
> He, doun the water, gies him thus guid-e'en:—

AULD BRIG.

> "I doubt na, frien', ye'll think ye're nae sheep-shank,
> Ance ye were streekit o'er frae bank to bank,
> But gin ye be a brig as auld as me,
> Though faith, that day I doubt ye'll never see,
> There'll be, if that day come, I'll wad a boddle,
> Some fewer whigmaleeries in your noddle."

NEW BRIG.

> "Auld Vandal, ye but show your little mense,
> Just much about it wi' your scantie sense;
> Will your poor narrow footpath of a street,
> Where twa wheelbarrows tremble when they meet,
> Your ruined, formless bulk o' stane and lime,
> Compare wi' bonnie brigs o' modern time?
> There's men o' taste wad tak the Ducat stream,
> Though they should cast the very sark and swim,
> Ere they wad grate their feelings wi' the view
> O' sic an ugly Gothic hulk as you."

AULD BRIG.

> "Conceited gowk, puffed up wi' windy pride!
> This mony a year I've stood the flood and tide;
> And though wi' crazy eild I'm sair forfairn,
> I'll be a Brig when ye're a shapeless cairn!
> As yet ye little ken about the matter,
> But twa-three winters will inform ye better.
> When heavy, dark, continued, a'-day rains,
> Wi' deepening deluges o'erflow the plains;

> When from the hills where springs the brawling Coil,
> Or stately Lugar's mossy fountains boil,
> Or where the Greenock winds his moorland course,
> Or haunted Garpal draws his feeble source,
> Aroused by blustering winds and spotting thows,
> In mony a torrent down his snaw-broo rowes;
> While crashing ice, borne on the roaring spate,
> Sweeps dams, and mills, and brigs a' to the gate;
> And from Glenbuck down to the Ratton-Key
> Auld Ayr is just one lengthened tumbling sea—
> Then down ye'll hurl, deil nor ye never rise!
> And dash the gumlie jaups up to the pouring skies,
> A lesson sadly teaching to your cost,
> That Architecture's noble art is lost!"

It came to pass as the Auld Brig predicted. The "conceited gowk" is no more, and another equally handsome bridge is "streekit o'er frae bank to bank" in its stead. In March, 1877, its masonry was found to be so rent and insecure that it was condemned, and ordered to be taken down, but it was not until the 5th of November same year that it was reduced to "a shapeless cairn." Then, its parapets and packing being removed, the arches were blown up with dynamite, and in the presence of a vast concourse of spectators assembled to witness its overthrow, it fell into the bed of the river, a shattered, formless mass of masonry.

Reader, do not smile at the writer's enthusiasm when he tells you that he not only crossed and re-crossed the Old Bridge, but curiously examined everything about it, and what is more, leaned over the weather-worn parapet and watched the water gliding from beneath the massive arches. He took a strange delight in doing so, for to be where the admired bard of his country found a theme for his muse gives one a more lively and vivid conception of the man, and a clearer insight into his master mind.

Despite the boast of the ancient edifice, its many good qualities are so far impaired that it is only traversed by foot-passengers now, but notwithstanding, it appears quite capable of bearing such "aboon the broo," and most likely will perform the degenerate duty for many, many long years,

---

* The "New" Bridge was a graceful, broad structure of five lofty, well-turned arches. On each of its sides were niches containing statues of heathen deities, and above the central spandril the armorial bearings of the town were displayed. On the whole, it was the handsomest public bridge in the county of Ayr.

and that too despite the assaults of time and the blustering wintry torrents which in the course of nature may lash themselves into foam against its buttresses.

After lingering by the celebrated edifice, I traversed a narrow, old-fashioned lane and entered the High Street— a well-paved thoroughfare containing many large shops and other places of business, and not a few buildings belonging to a former age. An observant pedestrian finds much to interest him in a bustling town, and objects to engage attention are not wanting in "the auld toon o' Ayr." Indeed, it will amply repay any person who has time to leisurely examine it, and although its store of antiquities is not great, yet they are worth hunting up and interesting when found.

For instance, I had proceeded but a short distance along this, the chief artery of the town, when my attention was attracted by a dumpy, ill-proportioned statue of the hero Wallace, peering in serio-comic fashion from a niche in the side wall of a corner tenement, which is said to occupy the site of the Tolbooth or prison-house in which "Scotia's ill-requited chief" languished after killing Lord Percy's steward. Blind Harry narrates the circumstances in "Buke Secund" of his metrical life of Wallace, and states that he was brought so low by damp and disease while immured that the gaoler during one of his visits considered him dead, and had him tossed over the prison wall like so much carrion. According to the minstrel, the gaoler's mistake was the means of preserving the patriot's life, for being found by "his first nurse," he was conveyed to her residence in Newton and concealed until health and strength were regained.

There are many curious old buildings in the vicinity of the tenement containing the statue referred to, but none more so than those situated in an adjacent alley named Isle Lane. One especially, which appears to have been the town residence of some noble family, carries one as far back as the Elizabethan period.

Entering Kirk Port, a narrow, but respectable lane branching off High Street nearly opposite Newmarket Street, I soon arrived at the gate of the quaint burying-place surrounding the old Parish Church, a venerable building of considerable interest, which stands on the site of the Grey Friars' Convent, an ecclesiastical edifice alluded to in a former chapter. The appearance of the Churchyard is very striking as you enter it from the peculiarly porched gateway which guards the entrance. Before you is the green uneven sward studded with memorials of the departed, and a little way off the church, a very plain, rude looking building with a jutting aisle which bears date 1654. An interesting fact connected with this place of worship is, that Oliver Cromwell contributed a sum of money towards defraying the expense of its erection when he sacrilegiously turned the historic church of Saint John (then the only place of worship in Ayr) into an armoury and built a portion of a fortification upon its burying-ground.

After surveying the exterior of this curious structure I entered by a door which was fortunately standing ajar and began to examine the interior without let or hindrance, for the place was entirely deserted. My footfalls echoed strangely through the vacant building, and the " dim religious light " which streamed through the stained glass windows had a solemnising effect upon me, but I reverently advanced and leisurely examined the surroundings. Although neither remarkable for beauty nor style of architecture, yet it is much to be regretted that the interior of this old church has been at various times altered so as quite to have changed its character. Indeed "improvements" have been carried on to such a degree that its ancient appearance is entirely obliterated by the introduction of "whigmaleeries" which new-fangled notions have suggested. It has three galleries, or lofts, which are designated the merchants', the trades', and the sailors'. That of the sailors had the model of a full-rigged ship hanging in front of it, but like every other characteristic feature, it is improved out of sight. On either side of the pulpit are large windows filled with stained glass of rich and interesting design. One is a memorial of John Welsh and William Adair, ministers of the church in olden times. The design illustrates the preaching of John the Baptist and the announcement of the Nativity by the angel to the shepherds of Bethlehem. One half of the other window is a memorial of Lady Jane Hamilton, and the other half is inscribed to Charles Dalrymple Gairdner. The Scriptural groups are delineated and wrought out with remarkable success, and the rich colouring, relieved by blending shades of white glass, sheds a mellow pure light upon the interior. The rest of the church need not detain us long. Besides these brittle, but brilliantly coloured memorials of good men, there are several monumental tablets on the walls which will repay examination, and also a fine organ behind the neatly fitted up pulpit.

After viewing the interior of the church, I began an interesting ramble through the churchyard, and there scanned the memorial stones of several men who were friends and associates of Burns, and others who have gained a kind of celebrity by being alluded to in his poetry. For instance, close to the southern wall of the church aisle rest the remains of the gentleman to whom the poet inscribed "the Brigs of Ayr." The tablet which marks the spot bears the following inscription :—"IN MEMORY OF JOHN BALLANTYNE, ESQR., OF CASTLEHILL, BANKER IN AYR, WHO DIED 15TH JULY, 1812, AGED 68." Judging from records on two old stones at the foot of the grave, the secluded nook seems to have been the burying-place of the Ballantynes for several generations. Robert Chambers sums up this gentleman's character in few words. He says :—"There could not have been a nobler instance of benevolence and manly worth than that furnished by Provost Ballantyne. His hospitable mansion was known far and wide, and he was the friend of every liberal measure."

Robert Aiken, the poet's earliest Ayr patron, rests near the worthy Provost; and within a railed enclosure by the side of the church are the graves of Drs. Dalrymple and M'Gill, the well-known heroes of "The Kirk's Alarm." The following is inscribed on the monumental slabs to their memory :—

"TO THE MEMORY OF THE REV. WILLIAM DALRYMPLE, D.D., MINISTER OF AYR, WHO DIED THE 28TH OF JANY., 1814, IN THE 91ST YEAR OF HIS AGE, AND THE 68TH OF HIS MINISTRY; AND OF SUSANNA HUNTER, HIS WIFE, WHO DIED THE 29TH NOVR., 1809, AGED 83. ALSO, OF THEIR CHILDREN ELIZABETH, M'CRAE, AND CHARLOTTE, WHO DIED INFANTS. OF RAMSAY, WHO DIED IN HER TENTH YEAR. OF JAMES, THEIR ONLY SON, WHO DIED IN HIS TWENTIETH YEAR. OF SUSANNA, WHO DIED 2ND JANY., 1817, IN HER 60TH YEAR; AND OF SUSANNA HUNTER STEWART, THEIR GRANDDAUGHTER, WHO DIED IN HER 12TH YEAR."

"TO THE MEMORY OF THE REVEREND WILLIAM M'GILL,

D.D., THIS MONUMENT IS ERECTED BY THE MAGISTRATES OF AYR, IN TESTIMONY OF THE SENSE WHICH THEY AND THE COMMUNITY THEY REPRESENT RETAIN OF HIS DISTINGUISHED WORTH IN THE DISCHARGE OF THE PASTORAL DUTIES OF THIS PARISH FOR A PERIOD OF 46 YEARS. HEAVEN CALLED HIM HENCE ON THE 30TH DAY OF MARCH, 1807, IN THE 76TH YEAR OF HIS AGE."

Dr. Dalrymple was senior, and Dr. M'Gill junior minister of the parish church of Ayr, and during the long period of their joint incumbency—forty-six years—the utmost cordiality existed between them.

Dr. Dalrymple is said to have been a man of extraordinary benevolence and worth, and many strange anecdotes are related regarding the philanthropic traits of his character, but it was more than hinted during his lifetime that his views regarding the Trinity were not altogether orthodox. Burns possibly had this in his mind when he penned the following stanza regarding him :—

> "D'rymple mild, D'rymple mild,
> Though your heart's like a child,
> And your life like the new-driven snaw;
> Yet that winna save ye,
> Auld Satan must have ye,
> For preaching that three's ane and twa."

As Dr. M'Gill raised the "heretic blast" which gave Burns the key-note of the celebrated satire "The Kirk's Alarm," a somewhat fuller notice may be accorded him. He was born at Carsenestock, in the parish of Penninghame, Wigtownshire, on the 11th July, 1731, and was early destined for the Church of Scotland. After receiving a preparatory education at the parish school, he entered the Glasgow University, and in due time was fitted for the ministry. Shortly after being licensed, he preached several times to the congregation of the Parish Church of Ayr during a vacancy in the second charge, and gave such universal satisfaction that at their earnest solicitation he was inducted to the living on the 22nd October, 1761. Some two years after his settlement he married Elizabeth Dunlop, a niece of his colleague Dr. Dalrymple—a lady of a somewhat capricious temperament, who had a small fortune of £700 ; but the sum being placed in the Douglas and Heron bank, it was unhappily lost when that unfortunate concern collapsed in 1772. To eke out his slender official income he received boarders into his house, and many country families whose sons were attending Ayr Academy availed themselves of the privilege of placing them under his excellent supervision. His life may be said to have passed without incident until the year 1786. Then he published a theological work entitled—*A Practical Essay on the Death of Jesus Christ, in two parts; containing* (1), *the History;* (2), *the Doctrine of His Death.* This bulky octavo volume of 550 pages is dedicated to his colleague, the Rev. William Dalrymple, D.D.; but it no sooner made its appearance than it was denounced as a heretical publication. It was said to favour Arian and Socinian doctrine, and declared contrary to the standard theology of the Church of Scotland. It was attacked by the clergy and laity, and replied to by pamphleteers. Indeed, many zealots in blind enthusiasm did their utmost to crush the writer, and stifle freedom of thought in matters of religion. Amid all this commotion, Dr. M'Gill remained silent, and never so much as deigned to explain or defend the opinions which the work contained until "Pebbles frae the water fit"—as Burns terms the Rev. William Pebbles, D.D., minister of Newton-upon-Ayr—published a sermon which he preached in commemoration of the Revolution on the 5th November, 1788. In this he spoke disparagingly of Dr. M'Gill and his work, and declared that "with one hand he was receiving the privileges of the church, while with the other he was endeavouring to plunge the keenest poignard into her heart"—a most unworthy charge certainly. War was now declared between hitherto warm friends. Dr. M'Gill at once replied by publishing the sermon which he delivered on the 5th November, and along with it an appendix, in which he defended what he had written, and severely censured his accuser. Up to this time the Presbytery exercised a prudent forbearance and took no notice of the controversy, but the instant it assumed such a flagrant form steps were taken to vindicate the standards of the church, and the case was laid before the Presbyterial Court of Ayr in April, 1789—exactly three years after the publication of the essay. Dr. M'Gill adhered to the opinions expressed in the work, and continued to defend them, but ultimately an elaborate report was drawn up which stated that the work contained heretical doctrines which were entirely opposed to the standards of the church. Afterwards the case was laid before the Synod which met in Glasgow on the 13th April, 1790 ; but, to the surprise of everybody, the Doctor requested that no further proceedings should take place, apologised, and gave an explanation of his views which entirely satisfied the assembled divines and ended the discussion.

The memory of this ecclesiastical squabble would have perished had not the satire of the bard rescued it from the oblivion which shrouds many a similar rupture. He had a keen relish for such conflicts, and doubtless watched this one with deep interest, for his noble nature rebelled against the gloomy Calvinism of his day. He wrote "The Kirk's Alarm" in the very heat of the dissension and circulated it in manuscript amongst his friends. In a letter to John Logan, Esq., which contained a copy of the satire, and shows in what direction his sympathies ran, he says : "If I could be of any service to Dr. M'Gill I would do it, though it should be at a much greater expense than irritating a few bigoted priests ; but as I am afraid serving him in his present embarass is a task too hard for me ;" and in a letter to his friend, Robert Graham of Fintry, containing another copy, he makes use of the following language regarding the persecuted doctor : "I think you must have heard of Dr. M'Gill, one of the clergymen of Ayr, and his heretical book. God help him, poor man ! Though he is one of the worthiest, as well as one of the ablest of the whole priesthood of the Kirk of Scotland, in every sense of that ambiguous term, yet the poor doctor and his numerous family are in imminent danger of being thrown out to the mercy of the winter winds."

This was the only eventful chapter in the life of Dr. M'Gill. Besides his "Practical Essay on the Death of Jesus Christ," he published various detached sermons, but none of them seem to have attracted much attention. Robert Chambers states that "he was a Socinian in principle, though not a disciple of Socinius, none of whose works he had ever read. In his personal and domestic character he was a strange mixture of simplicity and stoicism. He seldom smiled, but often set the table in a roar by his quaint remarks. He was inflexibly regular in the distribution of his time: he studied so much every day, and took his walk at the same hour in all kinds of weather. He played at golf a whole twelvemonth without the omission of a single week day, except the three on which there are religious services at the time of the communion. His views of many of the dispensations of Providence were widely different from those of the bulk of society. A friend told him of an old clergyman, an early companion of his own, who, having entered the pulpit in his canonicals, and on being about to commence service, fell back and expired in a moment. Dr. M'Gill clapped his hands together, and said—'That was very desirable; he lived all the days of his life.'"

Besides stones commemorating contemporaries of Burns, there are others of engrossing interest. One to the memory of the local martyrs mentioned in last chapter, who died for principle during the era of the Persecution, bears the following inscription:—"HERE LIES THE CORPSE OF JAMES SMITH, ALEXANDER M'MILLAN, JAMES M'MILLAN, JOHN STEWART, GEORGE M'KIRTNY, JNO. GRAHAM, AND JOHN MUIRHEAD, WHO SUFFERED MARTYRDOME AT AIR 27TH DECR., 1666, FOR THEIR ADHEREANCE TO THE WORD OF GOD AND SCOTLAND'S REFORMATION.

"THIS SMALL TRIBUTE TO THE ABOVE WAS DONE BY THE INCORPORATE TRADES OF AIR, ANNO DOMINI, 1814.

"FOR THE RIGHTEOUS SHALL BE KEEPIT IN EVERLASTING REMEMBERANCE.

"*Here lie seven martyrs for our Covenants,*
A sacred number of triumphant saints,
Pontius M'Adam th' unjust sentence past;
What is his own the world will know at last.
And Herod Drummond caus'd their heads affix,
Heaven keep a record of the fifty-six.
Boots, thumbkins, gibbits were in fashion then,
Lord let us never see such days again."

Close to the above stone is another to the memory of a Robert Cairns, shipmaster, Ayr, which bears the following quaint rhyme:—

"Though Boreas' blasts and heaving waves
   Has tost me to and fro,
Yet at the last by God's decree
   I harbour here below,

>   Where at an anchor I do rest
>   With many of our fleet,
>   Hoping for to set sail again
>   Our Admiral Christ to meet."

Before taking leave of the old church and its graveyard, a few anecdotes of Daft Rab Hamilton—a character of much local notoriety who was known the length and breadth of the shire, may be related. Although long dead, his face and figure are familiar to old people. He is described as having been an odd-like personage above the ordinary height and about sixty years of age—that was about the period of his death. He walked with a stoop and limped along with a shuffling gait, dragging as it were the one leg after the other. As to dress, he was in no way particular, for it depended very much upon chance and charity as to how he was clothed. He usually wore a battered and almost crownless hat, which he pressed down so far on his head that the upper portion of his face was all but concealed—a circumstance which caused him to blink and look upwards as if striving to peer through its rim. Although imbecile, he was quick at repartee, and often more pointed than pleasant in his remarks, but, upon the whole, inoffensive and harmless, even when "half seas over;" for he dearly lo'ed the whisky, and would, it is said, have drunk a pailful of water were he certain of securing a glass of the coveted liquid at the bottom. "Gude ale," he was not averse to, but "sour thing" he was extremely fond of, and drank amazing quantities when chance afforded.

In spite of his *penchant* for drink, Rab regularly attended church. He generally sat on the pulpit stair, and reverently listened to "the godly Maister Peebles" of the Newton, for in his estimation he was the best of preachers. On one occasion, however, he was persuaded to attend the Old Church of Ayr, and took up his position on the pulpit stair, as was his custom in what he termed his ain kirk. By some means he failed to catch the number of the psalm given out, and in his eagerness to procure the place he thrust his head through the stair rail to make the necessary enquiry at some people below. All went well; he got the information, but unfortunately, having put his head through a wide place of the rail and allowed his neck to slip down into a narrow place, he found himself fast, and although he rugged and tugged neither backward nor forward could he get. Ultimately, to the great amusement of the congregation, he yelled out, "Murder! murder! a man a-hanging in the house of God this day. Oh! that I sud hae left my ain guid, godly minister to come an' listen to an auld blether like you." Being assisted from his novel position, he picked up his hat and shuffled off, muttering that better could not have happened him for coming to hear the drones o' the auld kirk. Some time after the occurrence, Mr Auld asked him the reason of the disturbance, and having heard Rab's explanation, said, "Never mind, Robert, come again and here me preach." "Na, na," quoth he, "ye dinna preach, ye only read." Auld smiled.

On another occasion he was met by the same gentleman and asked how he was getting on. "O brawly," replied Rab, as he blinked from under the broken rim of his hat, "but I had an unco queer dream last nicht." "A dream?" said Mr Auld, "and what was it about, Robert?" "Atweel, sir," said he with a grin, "I thocht I was dead, an' that I was at the door o' heaven rappin' to get in, an' whan the door was opened the angel said, 'Whaur are ye frae?' 'Frae the toon o' Ayr,' says I. 'An' what kirk did ye gang to?' says he. 'To that o' the godly Maister Peebles o' the Newton,' said I. 'Ay, ay,' said the angel, 'come awa' in then, for there hasna been a body here frae the auld kirk o' Ayr sin' the days o' the gude Maister Walch.'" Having thus delivered himself, Rab hilched away, leaving Mr Auld to draw whatever conclusion he pleased. This dream became a favourite one and a source of profit to Rab, for he was often called upon to relate it. Once he was stopped on the New Bridge by a fop, who prevailed upon him to do so. While going on with the rehearsal, the would-be wit interrupted him at the word Heaven, and asked—"But what news from hell?" "Man," said Rab, as he laid his hand on his interrogator's shoulder, "they're expecting you there every day."

Upon one occasion a character from Glasgow named "Daft Jamie" paid a visit to Ayr, and having met with and found a kindred spirit in the redoubtable Rab, they agreed, being equally daft, to splice their odd coppers and celebrate their meeting with a drink of ale. Being "unco thick an' pack thegither," they repaired to a public house and called for a quart; but when the foaming tankard was placed before them

D

Rab laid hold of it and drank the contents without taking a breath. "There!" said he, as he placed the can on the table with a triumphant flourish, "there! that's the Ayr fashion." "An' there!" cried the astonished companion, as he picked up the empty measure and struck him a stounding blow on the head, "that's the Glasgow fashion;" and I suppose Rab thought it an odd one, but he afterwards apologised by saying that he would not have drunk the ale had he not been desirous of seeing the bonnie wee flower at the bottom.

Once when immured in the Poorhouse, Rab listened attentively to a local clergyman asking a blessing on the meagre breakfast set before the paupers. He said nothing, but seemingly thought much, for when it was concluded he edged up to the divine and dryly said—"'Deed, sir, I aye thocht there was a blessing wi' the puirshoose parritch, for when I tak a spoonfu' oot the hole aye fills up again."

Rab was very fond of money, and would have done anything for it. The offer of a coin generally caused him to smile all over; and its proper value he was fully alive to, as was shown one day when a gentleman presented a sixpence and a penny and told him to select whichever he pleased. Rab looked, smiled blandly, and said—"I'll no be greedy, I'll tak the little ane."

Waggery and poetry are often combined, and in Rab Hamilton they were not apart, for he had the reputation of being a maker of verses in a small way. It was glorious fun for the boys when they caught him on the street to compel him to jump over a straw or sing a song of his own composing. The poor fellow generally preferred the leap, but if there was no alternative he would whine, groan deeply, and cry—"Oh! de boys, de boys; oh! de boys," and then drawl away in a nasal manner at one of his favourite ditties. One was a kind of squib on a tailor who had offended him, and was entitled—"Ye ninth part o' a man." The following humorous fragment of this satire is remembered by a venerable friend of the writer who knew Rab and appreciated his drollery :—

> "Once upon a time a tailor neat an' fine
>   Spied a louse on his left shouther bane;
> He took up his shears and clippit off its ears ;
>   The louse gi'ed a roar, an' the tailor took the door ;

But he cam back wi' speed when he thocht the louse was deid:
  Hit it owre the back wi' an elwand,
An' the tailor drew stitch again, again.

Noo the tailor being crouse that he had killed a louse,
  Jumped up an' doon the floor, up an' doon the floor,
Crying—'I kill a louse, I kill a louse,'
  And what can a poor tailor do more?"

"Blackguard Jamie Jellie," as another of Rab's rhymes was styled, was composed on a small grocer who attempted to raise the price of meal during a period of great scarcity, but unfortunately it is irrecoverable, as also "Oswald's Cavalrie," a strain composed in praise of the deeds of the Ayrshire Yeomanry, who were at the time under the command of Oswald of Auchincruive. The poor demented creature's life was a hard one. He preferred to roam about and pick up a precarious livelihood rather than submit to the restraint of the poor-house. The foxes had holes and the birds of the air nests, but Rab had no fixed place of residence; he slept anywhere, and was in every sense of the word a child of chance. One night he might pass in a stable among straw, another in a hay-rick, or out of the way corner. Some days he fared sumptuously, and picked up many savoury scraps, and occasional waughts o' "sour yill," but there were others again when he scarce broke his fast. He was the only child of an excise officer, and was "born with a want." His father died when he was a stripling, and his mother—to whom, it is said, he was ardently attached—died some years afterwards. After the latter event there was no one to look after him, and he became a homeless wanderer, going hither and thither through the country as fancy directed.

After a contemplative ramble through this highly interesting churchyard, I passed through its quaint-looking porched gateway, and continued my journey.

CHAPTER VI.

THE WALLACE TOWER — THE TAM O' SHANTER INN — DROUTHIE CRONIES—SCENERY IN THE VICINITY OF AYR—THE CHAPMAN'S FORD—"THE MEIKLE STANE"—THE COT IN WHICH BURNS WAS BORN—ITS APPEARANCE AND DESECRATION—ITS ERECTION —WHEN AND HOW IT WAS TURNED INTO A PUBLIC-HOUSE— MILLAR GOUDIE—CURRAN'S VISIT—WHAT KEATS HAD TO SAY ABOUT "THE FLUMMARY OF A BIRTHPLACE"—THE FIRST BURNS CLUB.

THE name of Wallace appears to be greatly revered by the people of Ayr, for a little above Kirk Port, at the corner of a lane leading to the Ducat stream—as a ford referred to in "The Brigs of Ayr" is termed—there is a handsome Gothic tower one hundred and thirteen feet high to his memory. It is a striking object; but the lank, ungainly figure of the hero, peering from a niche in its front, is a decided failure as a work of art, for it has a closer resemblance to an inebriated individual assuming a sober appearance than to the burly wight who

"Dared to nobly stem tyrannic pride."

An old tower, with which several juvenile traditions of Wallace are connected, occupied the site, but in an attempt to repair it the walls gave way, and the whole was removed to ensure the safety of the lieges. It was a rude square block with arrow slits, and possibly was some place of strength in former times, for its situation was close to the site of a port or gate of the town. That Wallace was imprisoned in it is possible, but there is no authority but oral tradition for the statement.

A short distance above this memorial tower, and on the same side of High Street, an antique thatched-covered public house attracts attention. It is two storeys in height, and has a large oil painting over its doorway, the subject of which is Tam o' Shanter taking leave of his friend, Souter Johnnie. Tam is mounted on his mare Meg, and is gesticulating with his cronie, who, to all appearance, has somewhat more than "a wee drap in his e'e," while the landlord holds aloft a lantern, and the landlady shelters in the doorway. The daub is good enough in its way, but the following announcement is the bait to lure customers:—"THE HOUSE WHEREIN TAM O' SHANTER AND THE SOUTER HELD THEIR MEETINGS. CHAIRS AND CAUP ARE IN THE HOUSE." Now, what pilgrim to the land of Burns could resist the temptation of having a bicker of ale in what is stated to be the veritable house wherein " the Souter tauld his queerest stories," and Tam o' Shanter got "o'er a' the ills o' life victorious?" So it must be confessed that I yielded to temptation and entered, notwithstanding the fact that I have often looked upon relics which had the appearance of having been manufactured to serve the purpose. Being met on the threshold by a courteous, neatly-attired young lady, I was conducted up a narrow staircase, and ushered into a low-roofed oblong apartment in which a merry group of lads and lasses were seated, who to all appearance were "out for the day." A reaming measure being placed before me, I began to look round, and was not a little surprised to find the walls literally covered with pictures illustrating scenes in the life and writings of Burns, and also with masonic emblems sufficient to satisfy the most enthusiastic brother of "the mystic tie." From these my eyes wandered to the far end of the room, where, in a darkened window, stood a life-sized bust of Burns, and before it a small table with a quaint arm chair on each side, with brass plates affixed to their backs bearing quotations from "Tam o' Shanter," and the affirmation that the one was the favourite seat of the redoubtable Tam and the other that of his friend the Souter. There was also a moderately-sized silver-hooped wooden caup out of which the celebrated topers are said to have quaffed the "reaming swats that drank divinely," which was being merrily pushed about by the company referred to, but not in a selfish manner, for it was handed me, and I had the pleasure of drinking to the memory of Tam and the Souter. In the course of conversation I more than hinted that I was doubtful of the authenticity of the caup and chairs, but my scepticism being scouted, I took my departure rejoicing that the genius of Robert Burns exercises such an influence over the hearts of his countrymen that the remotest thing connected with him and his writings commands reverence.

That Burns had real personages in his eye when he wrote "Tam o' Shanter" has never been disputed, but who the personages were was long a matter of dispute, and, in fact, various individuals have been vain enough to aspire to the dubious honour of being one or other of the leading characters in the poem. However, this identity is now fully established, for it is agreed by all parties that Douglas Graham of Shanter—a farm between Turnberry and Culzean—was none other than the redoubtable Tam, and that his "drouthy cronie," Souter Johnny, was a shoemaker named John Davidson who dwelt in the immediate neighbourhood of the Shanter farm. Besides farming, Graham dealt in malt (for publicans brewed their own ale at the period) and to the business of shoemaking Davidson added that of a "dealer in leather." Being big men in a small way, their avocations brought them very often to Ayr, which then, as now, was the market town, and on such journeys they generally bore each other company. Davidson, after transacting his own business, often accompanied his neighbour, the malster, through his customers, for in every shop where he made a sale he was in the habit of calling a gill for "the good of the house," and to show gratitude for orders received. Having more liquor on these occasions than he could well make use of, there is little wonder

"That frae November till October
Ae market day *he* wasna sober,"

and was glad of the Souter or any other person to help him to consume it. Now, like all who tipple at the "barley bree," Graham had a favourite call-house—a tavern (possibly the one mentioned) at which he regularly put up. It was kept by a Carrick man named Benjamin Graham, who occasionally shared the good things of his table with them. To make some slight return for this hospitality, Graham and Davidson resolved to have "a nicht o't" at his house, and give him a treat in return. The time appointed arrived, and found the guidman o' Shanter

> "Planted unco richt,
> Fast by an ingle, bleezing finely,
> Wi' reaming swats, that drank divinely,
> And at his elbow Souter Johnny—
> His ancient, trusty, drouthy crony."

The social hours winged past, and about "the wee short hour ayont the twal" Graham mounted his mare and started home alone, amid a storm of wind and rain. When crossing Carrick Hills his bonnet blew off, but he was too far gone to recover it, it being as much as he could do to keep on the mare's back. Being "sensible drunk," however, he noted the place it fell, resolving to return and recover it before people stirred, for in its lining were secreted the bank-notes he had drawn the day before. Mrs. Graham was of a very superstitious turn of mind, and to account for the loss of his bonnet Tam trumped up a story about having seen a dance of witches in Alloway Kirk, and of being chased by them to the Bridge of Doon, where, thanks to the mare, he escaped with the loss of his bonnet. That there was a row in the farmhouse of Shanter no one need doubt; but the domestic storm would likely be allayed when the bonnet was found in a whin bush next morning with its contents uninjured.

This, courteous reader, according to Chambers and local authority, is the myth-divested story of Tam o' Shanter. Burns knew Graham, and doubtless heard of the exploit when he resided with his uncle at Ballochneil and attended school at Kirkoswald. Although but nineteen years of age then, he got introduced to the half-farming, half-smuggling class in the district—of whom the guidman o' Shanter was a specimen, and, to use his own words, "Here he first learned to fill his glass and to mix without fear in a drunken squabble."

Upon leaving the Tam o' Shanter inn I gleefully sped on to the birthplace of Burns, to

> "Gaze on the scenes he loved and sung,
> And gather feelings not of earth,
> His fields and streams among."

What a din there is at the top of the High Street of Ayr on a fine day! Every conceivable vehicle, and every skinful of bones about the town resembling a horse, seems to be brought into requisition to convey visitors to and from the monument on the banks of Doon. The car-men have quick eyes, and intuitively single out strangers from the passers by, but to their cry of "The Monument, the Monument!" I turned a deaf ear, and strove to get beyond the precincts of the town as quickly as possible; for dearer far to me are the hedge-bordered, foliage-shaded highways and byways of the open country, than the rattling of wheels and the busy hum of life in those hives of industry called towns. Gradually the business portion of Ayr was left behind, and the suburbs reached. Passing the cattle-market, and on through a toll-bar, and by several neat villa residences, a gorgeous natural panorama—which I enjoyed for some time as I strolled along—burst upon my vision. In the distance, Carrick Hill spread its brown bosom to the sunshine and formed a most romantic background to the wood-interspersed scene which lay between it and the town. The blue waters of the Frith and the wave-washed isle of Arran in the far distance, and the rugged margin of the bay sweeping into dim perspective, with the old castle of Greenan frowning over the surge "like a monarch, gray and grim," went to make up a scene of beauty which was doubly interesting from its historic and poetic associations. Of course the face of the country and the characteristics of the locality have undergone a great change since Burns wrote the glowing piece of descriptive imagery, but there are sufficient landmarks remaining to indicate the route pursued by worthy Tam o' Shanter, as he

> "Skelpit on through dub and mire,
> Despising wind, and rain, and fire;
> Whyles holding fast his guid blue bonnet;
> Whyles crooning o'er some auld Scotch sonnet;
> Whyles glow'ring round wi' prudent cares
> Lest bogles catch him unawares."

At Slaphouse—a neat farm-steading near the wayside—the road makes a gradual descent and passes over a bridge through which a burnie flows as it wimples on its way to the sea. Some 150 yards below the spot the celebrated

> ———— "Ford,
> Where in the snaw the chapman smoor'd,"

is still pointed out and shows that the road Burns had in his mind when penning "Tam o' Shanter" ran in a more westerly direction than the present modern and probably more commodious highway. After resting on the parapet of the bridge for a space, I moved slowly forward, but again stopped before proceeding many yards to note another point in the route of "honest Tam." It was the

——"Meikle stane
Where drucken Charlie brak's neck-bane."

This stone rests in a small garden which lies behind a rustic cottage and is easily perceived from the road, being little more than twenty yards distant. That an individual, who was oftener "the waur o't" than was either good for soul or body, actually broke his neck by stumbling over the obstacle when in such a condition that he could scarce

"Free the ditches,
Or hillocks, stanes, and bushes, ken aye
Frae ghaists and witches,"

tradition states; but who or what he was no one at this date knows. Having tarried rather long by the above-mentioned objects, I stepped out to make up for lost time. Machines to and from the Monument passed in quick succession and many pedestrians rubbed shoulders with me on the narrow footpath,

"For roads were clad frae side to side
Wi' mony a weary body
In droves that day."

I enjoyed the scenery very much as I plodded slowly along, holding converse with Nature and my own heart, feeling thankful that I was released from the cankering cares of life for the time being. When about two miles from town, the rounding of a slight curve in the road brought me somewhat unexpectedly to a row of humble cottages clustering together on the right hand side of the highway. The clanking of an anvil made known that a "Burnewin" was hard at work, and that some one was bringing

"Hard ower hip, wi' sturdy wheel,
The strong forehammer,
Till block and study ring and ree
Wi' dinsome clamour."

As I passed his door, I saw the flaming forge and heard the bellows blow; but did not linger, for—by the animated scene in front of a straw-covered cot a few yards off—I knew that I had reached the birthplace of Robert Burns, the bard whose name has gone forth through all countries. Indeed, while gazing on the bit biggin' and the fields which lie around it, I felt that I knew the poet better, and could hold closer converse with him than in his pages.

"The Cottage," as it is termed, is a low-roofed, one-storeyed structure of a very humble order, with rudely-lettered sign-boards on its front, of which the following is a facsimile :—

BURNS' COTTAGE.
ROBERT BURNS, THE AYRSHIRE POET,
WAS BORN UNDER THIS ROOF
ON THE 25TH JANUARY, A.D. 1759.
DIED 21ST JULY, A.D. 1796,
AGED 37½ YEARS.

A. HUNTER,

LICENSED TO RETAIL

WINES,

SPIRITS, & ALES,

The sound of mirth,

"And the loud laugh that spoke the vacant mind,"

issued from the interior as I entered and was shown into a small whitewashed, plainly-furnished apartment on the right, from which a company of holiday seekers were making their exit. The place was impregnated with the fumes of tobacco and whisky, but with my mind full of its associations I threw myself into a chair, laid aside my hat and stick, and began to look round.

The tables were strewn with empty measures and glasses, and swam with spilled liquor; but the most noticeable feature was that every portion of walls and ceiling were covered with names and addresses in pencil. Indeed, the very furniture was cut and initialed with jack-knives in a very wanton manner, and one table was so much hacked that it would have been difficult to have found space for another letter of the alphabet. Notwithstanding this scrawling on the walls, and the fact that repeated layers of whitewash concealed coatings of names, the room was scrupulously clean, and presented a rather tidy appearance.

A glance at the neatly-attired damsel who entered to attend to my wants was sufficient to convince me we had met before, but where I could not call to mind, nor did I until she mentioned the name of my family physician. In this instance the simple fact of being known was of immense service, for it not only procured a formal introduction to the amiable landlady, but the liberty of viewing the house and gathering such information regarding it and the district as is not usually accorded to strangers.

From the room described I passed into the memorial, or shrowroom, for it is fitted up with a counter and glass cases, in which are displayed photographs of the poet, albums, and a great assortment of ornaments "made of wood which grew on the banks of Doon," any of which can be purchased by visitors for a trifle, and carried away as souvenirs of a visit to a Mecca to which thousands of pilgrims annually flock. Here also is kept a ponderous "visitors' book," whose closely-written pages contain names by the thousand, which have been inscribed by individuals in all ranks of life and from all parts of the world. Truly great indeed is the genius of the peasant poet when the noble, the wise, and the beautiful come from all countries as pilgrims to the place of his birth.

After looking round the memorial chamber, I was next conducted to the most hallowed part of the cottage—namely, the kitchen, for in it, on a humble pallet, Robert Burns was ushered into the world. Its walls echoed the first tones of his voice, and its spacious hearth was the altar round which William Burness and his family assembled to hymn the Creator's praise. The bed in which the poet was born is in a recess in the wall, it being in Scotch parlance "set in." The fireplace is in its original form, but otherwise alterations of all kinds have been made in and about the cottage, which have materially interfered with its original appearance. With the exception of an old dresser which belonged to the poet's father there are no relics of importance shown.

This lowly kitchen has many associations. In it

"A blast o' Janwar win'
Blew hansel in on Robin."

and that so lustily that it threw down the gable of the house and whistled through the apartment in which the new-born poet lay in his mother's bosom. In it, too, the wayfaring gipsy "keekit" in his tiny loof, and predicted that whoever lived would

> "See the proof—
> The waly boy wad be nae coof,
> And thought they'd ca' him Robin."

Yes, and chalked out his future career pretty accurately—that is, if we are to believe what tradition and the "rantin', rovin' boy" have told us about the event. In it he spent the first seven years of his life, and gambolled and sported on its floor with youthful companions, and when his mind began to expand listened to old Betty Davidson as she unfolded her legendary store of ghost and witch stories.

While standing on the centre of the floor in silent contemplation I felt ashamed and humiliated that this humble but celebrated shrine of genius is converted into a common drinking shop—that it is the resort of the drunken, the thoughtless: yea of people who are incited by no higher feeling than that of vulgar curiosity. One freight of boisterous visitors no sooner left than another arrived. They wandered unceremoniously through the rooms, smoked, spat, and drank whisky in the kitchen, and behaved in such an unbecoming manner that I felt glad when the obliging hostess beckoned and ushered me into a handsome apartment designated "the hall." This spacious and beautifully fitted up room is an addition to the cottage, and was added with the idea of increasing its accommodation and extending its usefulness as an inn or house of entertainment. Its first stone was laid with masonic honours by the late much respected Maxwell Dick, Esq., Deputy Grand Master of Mother Kilwinning, on the 25th January, 1849. and since then its walls have rung with the mirth and plaudits of many a social gathering, and echoed many a eulogistic piece of eloquence in honour of the bard.

A very notable, and, it may be added, one of the most enthusiastic companies ever assembled in it was that which celebrated the Burns Centenary in 1859. The Rev. Hately Waddell presided on the occasion, and delivered a long and eloquent speech on the genius and character of him who could

> "alternately impart
> Wisdom and rapture in *his* page,
> And brand each vice with satire strong."

Besides a copy of the above oration, and six portraits and a bust of Burns, the walls are crowded with pictures illustrative of his writings, and with neatly framed pieces of verse composed in his honour or to his memory. Many of these are of considerable merit, but the most noteworthy are, "To a rose from Alloway Kirk," by Fitz Green Hallock; "Stanzas to the memory of Burns," by Eliza Cook; and "Lines written in Burns' Cottage," by R. S. Bowie, V.D.M., Dunfermline, which I quote.

LINES WRITTEN IN BURNS' COTTAGE.

> O Burns! the matchless, deathless, and divine,
> Here in the "cottage" to thy mem'ry dear,
> We sit and ponder o'er that life of thine
> Which oft hath made us shed the silent tear.
> O Bard of Scotia!—nay, of all the earth—
> Here pilgrims from all lands together meet
> To do obeisance at the shrine of worth;
> Here strangers rest and hold communion sweet
> With those ne'er known before, because of thee!
> O! how thy songs can melt auld Scotland's faes,
> And make them in her sons their brothers see;
> Aye, e'en the flowers that bloom on Doon's sweet braes
> Are loved and honoured for the poet's sake,
> And in our hearts their best emotions wake.*

It need scarce be chronicled that I lingered some time in this apartment examining the many interesting objects which it contains, or that I drank to the immortal memory of of Burns before leaving. But as "nae man can tether time or tide," I was compelled reluctantly to depart, for several miles had to be traversed before "a blink o' my ain fireside" would be obtained. When taking leave of my new friends at the cottage door, I was surprised at the number of

---

* Besides this neat sonnet, Mr. Bowie is the author of many highly meritorious pieces of verse, and has given to the world a small volume, entitled "Fireside Lyrics;" also, a Hymnal "respectfully dedicated to all who believe in the fatherhood of God and the brotherhood of man," which contains many pieces from his pen of a truly graceful and devotional character which will bear favourable comparison with the productions of our best hymn writers. It is a pity that he is so little known.

visitors passing in and out, and at the number who lovingly lingered "ower a wee drappie o't." By a side glance I noticed that the room I first entered was full, and that while stentorian voices sang "There was a lad was born in Kyle,"

> " Drink gaed round in cogs and caups
> Among the forms and benches :
> And cheese and bread frae women's laps
> Was dealt about in lunches
> And dauds that day."

My thoughts and opinions are of little consequence, but I must give expression to them in this instance. A mausoleum in St. Michael's Churchyard, Dumfries, has been reared to the memory of our national poet, as also statues in Edinburgh, Glasgow, and America, not to speak of the beautiful monuments on the banks of the Doon and at Kilmarnock. All this has been done by the liberality of his countrymen, but why the cot wherein he first drew the breath of life has not been rescued and raised to something better than a road-side public house I know not. Englishmen have done for Shakespere what Scotchmen have failed to do for Burns—they have saved his birthplace from degradation and secured it not only for the present age but for posterity. Why is this? Can the banks of the Avon be considered more sacred than those of " bonnie Doon" and gurgling Ayr ? Certainly not ; so the sooner the clay biggin' is retrieved from its present position the better, or else people of good taste and feeling will begin to look upon it with disgust. A brief summary of the history of the cottage will form a fitting conclusion to this chapter.

Some time after settling in Ayrshire, William Burness, the poet's father, wooed and won the daughter of a Carrick farmer named Agnes Brown. Before being united to her he leased seven acres of land, and built upon it, with his own hands, a house wherein to lodge his bride. The walls were of clay, and the roof of thatch ; but to convey to the reader an accurate description of " the biggin'," it will be as well to quote what Gilbert Burns has said regarding it in a communication to Dr. Currie :—" That you may not think too meanly of this house, or my father's taste in building, by supposing the poet's description in the " Vision " (which is entirely a fancy picture) applicable to it, allow me to take notice to you that the house consisted of a kitchen in one end and a room in the other, with a fireplace and chimney; and that my father had constructed a concealed bed in the kitchen, with a small closet at the end, of the same materials with the house, and when altogether cast over, outside and in, with lime, it had a neat comfortable appearance, such as no family of the same rank, in the present improved style of living, would think themselves ill-lodged in." To this humble edifice, in December, 1757, William Burness led his bride, and in thirteen months thereafter, within its precincts, Robert Burns their illustrious son was born. When William Burness leased the ground, he did so with the idea of carrying on business as a market gardener, but this he shortly afterwards abandoned, and became gardener on the estate of Doonholm. After an eight years' residence in "the clay biggin'," the worthy man removed with his family to Mount Oliphant, a cold-soiled farm about two miles distant, but after a twelve years' struggle with poverty and a bad bargain, he removed to Lochlea—a more genial farm in the parish of Tarbolton. Either from straitened circumstances or a desire to break his connection with the district of Alloway, he then disposed of the cottage and grounds to the corporation of shoemakers in Ayr for £120, and to them it still belongs.* Since the days of Burns the clay cot has undergone may changes, and, as already stated, is now incorporated with other buildings similar in construction and appearance.

The idea of turning the cottage into a public-house originated in the fertile brain of a person known as "Miller Goudie." He was born at Riccarton Mill on the banks of the Irvine, a short distance from Kilmarnock, but at an early age left the paternal roof and settled in Alloway, having obtained employment in the mill of that district. He married a sharp little woman named Flora Hastings, who made good the old adage, that "The grey mare is often the better horse." After their union they started "The sign of the bush" in a small thatched cottage that stood close to the auld brig o' Doon, and continued in it for a long series of years, but about the beginning of the present century, in response to what was to them a lucky idea, they removed their business to Burns cottage, and turned the interest it possesses in the eyes of

---

* Its present rental is £110 a year.

travellers into a profitable speculation, and since then it has continued to be a house of entertainment. Flora took care of the cash and managed the business, and left her husband no other duty to perform than that of helping customers to consume surplus liquor. The consequence was that he was seldom or ever sober, and must have been in his wonted state of inebriety when Curran, the Irish orator, visited the cot in 1810. "We found," says he in his account of the visit, "the keeper of it tipsy. He pointed to the corner on one side of the fire, and, with a most *mal-a-propos* laugh, observed—'There is the very spot where Robert Burns was born.' The genius and the fate of the man were already heavy on my heart; but the drunken laugh of the landlord gave me such a view of the rock on which he foundered, I could not stand it, but burst into tears." Since then full many a sympathetic admirer of the poet's genius has shared the same feelings, and left the place overcome with disgust and shame.

On a lovely July morning in 1818, John Keats, the poet, walked from Maybole to Ayr. As he crossed Carrick hills and came down by the old bridge of Doon, he was fairly enchanted with the scenery; but, alas! his enthusiasm received a check when he crossed the threshold of the cottage. "A prophet," he writes, "is no prophet in his own country. We went to the cottage, and took some whisky. I wrote a sonnet for the mere sake of writing some lines under the roof: they are so bad I cannot transcribe them. The man at the cottage was a great bore with his anecdotes. I hate the rascal. His life consists in fuzy, fuzzy, fuzziest. He drinks glasses, five for the quarter, and twelve for the hour; he is a mahogany-faced old jackass who knew Burns: he ought to have been kicked for having spoken to him. He calls himself 'a curious old ———,' but he is a flat old dog. I should like to employ Caleb Vathek to kick him. Oh, the flummary of a birthplace!" "The Miller" appeared sensibly clear on one point, and that was that he had often seen and conversed with the poet. "The last time I saw him," he used to tell, "was whan he cam' through frae Dumfries to tak' his fareweel o' here awa. We met roun' by the auld kirk-yard dyke there, and he was walkin' unco slow an' dowie like. We gaed down to my bit house beside the auld brig an' had just three gills, but I drank the maist o' them, for he spak' little, an' only askit a question noo an' than about auld ne'bours as he sat wi' his brow restin' on his hand." There was little wonder that the greater portion of the three gills fell to "the miller," for the thoughts that passed through the mind of Burns on the occasion must have been of the most saddening description.

"The miller" died in 1843, at the advanced age of eighty. His wife survived him a few years. Any reader wishing to see what the old couple looked like may turn up Blackie's edition of Burns, where correct portraits of them will be found in the picture of "John Anderson my Joe, John."

The first meeting to celebrate the anniversary of the Poet's birth was held in the cottage on the 25th January, 1801. The Rev. Hamilton Paul, who was present, says :—"The party was small but select, and formed a most interesting group from the circumstance of nearly one half of the company having their names associated with some of the most gratifying particulars in the poet's history. The meeting consisted of the following friends and admirers of their far famed countryman : —William Crawford, Esq. of Doonside, by whose father the father of Burns had been employed in the capacity of a gardener; John Ballantyne, Esq., to whom Burns addressed 'The Twa Brigs;' Robert Aitken, Esq., to whom he dedicated 'The Cottar's Saturday Night;' Patrick Douglas, Esq. of Garallan, by whose interest he was to have obtained a situation in Jamaica had he followed out his intention of repairing to that island; Primrose Kennedy, Esq. of Drumellan; Hew Ferguson, Esq., Barrackmaster, Ayr; David Scott, Esq., Banker, Ayr; Thomas Jackson, Esq., LL.D., Professor of Natural Philosophy in the University of St. Andrews; and the Rev. Hamilton Paul." This, the oldest Burns Club, is still in existence, and meets annually in the hall attached to "The Cottage" to

"Honour Scotia's Bard,
And toast his name with feelings warm,
For oh! though many a lyre is heard,
'Tis his that yields the sweetest charm."

The business carried on in "the cottage" has changed hands several times since the decease of "Miller Goudie," but no landlord appears to have thriven by it. One is said to have shot himself, and another to have cut his throat. The land belonging to it is curtailed to five acres, and a sum of £3000, it is affirmed, has been asked for the whole. Some gentlemen, I am informed, offered £2000 for the house and land, in order that they may be kept in a creditable manner, and that the cottage of the pious father of the "Cottar's Saturday Night" may be saved from further degradation. Unfortunately, they failed to procure it; but I trust the time is not far distant when the classic little property will fall into the hands of some respectable person, instead of being continued as a low public house, the disgust of the neighbourhood and of all strangers visiting a spot hallowed by so many interesting and affecting associations.

[The birthplace of Burns is now (February 1879) in the hands of Mr Thomas Morley, a retired soldier—and very curiously an Englishman—who deserves more than a passing notice, from the circumstance that he took part in the charge of the Light Brigade at Balaclava, and with the last remnant of that ill-fated squadron under his command cut his way through the Russian lines and rejoined the British forces when the blundering order which almost annihilated his regiment had been fulfilled. Finding that this and other heroic achievements performed by him during the arduous campaign were slightingly passed over by the War Department, he joined the American Army, and during the civil war of that country rose to the post of Captain. When peace was restored, he returned to this country and became Regimental Sergeant-Major of the Ayrshire Yeomanry Cavalry, and latterly tenant of "The Cottage." Under his judicious management, drink is no longer dispensed within its precincts, but is wholly confined to the adjoining slated house, where all visitors desirous of indulging must consume their potations.]

CHAPTER VII.

FROM "THE COTTAGE" TO MOUNT OLIPHANT—THE APPEARANCE OF THE STEADING—GOSSIP, ETC.—PRIVATIONS ENDURED BY THE PARENTS OF BURNS WHEN RESIDING AT MOUNT OLIPHANT—THE POET'S FIRST SWEETHEART — THE FLITTING — "THE FESTIVAL" ON THE BANKS OF THE DOON—ALLOWAY KIRK—A LEGEND—THE GRAVE OF THE POET'S FATHER—OLD STONES.

FROM December, 1757, to Whitsunday, 1766, the parents of Robert Burns lived a contented, happy, and comparatively prosperous life in the cottage, and would have continued to do so had they not been ambitious to improve their condition and make a better provision for their family. In an evil hour his father resolved to become a farmer, and with this object in view applied to Mr. Ferguson of Doonholm—to whom he had proved a faithful servant—for a lease of Mount Oliphant, a then tenantless farm on his estate. The request was generously granted, but with its acceptance a series of misfortunes commenced which pursued the worthy man to his grave.

Being aware that this farm is only some two miles distant from the poet's natal cot, I resolved to visit it, and for the purpose turned into a pleasant rural lane which branches off the highway some fifty yards beyond the celebrated "biggin'." As the braes over which this old lane winds is climbed, the landscape becomes more varied and picturesque, and a wide expanse of country lies around, which, when once seen, can never be forgotten. Even now I can picture it, and in fancy scan the view. Yonder are the heights of Arran towering from the glistening bay; nearer are the Heads of Ayr, and the old Castle of Greenan standing out on the verge of the wave, while stretching inland are the brown rugged hills of Carrick, and on the table land below the shady woods of Newark, Doonholm, and Mountcharles, with their mansion-houses peering above the tree-tops; but the most interesting of all the objects on which the eye rests is the cottage in which the poet was born, the monument to his memory, and "Alloway's auld haunted Kirk," the scene of Tam o' Shanter's adventure with the witches.

There is no saying how romantic one might become over a delightful prospect; but, suffice it to say, a broad traffic-worn cross road was soon reached by whose side a burnie murmured, and along which a man was driving a flock of sheep. Here I rested on a small stone bridge over which the lane passes, and looking down into a clear brook, listened to its sweet babbling music, and the birds singing in gladsome minstrelsy in the rich foliage draping the bank. After lingering by the delightful scene for a space, a sharp uphill walk brought me to a by-road which proved rugged and steep, and ultimately to Mount Oliphant, the farm on which the parents of our poet toiled and suffered for the long period of eleven years.

The humble buildings which constitute this steading are compactly built round a spacious quadrangular courtyard, opening to the road, but there is nothing about them to interest the visitor. A number of hens were gathered round the kitchen door, clucking and cackling over the corn which a rosy-faced, bare-armed milk-girl was throwing them, and a collie, not unlike the one whose

> "honest, sonsie, baws'nt face,
> Aye gat him friends in ilka place,"

lay basking in the sun. As I approached it rose, and after sniffing curiously about me, began to fawn and frisk in such a way that I wished him at a safe distance. How far this familiarity would have extended it is hard to say had not an elderly dame appeared on the scene and told him to "gang an' lie doun"—an order which, to all appearance, he intended to obey when it suited him. To my question, "Is there aught of interest here in connection with Robert Burns?" she replied—"'Deed no. There used to be an auld crab-tree at the mouth o' the close there that he used to play below when he was a bairn, but it was blawn doun ae windy nicht short syne. The house, did you say? Weel, like every ither thing it's changed too, an' I dinna think there's a stane stan'in' that was in it in his father's time." To all appearance the statement was true, so the reader need not be troubled with more than the burden of our conversation. During the summer months they have many visitors, "maistly gentry," and one man, she affirmed, who had been sent by some society in America to view the place, was so enthusiastic that he sat in the kitchen and wrote for upwards of an hour, and told them things about Burns and his parents that they never knew. "He was an extraordinar' body," she remarked, "an' muckle ta'en up wi' everything here awa." According to her, the rent of Mount Oliphant is seventy pounds a year. The poet's father had it at forty-five pounds, and found it all but impossible to wring the amount from the ungenial glebe, but now, with an improved system of husbandry, the first-mentioned sum is considered the reverse of excessive.

From its elevated situation Mount Oliphant is conspicuous from a great distance, and consequently commands a wide range of scenery which has undergone very little change since the boy poet wandered in its midst. Indeed the eye of man has seldom rested on a more pleasing or extensive prospect than that witnessed from this eminence. Beautiful as it is, however, it brought neither peace nor contentment to the Burns' family. The soil of Mount Oliphant was poor and the rent high, and, to add to the discomfiture of a bad bargain, they entered upon it burdened with a debt of a hundred pounds. Hard labour and rigid economy were vainly opposed to the tide of misfortune by which they were overtaken, but allow Gilbert Burns, the poet's brother, to tell the sorrowful tale in his candid, simple way. In a letter to Mrs Dunlop, he says: "For several years butcher's meat was a stranger in the house, while all the members of the family exerted themselves to the utmost of their strength, and rather beyond it, in the labours of the farm. My brother, at the age of thirteen, assisted in thrashing the crop of corn, and at fifteen was the principal labourer on the farm, for we had no hired servant, male or female. The anguish of mind we felt at our tender years, under these straits and difficulties, was very great. To think of our father growing old (for he was now above fifty), broken down with the long-continued fatigues of his life, with a wife and five other children, and in a declining state of circumstances—these reflections produced in my brother's mind and mine sensations of the deepest distress." Notwithstanding incessant labour, and the retrenchment of expenses, the worthy father managed to give his boys several snatches of education, and by the time Robert was twelve years of age he was "a critic in substantives, verbs, and particles."

It was at Mount Oliphant that our poet first "committed the sin of rhyme." He says—

> "Amaist as soon as I could spell,
> I to the crambo-jingle fell,
>   Though rude and rough;
> Yet crooning to a body's sel'
>   Does weel enough."

And again, in some noble verses, we have the following passage:—

> "I mind it weel in early date,
> When I was beardless, young, and blate,
>   And first could thrash the barn,
> Or haud a yoking at the plough;
> An' tho' forfoughten sair enough,
>   Yet unco proud to learn;
> When first amang the yellow corn
>   A man I reckoned was,
> An' wi' the lave ilk merry morn
>   Could rank my rig and lass:
>   Still shearing and clearing
>   The ither stookit raw,
>   Wi' clavers and havers
>   Wearing the day awa.
>
> "E'en then a wish (I mind its power),
> A wish that to my latest hour
>   Shall strongly heave my breast,
> That I for poor old Scotland's sake
> Some usefu' plan or beuk could make,
>   Or sing a sang at least.
>   The rough bur-thistle, spreading wide
>   Amang the bearded bere,
>   I turn'd the weeder-clips aside,
>   And spared the symbol dear."

He speaks here of ranking his "rig and lass." Who was the lass? Let us see. In a letter to Dr. Moore he says—"You know our country custom of coupling a man and woman together as partners in the labours of harvest. In my fifteenth autumn my partner was a bewitching creature, a year younger than myself. My scarcity of English denies me the power of doing her justice in that language; but you know the Scottish idiom, 'she was a bonnie sweet sonsie lass.' In short, she altogether, unwittingly to herself, initiated me in that delicious passion which, in spite of acid disappointment, gin-horse prudence, and book-worm philosophy, I hold to be the first of human joys, our dearest blessing here below! How she caught the contagion I cannot tell. You medical people talk much of infection from breathing the same air, the touch, &c.; but I never expressly said I loved her. Indeed, I did not know myself why I liked so much to loiter behind with her, when returning in the evening from our labours; why the tones of her voice made my heart-strings thrill like an Æolian harp; and, particularly why my pulse beat such a furious ratan when I looked and fingered over her little hand to pick out the cruel nettle-stings and thistles. Among her other love-inspiring qualities she sang sweetly; and it was her favourite reel to which I attempted giving an embodied vehicle in rhyme. I was not so presumptuous as to imagine that I could make verses like printed ones, composed by men that had Greek and Latin; but my girl sang a song which was said to be composed by a country laird's son, on one of his father's maids, with whom he was in love; and I saw no reason why I might not rhyme as well as he; for, excepting that he could smear sheep and cast peats, his father living in the moorlands, he had no more scholar-craft than myself. Thus with me began love and poetry." Yes, they were kindled on the braeside of Mount Oliphant, and burned brightly until quenched by the cold hand of death in the little tenement in Mill Street, Dumfries.

The damsel, so affectionately referred to in the above extract, was named Nelly Kilpatrick, and although, in after years, he characterised the song in her praise as "a very puerile and silly performance," it contains several good lines, as the following will show:—

"A bonnie lass, I will confess,
 Is pleasant to the e'e,
But without some better qualities
 She's no the lass for me.

"But Nelly's looks are blythe and sweet,
 An', what is best of a',
Her reputation is complete,
 An' fair without a flaw.

"She dresses aye sae clean and neat,
 Both decent and genteel,
An' then there's something in her gait
 Gars ony dress look weel."

The difficulties and privations undergone by the parents of

the poet while on this farm served to bring out the sterling qualities of their gifted son, for he shrank not from sharing their hardships and doing his utmost to alleviate them. He, the child of poverty and toil, when a mere boy, performed the work of a man, and when his compeers in the towns and villages were attending school and fully occupied with the games and pursuits of youth, he followed the plough, or made the grain dance under his flail on the barn floor.

In 1777 the poet's father succeeded in ridding himself of the lease which bound him to the sterile soil of Mount Oliphant, and removed to Lochlea—a farm in the parish of Tarbolton. The Rev. Hately Waddel gives a beautiful imaginative description of the "flitting" in his elaborate edition of the poet's works. It is as follows:—"Best tables, chairs, and presses piled carefully aloft on all available carts or cars about the steading; friendly neighbours assisting with horses and gear; Agnes and the 'weans' securely nestled among bedding and straw; Robert or his father at the horse's head, solemn; and Gilbert with 'Luath' at his heels contemplative, like the forerunners of the patriarch, in charge of the 'beiss' before. Thus marshalled in succession, they take leave of Mount Oliphant in the morning—a blossom or two torn off from the old crab tree in the close for a keepsake, as they go; and pitch, after noon, at Lochlea."

There are many pleasant rambles in the vicinity of Mount Oliphant to repay those who have time to seek for them. For my part, I retraced my steps, and in a short time found myself once more in the vicinity of the cottage in which Robert Burns was born. People hurried out and in its door, and flocked past to view the classic scenes in its immediate vicinity, but my mind was too much occupied to notice their various peculiarities, so, with a last fond look at the lowly dwelling, I leisurely strolled towards Alloway Kirk, which I found to be something less than a quarter of a mile distant. When it is first sighted, it bears a closer resemblance to a roofless barn than a time-shattered sanctuary; but with Hew Ainslie it may be said—

> "Alloway, that night ye were
> Hell's place o' recreation—
> Baith heez'd an' dignified ye mair
> Than a' your consecration.

> "The bit whar fornicators sat
>   To bide their pastor's bang
> Is now forgotten for the spat
>   Whar Nanny lap an' flang.
>
> "The pu'pit whar the gude Mess John
>   His wig did weekly wag,
> Is lightlied for the bunker seat
>   Whar Satan blew his bag."

Yes, the old building is hallowed by the muse of Burns, and on that account is better known throughout the civilized world than Melrose Abbey and other ecclesiastical edifices whose sculpture-bedecked walls lie prostrate at the feet of Time.

As I moved towards the celebrated ruin, I passed the field in which the first public demonstration in honour of Burns took place. It occurred on Tuesday, the 6th August, 1844, and was attended by a concourse of 80,000 persons of all ranks and conditions in life, who had come from all parts of the United Kingdom to do honour to the memory of the ploughman poet. A temporary erection of sufficient dimensions to accommodate 2000 individuals was put up in the field, as also tents wherein visitors could obtain rest and refreshments; but the gathering together of the greater bulk of the vast assemblage took place in the Low Green, Ayr, at ten o'clock forenoon. There the various societies taking part in the demonstration formed in procession, and with their bands, banners, and devices marched to the place of festivity. To quote from a report of the proceedings published in Glasgow at the time:—

"When fully marshalled, the immense body moved onwards, the bands striking up the well-known air of 'A man's a man for a' that,' along the south side of Wellington Square. The procession was formed three deep, and extended nearly a mile in length. It had a very imposing effect. On going down Sandgate, up the High Street, and on to the Maybole road, every window was thronged with onlookers, and the streets were densely crowded. As they proceeded, the bands played the national airs of 'Green grow the rashes,' 'This is no' my ain house,' 'My love she's but a lassie yet,' 'Wat ye wha's in yon town,' &c. The road all along was greatly crowded; so much so that it was with difficulty the mass

could keep moving. The walls, houses, and gates were everywhere lined with anxious observers, and various platforms were constructed for the accommodation of ladies. On approaching the cottage where the poet was born, and where, as already mentioned, a splendid triumphal arch was erected, the bands struck up 'There was a lad was born in Kyle;' and the procession, uncovering, lowered their flags as they passed the humble but much endeared spot. . . . . .
As the long extended line approached Kirk Alloway, the bell (which still occupies the belfry) was set a-ringing, and continued so while the procession passed on under the triumphal arch along the New Bridge. Deploying round towards the Old Bridge, the circling line, partially obscured by the houses and trees, had a truly picturesque effect. The waving banners, the music of the bands, mellowed and echoed by the 'Bank and braes o' bonnie Doon,' imparted an inexpressibly agreeable sensation. On reaching the triumphal arch of the 'Auld Brig,' venerable and grey with age, the bands struck up the air of 'Welcome, royal Charlie,' while the procession, uncovering and lowering their flags, passed over the rustic bridges in front of the platform, whereon the sons of Burns were elevated. On the platform, beside the Earl of Eglinton and Professor Wilson, we observed H. Glassford Bell, Colonel Campbell, Sir D. H. Blair, H. Onslow, R. Chambers, Mrs. General Hughs, W. A. Cunninghame; A. Boyle, Lord Justice General; Alexander Hastie, M.P.; A. Buchanan, J. O. Fairlie, and a number of ladies. The sons of Burns seemed to feel deeply the compliment paid to them, and acknowledged it most cordially. The immense crowd which surrounded the platform seemed highly gratified by the opportunity afforded them of feasting their eyes upon the lineaments of the sons, where they sought to trace those of the father. The procession occupied at least an hour in passing from the New Bridge into the field, on entering which the whole of the bands played the tune of 'Duncan Gray,' followed by 'The birks of Aberfeldy.' A large circle was then formed round the platform for the musicians in the field, and the whole company, led by professional vocalists, joined in the singing of 'Ye banks and braes o' bonnie Doon,' and 'Auld Langsyne.' The bands were afterwards stationed in various quarters throughout the field —the regimental and Glasgow St. Andrew's bands in the

centre of the field, and the Kilwinning and Cumnock bands at the cottage, the bagpipes playing at a distance from the Pavilion. There were two inclosures for dancing—one towards the head of the field, and the other at the brow overlooking the water of Doon. Immediately after the procession was over, the crowd were astonished by the sudden appearance of Tam o' Shanter, 'weel mounted on his grey mare, Meg,' and a flight of witches in full pursuit of him. Tam approached from the plantation near the cottage, and jogging along the road, put spurs to his 'noble Maggie' opposite the 'auld haunted kirk,' when 'out the hellish legion sallied.' Maggie, of course, reached the 'key-stane of the brig' in safety, but there left behind her 'ain grey tail.' The enactment of this characteristic interlude created much amusement. The company began to enter the Pavilion almost immediately after the close of the procession, and the chair was taken about two o'clock."

Nearly all the celebrated individuals mentioned in the above extract are now dead, and the great majority of that vast, enthusiastic assemblage have shared a like fate. The late Earl of Eglinton occupied the chair, and among other things said :—" This is not a meeting for the purpose of recreation and amusement; it is not a banquet at which a certain number of toasts printed on paper are to be proposed and responded to, which to-day marks our preparations; it is the enthusiastic desire of a whole people to pay honour to their countryman; it is the spontaneous offering of a nation's feelings toward the illustrious dead, and add to this the desire to extend a hand of welcome and friendship to those whom he has left behind. Here, on the very spot where he first drew breath—on the very ground which his genius has hallowed, beside the Old Kirk of Alloway which his verse has immortalized, beneath the Monument which an admiring and repentant people have raised to him, we meet, after the lapse of years, to pay our homage to the man of genius. The master mind who has sung the 'Isle of Palms,' who has revelled in the immortal 'Noctes,' who has already done that justice to the memory of the bard which a brother poet can alone do—Christopher himself—is here, anxious to pay his tribute of admiration to a kindred spirit. The historian who has depicted the most eventful period of the French empire, the glorious triumphs of Wellington, is here—Clio, as it were, offering up a garland to Erato. The distinguished head of the Scottish bar is here—in short, every town and every district, every class, and every sex, and every age has come forward to pay homage to their poet. At his name every Scottish heart beats high. He has become a household word alike in the palace and the cottage. Of whom should we be proud—to whom should we pay homage—if not to our immortal Burns!"

At the conclusion of the addresses the assemblage joined the noble chairman in pledging one overflowing bumper to "The memory of Burns." When the deafening shouts of applause which followed ceased, Mr. Robert Burns, the poet's son (now dead) made a suitable reply, and was followed by the world-famous Professor Wilson of Edinburgh, who gave a long and vigorous speech, which was characterised throughout by masterly eloquence and fervour of feeling.

Toasts, songs, and speeches followed in quick succession, which I would fain chronicle did space allow; but suffice it to say, the "Festival," as this demonstration is commonly termed, was one of the finest attestations to genius ever witnessed.

A very pleasing glimpse of the Monument to the memory of Burns is obtained by the pedestrian as he nears the flight of steps leading to the stile or opening in the wall which admits visitors to Alloway Kirkyard. I paused on their landing and reverentially viewed the scene, but visitors in general seemed less impressed, for many romped amongst the grave-stones, and others cracked jokes at the expense of an odd-like personage attired in a broken-rimmed straw hat and rather soiled apparel, who, in a good round brogue, recites passages from "Tam o' Shanter," and exhibits the rather weird objects of interest over which he appears to be the presiding genius. His story is always the same, and, however interrupted, he goes through it like a school-boy rehearsing a psalm. He evidently considers himself a part of the place, and indeed is so much a part of it that it would be unjust to describe it and omit him. Seemingly he picks up a scant livelihood by waiting on visitors, so, far be it from me to pen a word to injure him in their eyes.

The ruin consists of two gaunt gables, and a front and back

wall of rude masonry, some seven feet in height. The gable fronting the entrance is surmounted by a belfry, which still retains its bell. In its centre is a small window divided by a thick mullion, which Burns refers to as the "winnock bunker in the east." Around the walls are other windows which are built up, but on the south side one is pointed to as that through which Tam o' Shanter is supposed to have witnessed the witches' carnival and all the horrors of their orgies. One thing, however, struck me forcibly when looking into the interior, and that was the fact that his Satanic majesty must have had an insecure seat and his emissaries a very small place wherein to hold a revelry like that which the poet describes. Every scrap of wood about the building was carried off many years ago. Some half-dozen arm chairs have been made out of its rafters, but when one thinks of the enormous quantity of snuff-boxes and similar articles said to be made out of the same materials, the wood seems to have strongly resembled that of "the true Cross." The interior is divided by a partition wall and used as a place of burial by the Cathcarts of Blairston, the Crawfords of Doonside, and others. The date of its erection (1516) is inscribed above a doorway, but its history is void of interest.

At one time a manse and glebe were attached to Alloway Kirk, but the stipend of the minister being only £32 a year, the parish was added to that of Ayr about the close of the seventeenth century and the sum divided between its ministers. After that the building became untenanted and ruinous, and on that account was considered to be the resort of witches and things uncanny—indeed, it is on record that people who passed it after dark saw "unco sichts" and heard sounds of a supernatural description. Burns was familiar with many of its legends, and on the following founded the tale of "Tam o' Shanter":—

"On a market day in the town of Ayr, a farmer from Carrick, and consequently whose way lay by the very gate of Alloway Kirkyard, in order to cross the river Doon at the old bridge which is about two or three hundred yards further on than the said gate, had been detained by his business till, by the time he reached Alloway, it was the wizard hour, between night and morning. Though he was terrified with a blaze streaming from the kirk, yet, as it is a well-known fact that to turn back on these occasions is running by far the greatest risk of mischief, he prudently advanced on his road. When he had reached the gate of the kirkyard he was surprised and entertained through the ribs and arches of an old Gothic window, which still faces the highway, to see a dance of witches merrily footing it round their old sooty blackguard master, who was keeping them all alive with the power of his bagpipe. The farmer, stopping his horse to observe them a little, could plainly descry the faces of many old women of his acquaintance and neighbourhood. How the gentleman was dressed tradition does not say, but that the ladies were all in their smocks; and one of them happening unluckily to have a smock which was considerably too short to answer all the purpose of that piece of dress, our farmer was so tickled that he involuntarily burst out, with a loud laugh, 'Weel luppen, Maggie wi' the short sark!' and recollecting himself, instantly spurred his horse to the top of his speed. I need not mention the universally known fact that no diabolical power can pursue you beyond the middle of a running stream. Lucky it was for the poor farmer that the river Doon was so near, for, notwithstanding the speed of his horse, which was a good one, against he reached the middle of the arch of the bridge, and consequently the middle of the stream, the pursuing vengeful hags were so close at his heels that one of them actually sprang to seize him; but it was too late. Nothing was on her side of the stream but the horse's tail, which immediately gave way at her infernal grip, as if blasted by a stroke of lightning, but the farmer was beyond her reach. However, the unsightly, tailless condition of the vigorous steed was, to the last hour of the noble creature's life, an awful warning to the Carrick farmers not to stay too late in Ayr markets."*

After leisurely examining the scene of this legend, and listening to the prosy descriptions and nasal recitals of the curious specimen of humanity referred to, I began to stray through the unkept burying-ground, and note the humble gravestones of the unknown poor and the more pretentious tombs of the rich. Small as the place is, it is absolutely crowded with memorial stones of one description and another. Many of these are modern, and several mark the resting-places

---

* See letter from Robert Burns to Francis Grose, Esq., F.S.A.

of individuals whose remains have been brought from considerable distances to moulder with those of the rude forefathers of the hamlet. A plain upright stone which heads, and a tablet which covers a grave near the entrance, attract universal attention. And why? Because there rest the ashes of our Poet's father—that admirable man who now lives in the memory of men as the original of "The Cottar," whose "Saturday Night" is so picturesquely sketched. It was the old man's desire that he should repose in this churchyard, and it was lovingly complied with, although the place where he breathed his last was distant nine miles. A small headstone was erected over the grave by the family, but it was chipped to pieces and carried away by relic-hunters. The one occupying its place bears the following inscriptions:—

(Back).
" Oh ye, whose cheek the tear of pity stains,
  Draw near with pious rev'rence and attend!
Here lie the loving husband's dear remains,
  The tender father, and the gen'rous friend.
The pitying heart that felt for human woe;
  The dauntless heart that feared no human pride;
The friend of man, to vice alone a foe;
  'For even his failings leaned to virtue's side.'"

(Front).
"SACRED TO THE MEMORY OF WILLIAM BURNESS, FARMER IN LOCHLIE, WHO DIED ON THE 13TH FEB., 1784, IN THE 63D YEAR OF HIS AGE. AND OF AGNES BROWN, HIS SPOUSE, WHO DIED ON THE 14TH JANY., 1820, IN THE 88TH YEAR OF HER AGE. SHE WAS INTERRED IN BOLTON CHURCHYARD, EAST LOTHIAN."

This inscription is continued on the slab over the grave, and reads thus:—

"ALSO, OF ISABELLA, RELICT OF JOHN BEGG, THEIR YOUNGEST DAUGHTER. BORN AT MOUNT OLIPHANT, 27TH JUNE, 1771. DIED 4TH DECEMBER, 1858. MUCH RESPECTED AND ESTEEMED BY A WIDE CIRCLE OF FRIENDS TO WHOM SHE ENDEARED HERSELF BY HER LIFE OF PIETY, HER MILD URBANITY OF MANNER, AND HER DEVOTION TO THE MEMORY OF HER GIFTED BROTHER."

Burns often expressed a wish that his bones should rest with those of his father; and so anxious were two of his Ayr friends that it should be complied with that they went to Dumfries and offered to bear the expense of transmitting his remains, but they were too late in arriving, arrangements having been made for his interment in St. Michael's church-yard. As it is, a path worn by many feet encircles the grave, and the rank grass which covers the uneven sward in its vicinity is trampled and interspersed with bare patches—a sure sign that it is the peculiar prerogative of genius that it attracts the attention of the world not only towards itself but towards everything that is connected with it.

The above is the only grave of interest in Alloway Kirkyard, but several weather-worn memorials are to be met with which may be briefly referred to. One marks the burial place of Haire of Rankinstone, and bears date 1621; while another, decked with heraldic devices and dated 1665, covers that of the Hunters of Broomberry. Near to the grave of the Poet's father there are several bearing curious sculptured devices. One has a representation of Justice holding a balance which a figure is bearing down; another the motto *Post mortem spero vitam*, and the figure of a horse in the act of being shod, and also the instruments of farriery; while a very curious but much defaced slab, without name or date, has the following all but obliterated verse:—

> " Passenger, we here who lye
> Own it is just that man should die,
> And bless God, who freely gave
> That faith which triumphs o'er ye grave.
> When glorious Jesus Christ shall come,
> We rest in hope that this our dust
> Shall then rise with him from the tomb."

A stone to the memory of " the last person baptised in Alloway Kirk" attracts considerable attention, as also one which the exhibitor represents as marking the grave of Souter Johnnie. That an individual who *aspired* to the dubious honour of being Burns's ideal of that character is buried in the grave he indicates is correct, but he was not the prototype of the Souter; and it is astonishing to see how many visitors are deceived by the statement. Evidently the majority hear and believe, and visit places associated with literary and other celebrities more from the impulse of fashion than admiration for what they have achieved.

Passing through the kirkyard stile I entered the roadway and crossed to the new Kirk of Alloway—a neat little building, to which a cosy manse is attached. It was built in 1857, but not before the admirers of Burns had done everything in their power to induce the late Mr Baird of Cambusdoon to change the site, for they considered that the erection would materially interfere with the view of the Monument. He proved inexorable, however, and in spite of public meetings and memorials the building was gone on with.

A few yards further on I reached the entrance to the grounds of the Monument, and paused to look upon the busy scene in its vicinity. Vehicles arrived and departed in quick succession, and visitors hurried hither and thither or sauntered about in little groups in the most enjoyable manner, as if gratified at being surrounded by scenes of which the Scottish heart might well be proud. The promiscuous throng seemed to be composed of all classes of society, and in waiting were all manner of conveyances. Here might be seen the smart equipage, there the hired carriage or cab, and close to them the commodious "brake" and common cart fitted up with temporary seats for the accommodation of the more humble class of visitors from a distance.

On the right hand side of the highway is Doonside cottage, within the enclosed grounds of which

"The thorn aboon the well,
Where Mungo's mither hang'd hersel',"

is still to be seen. It was the residence of the late David Auld, an enthusiastic admirer of Burns, who, after acquiring a competency in Ayr, purchased land at Doonbrae, and on it erected the commodious and well-built hotel opposite. Along the road is the new Brig o' Doon, and a splendid panorama of hills, and to the left, the road down which Tam o' Shanter is supposed to have dashed when pursued by the witches.

The busy scene in the vicinity of the Monument somewhat surprised me, but I learned from a "cabbie" with whom I entered into conversation that it was nothing unusual. "Visitors come," said he, "from all parts and at all seasons, but more especially during the summer months. Then they arrive in little parties of ten or a dozen, and come in carriages and carts of every description, and many like yourself, sir," he added, with a significant glance at my dusty boots, "come on foot, but the fact is, people never cease nor seem to weary of coming, for I have noticed the same individuals three or four times during a season. O yes, the monument is a favourite resort for all. Family parties, wedding parties, and excursion parties arrive almost daily from Maybole, Ayr, Troon, Irvine, and Kilmarnock, and there are often excursions from Glasgow and other places; but Americans are the most enthusiastic of all visitors. They never drink; no, it is all business with them, and I can assure you they delight in everything connected with Burns and his works—they wish to see everything that is to be seen, and when they see it they are off; yes, a fine class of people are the Americans. I have driven them all round here often. But have you been in the monument? No—well, in you go and see the show, for there is too much of that about it."

Following his advice, and a merry party of lads and lasses, I presented myself at the gate of the grounds which encircle the handsome tribute to the Poet's memory, and was admitted upon paying twopence, for such is the amount levied on each visitor for the purpose of defraying the necessary expense of keeping the Monument in proper order.

CHAPTER VIII.

The Monument on the Banks of Doon—Its External and Internal Appearance—Relics of the Poet—Highland Mary's Bible—Scenery—The Statues of Tam O' Shanter and Souter Johnny—The Scheme for Erecting the Monument and How it Originated—Laying the Foundation Stone—Mr. Boswell's Address, etc.

The grounds surrounding the Monument on the banks of Doon, although barely an acre in extent, are quite paradisiacal in appearance, being beautifully laid off and well stocked with shrubs and choice flowers. The tribute to the Poet's memory is situated in the centre, and towers far above its surroundings, being sixty feet high. The basement, which is triangular in form, contains a small chamber and supports a circle of nine fluted columns thirty feet in height which bear up a copula crowned by three inverted dolphins and a gilt tripod. Altogether, it is a handsome piece of masonry and worthy of the object to which it is devoted.

After conversing with the courteous superintendent, I entered the circular chamber in the basement of the pile which was literally crowded with visitors intently examining relics of the poet that are preserved in glass cases. On a table lay a ponderous ledger or "Visitors' book," round which a knot were gathered anxiously waiting to add their names to the many thousands its pages contained; but from it my eye wandered round the apartment, and rested on a well-executed portrait of Burns from the celebrated painting by Naismyth, and also upon several spirited sketches illustrating happy passages in his poems. These adorned the walls, but a masterpiece of art, in the form of a bust of Burns, arrested universal attention by its life-like appearance. It is a souvenir of the genius of the late Patrick Park, R.S.A., a Scottish sculptor of considerable merit, who died on the threshold of Fame's temple. These in themselves are very interesting, but the "Burns relics" are more attractive by far, and in consort with other enthusiasts I looked upon them with feelings akin to veneration. The following is a list of the most noteworthy:—The Bible presented by Burns to "Highland Mary;" "Bonnie Jean's" (Mrs. Burns') wedding ring, presented by Mrs. Hutchison, a grand-daughter of the poet; two rings, containing portions of the hair of Burns and his devoted wife, presented by their son, James G. Burns; two drinking-glasses presented by Burns to Clarinda; a snuff-box made from the rafters of "Alloway's auld haunted kirk;" and a caup said to have been used by the "randie, gangrel bodies" who frequented the establishment of Poosie Nancy. Beside these, there is a copy of the original Kilmarnock edition of Burns' poems, and one of the Edinburgh edition; but the greatest literary curiosities are those in the German and French languages. There are also to be seen a letter from Burns to Captain Millar of Dalswinton, and *fac similes* of the MSS. of "Scots wha hae," and "The Jolly Beggars." The Bible which the poet presented to his "Highland lassie" when they parted for ever on the banks of the Ayr, consists of two small volumes, and bears the following in his unmistakeable handwriting:—Vol. I.—"And ye shall not swear by my name falsely, I am the Lord. Levit. 19th chap. 12th verse." In the centre of the opposite fly-leaf there is a mystical Free Mason mark. Vol. II.—"Thou shalt not forswear thyself, but shalt perform unto the Lord thine oath. Matth. 5th ch. 33d verse." On the top of the opposite fly-leaf are "Robert," and two indistinct words, which possibly are Burns and Mossgiel.

The history of this Bible is somewhat singular. After Mary's death, her father forbade the name of her lover to be mentioned in the family. Her mother, however, was more relenting, and with fond memories of her child treasured the volumes, and shortly before her own demise, which occurred in Greenock in 1828, presented them to her daughter, a Mrs. Anderson; but from her they passed from one sister to another, and ultimately came into the possession of her son, William Anderson, mason, Renton, Dumbartonshire. In 1834 he emigrated to Canada and took the volumes with him. For a long time thereafter all traces of them were lost; but being accidentally heard of by a few patriotic Scots in Montreal,

"*These* records dear of transports past"

were purchased for £25, and generously sent to the old country to be placed in the Monument with the memorials mentioned above.

From the chamber in which the relics are preserved a narrow stair leads to a platform within the prestile. When I emerged from it I found several visitors, leaning on the balustrade upon which the columns rest, intently gazing upon the extensive and highly-interesting landscape which comes within the range of vision from the elevated position. I also found myself leaning on the stone work and as deeply engrossed with the matchless views as any one, for in whatever direction the eye turned it rested on objects consecrated by the Poet's genius and upon scenery unsurpassed for richness and beauty. I could have " gazed myself away," as Wordsworth has it, but the afternoon was well spent, and to guard against being " catch'd wi' warlocks in the mirk," I descended with the intention of taking a turn through the grounds before leaving.

While admiring the flowers and neatly-bordered walks, I stumbled on a grotto containing "Tam o' Shanter" and " Souter Johnny "—two life-sized stone figures from the chisel of the late James Thom, an amateur sculptor of some celebrity, who travelled and exhibited them in the principal towns of Great Britain and Ireland before being deposited where they now are. The figures, which are natural and life-like, are represented sitting in chairs with a can of " reaming swats " between them which appear to be of divine quality, for as Tammie holds his bumper, the very smile on his face would make one believe that he was about to pronounce the old toast, "Here's to ye." Johnnie looks quite pleased also, and in every way as jolly and happy as his prototype, " Laird M'Pherson," was when in the flesh. The " Laird " was a Symington cobbler whom Thom modelled so cleverly that an urchin from the village was nearly frightened out of his wits when he first peered in at the grotto door.

Before leaving the Monument, a word may be said about its inauguration. The honour of originating the scheme for its erection is wholly due to the late Sir Alexander Boswell of Auchinleck—a gentleman who was not only an enthusiastic admirer of the bard, but a poet of decided merit, and a patriot who took a deep interest in everything connected with the weal of his native land. He knew how the Scottish heart beat towards Burns, and in the belief that an appeal for funds to erect a memorial for him on the banks of classic Doon would be heartily responded to, he ventured to call a public meeting in Ayr for the purpose of having his proposal taken into consideration. The day came, and the hour of meeting arrived, but not a single individual but Mr Boswell (his title was not then conferred upon him) and a friend put in an appearance, so utterly regardless seemed the community about the matter. This was disheartening enough, but it did not damp the enthusiasm of Boswell, for he believed with his friend that the matter only required to be known and Scotchmen in all parts of the globe would give it countenance. With due formality, the same friend voted him to the chair and proposed that a subscription should be commenced for the purpose of raising a monument to the poet Burns on the banks of Doon. It is needless to say that the resolution met with no opposition. A minute of the proceedings being signed by the chairman, the meeting broke up. The friends next advertised in the public journals that such a meeting had been duly called, and that said resolution had been unanimously carried at it. £1600 was soon collected, and with this sum it was resolved to commence building the memorial. On the anniversary of the poet's birthday, the following year (1820), a great demonstration—in which large deputations from all the Masonic lodges in Ayrshire took part—was held in honour of the laying of the foundation stone. The day was anything but favourable for the occasion, but despite the inclemency of the weather the procession with music playing and banners flying marched from Ayr to the site—and where could there have been a more appropriate one found? An extensive circle being formed round it, the stone was laid with Masonic honours by Mr Alexander Boswell; and within a cavity were deposited the coins of the realm, the local newspapers, and a brass plate bearing the following inscription :—" By the favour of Almighty God, on the twenty-fifth day of January, A.D. MDCCCXX, of the era of Masonry 5820, and in the sixtieth year of the reign of our beloved Sovereign George the Third, His Royal

Highness, George Prince of Wales, being Regent of the United Kingdom, and a munificent subscriber to the edifice, the foundation stone of this monument, erected by public subscription in honour of the genius of Robert Burns, the Ayrshire poet, was laid by Alexander Boswell, Esq., Auchinleck, M.P., Worshipful Depute-Grand Master of the Most Ancient Mother Lodge of Kilwinning (attended by all the mason lodges in Ayrshire) according to the ancient usages of masonry. Thomas Hamilton, jr., Edinburgh, architect. John Connell, jr., builder and contractor." At the conclusion of the ceremony the Grand Master delivered the following brief but beautiful oration:—

"BRETHREN,—May corn, wine, and oil abound; may all that is useful and ornamental be cultivated amongst us; and may all that can invigorate the body or enliven the soul shed their blest influence on our native land. We have at length assembled to pay a grateful, although a tardy, tribute to the genius of ROBERT BURNS, our Ayrshire poet and the bard of Coila. There surely lives not the man so dull, so flinty, or phlegmatic, who could witness this event without emotion. But to those whose heart-strings have thrilled responsive to the chords of the poet's lyre—whose bosoms have swelled, like his, with love and friendship, with tenderness and sympathy, have glowed with patriotism, or panted for glory—this hour must be an hour of exultation. Whether we consider the time, the place, or the circumstance, there is enough to interest in each; but these combined, and at once in operation on our feelings and our fancies—his muse, alas! is mute, who could alone have dared to paint the proud breathings of such an assembly at such a moment. When we consider the time, we cannot forget that this day is the anniversary of that which gave our poet to the light of Heaven. Bleak is the prospect around us; the wood, the hawthorn, and 'the birken shaw,' are leafless; not a thrush has yet essayed to clear the furrowed brow of winter; but this we know shall pass away, give place, and be succeeded by the buds of spring and the blossoms of summer. Chill and cheerless was our poet's natal day; but soon the wild flowers of poesy sprung as it were beneath his boyish tread; they opened as he advanced, expanded as he matured, until he revelled in all the richness of luxuriance. Poverty and disappointment hung frowning around him, and haunted his path; but soothed and charmed by the fitful visits of his native muse, and crowned, as in a vision, with the holly wreath, he wantoned in a fairy land, the bright creation of his own vivid and enrapt imagination. His musings have been our delight. Men of the loftiest talents and of tastes the most refined have praised them—men of strong and swelling but untutored intellect have admired them—the poet of the heart is the poet of mankind. When we consider the place, let us remember that these very scenes which we now look upon, awakened in his youthful breast that animating spark which burst upon the world in a blaze of inspiration. In yonder cottage he first drew breath. In that depository of the lowly dead sleeps the once humble now immortal model of the cottage life—there rests his pious father—and there it was his fond and anxious wish that his dust should have been mingled with the beloved and kindred ashes. Below us flows the Doon, the classic Doon, but made classic by his harmony; there gliding through the woods, and laving his banks and braes, he rolls his clear and 'far-fetch'd waters' to the ocean. Before us stand the ruins of Kirk Alloway, shrouded in all the mystic imagery with which it is enveloped by his magic spells—Kirk Alloway! to name it is enough. If, then, the time and place are so congenial with our fond impressions, the circumstances which have enabled us to carry into effect this commemoration of our bard must give delight to every enthusiastic mind. In every region where our language is heard, the songs of Burns give rapture—and from every region, and from climes the most remote, the votive offerings have poured in to aid our undertaking; and the edifice which we have now begun shall stand a proud and lasting testimony of the world's admiration. Not on the banks of Doon alone, or hermit Ayr, or the romantic Lugar, echo repeats the songs of Burns; but amidst the wild forests of Columbia, and scorching plains of Hindostan—on the banks of the Mississipi, the St Lawrence, and the Ganges, his heart-touching melodies float upon the breeze. This monument rises like a pile cairn over our warriors of old—each man casts a stone; and in honour of him, the son of a cottar, and himself a ploughman, our Prince, with the true feelings of true greatness, and more illustrious by this act of generosity, pays here his tribute at the shrine of genius. May the work prosper;

and when happily completed, then may it tell to future generations that the age which could produce a Burns was rich also in those who could appreciate his talents, and who, while they felt and owned the power of his muse, have honoured his name."

After the applause which followed this eloquent speech had subsided, the Rev. Hamilton Paul of Broughton closed the proceedings with an appropriate prayer, and with three hearty cheers the assemblage commenced the return journey to the town.

Towards evening the Grand Lodge was "opened" in the King's Arms Hall, and many patriotic toasts were proposed and heartily responded to, but the toast of the evening was "The Admirers of Burns." When proposing it, the Grand Master (Mr Boswell) mentioned some particulars regarding the subscriptions raised for the erection of the Monument, and, amongst other things, said that its success was in a great measure due to the exertions of Sir James Shaw and William Fairlie of London, for they had remitted large sums in furtherance of the undertaking which they had been instrumental in collecting in London, America, and the East Indies, where, he affirmed, a greater enthusiasm prevailed in favour of Burns and his writings than in his native country. After the toast had been duly honoured, the Grand Master sang the following song which he had composed for the occasion :—

"Vain thought! but had Burns ever witnessed a meeting
   Of souls so congenial, and warm'd with such fire,
The wild flow of fancy in ecstasy greeting,
   Ah! what might have been the bold notes of his lyre?

As rays by reflection are doubled and doubled,
   His bosom had swelled to your cheering reply,
Soft sympathy soothing the heart that was troubled,
   A smile for his mirth, for his sorrow a sigh.

Admir'd but unaided, how dark was his story,
   His struggles we know, and his efforts we prize ;
From murky neglect, as the flame bursts to glory,
   He rose, self-embalm'd, and detraction defies.

A ploughman he was : would that smiles of false favour
   Had never decoyed him from home and his team,
And taught all his hopes and his wishes to waver,
   And snatching reality, left him a—dream.

> To rank and to title, due deference owing,
>   We bow, as befitting society's plan;
> But judgment awaken'd, and sympathy glowing,
>   We pass all distinctions, and rest upon—man.
>
> And from the poor hind, who, his day's task completed,
>   With industry's pride to his hovel returns,
> To him who in royalty's splendour is seated,
>   If soul independent be found, 'twas in Burns.
>
> His birthright, his muse! like the lark in the morning,
>   How blithely he caroll'd in praise of the fair;
> With Nature enraptur'd and artifice scorning,
>   How sweet were his notes on the banks of the Ayr!
>
> And near to that spot where his kindred dust slumbers,
>   And mark'd by the bard on the tablets of fame,
> And near the thatch'd roof where he first lisp'd his numbers,
>   We'll raise a proud tribute to honour his name."

On the 4th of July, 1823, Mr Fullarton of Skeldon—in presence of a vast assemblage of Freemasons and subscribers—placed the tripod on the summit of the Monument, and pronounced it finished. He afterwards delivered an appropriate address.

> "But what to us the sculptor's art,
>   His funeral columns, wreaths, and urns?
> Wear we not graven on our heart,
>   The name of ROBERT BURNS?"

CHAPTER IX.

THE HOTEL AND SHELL PALACE—THE AULD BRIG O' DOON—THE NEW BRIG AND ITS PETITION—VIEW FROM THE HEIGHTS IN ITS VICINITY—NEWARK CASTLE—GREENAN CASTLE—THE RETURN JOURNEY.

It has been said that a toothache would speedily bring to earth the loftiest flight of the philosopher, and certainly hunger and fatigue would speedily dispel the enthusiasm one feels when visiting celebrated places. There is no use denying it, a good inn or hotel is occasionally essential, and I never stood in greater need of the comfort one or either affords than I did on the occasion of my visit to the banks of Doon.

The hotel referred to in last chapter was completely crowded with excursionists, and it was not without considerable jostling that I managed to get into a room, where, despite an atmosphere of tobacco smoke and the music of a party who persistently sang—

> "Landlady count the lawen,
> The day is near the dawin:
> Ye're a' blind drunk, boys,
> And I'm jolly fu',"

I managed to enjoy the rest and refreshment which my long walk had rendered necessary. My stay was short, but before leaving I paid a visit to "The Shell Palace," as a small grotto in the grounds of the establishment is termed. It is a curiosity in its way, being clad on the inside with countless shells and decked with mirrors, in which the visitor finds his form reflected again and again; but beyond the chair made out of the prolific rafters of Alloway Kirk, it contains nothing of interest. The garden, however, is delightfully situated between the Old and New Brigs o' Doon, and commands an excellent view of both structures.

Turning the corner of the hotel, I strolled down to the Auld Brig, which is only some five minutes' walk from the Monument gate. On my right lay the carefully enclosed grounds of the hotel, and on my left those of the Monument; and in front the "banks and braes o' bonnie Doon," blooming as fresh and fair as they did when Burns wandered by them or

> "Walked in glory and in pride,
> Following his plough upon the mountain side."

Visitors sauntered in the path as if unwilling to bid adieu to the fascinating scene, but one happy chap, reclining on the verdant bank with his arms about his dearie, I really envied, for to all appearance he was so absorbed in love-making that he cared not although

> "Worldly cares and warldly men
> Should a' gae tapsalteerie."

The road makes a rather abrupt turn towards the bridge and rises steeply over its arch, but it was not until it was neared that I discovered that the strains of a fiddle, and peals of merriment which smote my ear, proceeded from its centre—yea, from the spot where Maggie

> "Brought aff her maister hale,
> But left behind her ain grey tail."

Sure enough a group of lads and lasses were busy going through the intricacies of a Scotch reel, and as the arm of the musician played "jink and diddle,"

> "They reeled, they set, they cross'd, they cleekit,"

and gleefully danced to the notes of his instrument. As I approached the fun grew "fast and furious," and it was with the utmost difficulty I kept my legs from flying into the air like those of a jumping jack, so influenced were they with the surplus music of the party. But it came to an end, and by way of finale the mirth-loving throng struck up "Ye banks an' braes o' bonnie Doon," which I think was never sung with greater effect, for Echo took up the strain and beautified the melody. Leaning upon the parapet of the bridge I watched the placid water rippling over the pebbly bottom of the stream, and was soon oblivious to all save the superb scene through which it flows.

Above the old bridge the scene has lost none of its beauty since the time of Burns, but below it has undergone a very great alteration indeed. The new bridge—a handsome structure, some hundred yards distant—has been erected, and every building, save Alloway Kirk, is comparatively modern. But notwithstanding this radical change, the whole locality remains a picture of unsurpassed loveliness.

The auld brig o' Doon is a narrow, inconvenient structure of one lofty, well-turned arch, and is chiefly interesting as the closing scene of Tam o' Shanter's adventure with the witches.

> " Now, do thy speedy utmost, Meg,
> And win the key-stane o' the brig ;
> There at them thou thy tail may toss,
> A running stream they darena cross.
> But ere the key-stane she could make,
> The fient a tail she had to shake ;
> For Nannie, far before the rest,
> Hard upon noble Maggie prest,
> And flew at Tam wi' furious ettle ;
> But little wist she Maggie's mettle—
> Ae spring brought aff her maister hale,
> But left behind her ain grey tail ;
> The carlin claught her by the rump,
> And left poor Maggie scarce a stump."

James Paterson, in his account of the parish of Maybole, states that this bridge was erected by Bishop Kennedy in 1466, but other equally trustworthy authorities affirm that its age is unknown. From the high sweep of its arch, however, and the appearance of its masonry, and the fact that the Burgh of Ayr contributed towards having it repaired 300 years ago, there is every reason for supposing that it was reared at a very early date. In 1810 the Trustees of the roads in the County of Ayr agreed to erect a new bridge across the Doon, and demolish the ancient structure, but the very mention of this act was sufficient to rouse the indignation of the admirers of Burns and produce a movement for its preservation. "The old bridge," it was represented, " boasts a very high antiquity, and is considered one of the finest in Europe, being in height and span equal, if not superior, to the Rialto at Venice. It also forms an interesting feature in that exquisite picture of his native scenery drawn by Burns in his 'Tam o' Shanter.' The cottage in which he was born, Alloway Kirk, and the auld brig are objects which give such a charm to the landscape in the eye of the stranger who has read and admired the writings of Coila's Bard that the annihilation of any of them would prove the object of general regret." Under these impressions a subscription was set on foot with a view to raise a fund to purchase and preserve the venerable edifice, but the following appeal from the pen of the Rev. Hamilton Paul had the desired effect :—

"*Unto the Honourable the Trustees of the Roads in the County of Ayr, the petition and complaint of the Auld Brig o' Doon.*

"Must I, like modern fabrics of a day,
Decline unwept, the victim of decay?
Shall my bold arch, that proudly stretches o'er
Doon's classic stream, from Kyle's to Carrick's shore,
Be suffered in oblivion's gulf to fall,
And hurl to wreck my venerable wall?
Forbid it! every tutelary power!
That guards my keystane at the midnight hour.
Forbid it ye who, charmed by Burns' lay,
Amid these scenes can linger out the day!
Let Nannie's sark, and Maggie's mangled tail,
Plead in my cause, and in that cause prevail.
The man of taste, who comes my form to see,
And curious asks, but asks in vain for me,
With tears of sorrow will my fate deplore,
When he is told 'The Auld Brig is no more.'
Stop then, O stop the more than Vandal rage
That marks this revolutionary age,
And bid the structure of your fathers last,
The pride of this, the boast of ages past;
Nor ever let your children's children tell
By your decree the ancient fabric fell.

"May it therefore please your honours to consider this petition, and grant such sum as you may think proper for repairing and keeping up the Old Bridge of Doon.
(Signed) " ———————
For the Petitioner."

The gentleman to whom the petition was presented explained that they had no powers to expend public money on a disused road, but being amused with the novel document, they subscribed handsomely towards having the bridge repaired and preserved. The old structure is used by foot passengers, and is in excellent preservation, and, to every appearance, will prove as durable as its usurper.

The goal of my journey being attained, I lingered in its vicinity and

"Roved by bonnie Doon
To see the rose and woodbine twine."

"But pleasures are like poppies spread." Train time was but three hours distant, and a long road lay between me and the railway station at Ayr. There was no help for it though, so I reluctantly left the classic scene, and with a fond adieu to its numerous fascinations, entered the road along which Tam's tailless mare galloped after making the prodigious spring that carried its rider beyond the vengeful clutch of Cutty-sark and the horde of witches in her wake. It is hard to determine the course this road pursued when Burns traversed it, but, at this date, it sweeps round a gentle curve at no great distance from the bridge and joins the new road to Maybole at a toll-bar, from which there is a splendid view of the woods of Newark Castle and the rugged chain of hills which rise abruptly from the vale. The old toll-keeper was enjoying his afternoon pipe at the door of his cot in the most complaisant manner, and was not the least diffident to converse. He proved racy of speech, and well acquainted with the district ; but our conversation was abruptly brought to a close by the approach of a company of young men with japanned tin cases slung over their shoulders, who stopped to examine a plot of weeds in the taxman's triangular garden. It was evident that they were amateur botanists, so, to watch their operations, I accompanied them fully half a mile along the road, but failed to increase my stock of botanical knowledge despite their efforts to make me comprehend the technicalities of the science. I love wild flowers, and can at all times see beauty in a worthles weed, but I can see no reason why the classification, construction, and properties of plants should be concealed from the illiterate in a mist of to them unintelligible terms. Still, without such scientific knowledge,

"God's wondrous power the mind can read,
In valley, mountain, plain, and hill ;
While in the humblest wayside weed
We may perceive His wondrous skill."

Taking leave of this little company, I commenced my homeward journey, and from the height, almost unconsciously attained, beheld one of the most beautiful and picturesque prospects ever witnessed. In the foreground lay Alloway Kirk, the Monument, and the Auld Brig o' Doon; a little further on, The Cottage; and between them and the town of Ayr—which is seen to great advantage—the space appeared dotted with elegant mansions, snug cottages, and embowering trees. To the left, the Frith of Clyde gleamed round the dark hills of Arran like a sea of molten silver, and stretched away in the distance until its waters seemed blended with the fleecy clouds. To the right, the distant hills of Cumnock and Muirkirk were mapped out; but the scene must be seen to be appreciated, and I trust that every reader who visits the Monument will not leave the locality before ascending these rugged heights.

A brisk walk brought me back to the toll-bar. From it I moved in the direction of the new Bridge, and turned down a shady avenue to the left. The walk is a lonely one, and in many parts literally canopied with foliage. Here I passed Newark Castle, a charming residence nestling in a perfect bower of wood at the foot of the range of hills already mentioned. It is greatly modernised, and is memorable as the place where Queen Mary passed the night after the disastrous battle of Langside.

Although travel-worn, I trudged cheerfully onward, and soon arrived in a commodious highway running parallel with the shore. To the west was the beautiful bay, and north and south an extensive track of coast scenery; but the most prominent, and in my eyes the most picturesque, object on the landscape was the shattered remnant of Greenan Castle frowning from a cliff on the verge of the watery waste. It being but a field's breadth from where I stood, the temptation to pay it a visit was so great that I instinctively yielded to the impulse and sought the lane leading to the farmsteading in its vicinity. The approach was a little circuitous, but when it was traversed I bounded down the embankment, and boylike watched the rippling waves of the fast receding tide as they rolled backward and forward in apparent anxiety to lave my weary feet. The splashing of the oars of a passing boat, and the merry laughter and shouts of a company of children on the sands, fell like music on my ear as I gazed upon the deep, and on the ruined stronghold frowning from the edge of a high and almost perpendicular rock by my side. The scene was beautiful, but to enjoy it more fully I climbed a verdant slope and began to stray over some grass-covered foundations near the shattered remnant of former greatness. Approaching the edge of the precipice on which the ruin stands, I passed through a low doorway and entered a vault-like chamber with an arched roof, but neither in it nor in another ruined apartment at the top of a wrecked staircase did I find anything to reward my intrepidity. In fact, my blood ran cold when I looked through an arrowslit in the back wall, and beheld the chasm over which the fabric hangs.

Very little is known regarding Greenan Castle. Over the door of the tower the letters "J. K.," and the figures "1603" are still discernable; but that an older building occupied the site is evident from the stronghold being mentioned in a grant of the Doon Fisheries, which was drawn up during the reign of William the Lion. The following verses are selected from an address to the old pile which may be found in a meritorious volume of verse published in Ayr in 1841:—

"It frowns upon the steep
  Like a monarch grey and grim,
To its feet the mighty deep
  Bears a never failing hymn;
And proudly o'er the billow,
  Looks the tower the sunshine through,
When the sailor on his pillow,
  Dreams of home and love so true.

"I have heard the rude winds railing
  O'er the bosom of the sea,
And the mariners assailing
  In their mischief-making glee;
But disdainful through the haze,
  While the drift flies gloomy past,
And the frightened seaman prays,
  Frowns the ruin on the blast.

"Old Time, with heedless hand,
  In the city and the wood,
Strews oblivion's darkest sand
  O'er the lovely and the good;
And they moulder on the hill,
  And they fade within the heart,
But the ruin lingers still,
  Though the fair and young depart."

From Greenan Castle I passed down to the shore and walked

sharply towards Ayr—the tide being far out and the sand firm and pleasant to walk upon. At the confluence of the Doon I was brought to a standstill, for to cross dry-shod appeared impossible, and to go round by the Low Bridge was to take up too much time. However, I got over the difficulty and the river together by wading across with my boots and stockings suspended across my shoulder at the end of my stick, and after a lengthy but pleasant walk reached the Low Green—a large level park in which games of cricket and football were progressing with great spirit. Thence I passed the County Buildings and hurriedly sought the Railway Station, but not a moment too soon, for I had no sooner procured a ticket and taken a seat than the train moved off. The journey to Kilmarnock was as free from incident as such journeys generally are; so, courteous reader, we will start together in next chapter, and in fancy accompany each other in a ramble to the farm of Lochlea and other places in the vicinity of Tarbolton.

CHAPTER X.

From Kilmarnock to Coilsfield—Riccarton Graveyard—An Eccentric Miser—A Burns Worthy—Craigie Road—Scargie—Howcommon—A Good Joke—Scenery—The Farm of Lochlea and Crannog—The Old Dwelling House and New Barn—The Death of the Poet's Father—Wild Flowers—The River Ayr—Failford, etc,

After visiting "The banks and braes o' bonnie Doon," I resolved upon a pilgrimage to the farm of Lochlea and the various places of interest in its immediate vicinity, for to it, as we have seen, the Burns' family removed after a protracted struggle with adverse circumstances in the locality which formed the goal of last ramble. The day set apart for the journey being favourable, I crossed the old bridge at Riccarton, and passed up the village street as the clock in the church spire announced the hour of ten. Finding the gate of the churchyard open, I entered and sought out the grave of the Rev. Alexander Moodie, a Burns hero, "who," as the weather worn stone states, "died 15th Feb., 1799, in the 72nd year of his age, and the 40th of his ministry." He was a zealous auld light preacher, and figures as one of the herds in the "Holy Tulzie"—a satire on an unseemly quarrel between him and the Rev. John Russell of Kilmarnock :—

> "Oh, Moodie, man, and wordy Russell,
> How could you raise so vile a bustle?
> Ye'll see how New Light herds will whistle,
>   An' think it fine;
> The L——'s cause ne'er got sic a twistle
>   Sin' I hae min'.
>
> "O, sirs! whae'er wad hae expeckit,
> Your duty ye wad sae negleckit,
> Ye wha were ne'er by lairds respeckit,
>   To wear the plaid ;
> But by the brutes themselves eleckct,
>   To be their guide.

> "What flock wi' Moodie's flock could rank,
>   Sae hale and hearty every shank !
>   Nae poisoned sour Arminian stank
>   He let them taste ;
>   Frae Calvin's well, ay clear, they drank—
>   Oh, sic a feast !"

In referring to the dispute, Robert Chambers makes mention of its origin. "It happened," says he, " that a dryness arose between them. The country story is, that as they were riding home one evening from Ayr, Moodie, in a sportive frame of mind, amused himself by tickling the rear of his neighbour's (the Rev. John Russell's) horse. The animal performed several antics along the road, much to the amusement of the passing wayfarers, but greatly to the discomfiture of black Jock, who, afterwards learning the trick, could not forgive Moodie for it. Afterwards a question of parochial boundaries arose between them. It came before the Presbytery for determination. 'There, in the open court,' says Mr. Lockhart, 'to which the announcement of the discussion had drawn a multitude of the country people, and Burns among the rest, the reverend divines, hitherto sworn friends and associates, lost all command of temper, and abused each other *coram populo*, with a fiery virulence of personal invective such as has long been banished from all popular assemblies, wherein the laws of courtesy are enforced by those of a certain unwritten code. This was too much temptation for the profane wit of Burns. He lost no time in putting the affair in allegorical shape."

The Rev. Mr. Moodie is also mentioned in "The Kirk's Alarm," and his style of oratory is hit off to a nicety in the following verses of "The Holy Fair" :—

> "Now a' the congregation o'er
>   Is silent expectation,
> For Moody spiels the holy door
>   Wi' tidings o' d——tion.
> Should Hornie, as in ancient days,
>   'Mang sons o' God present him,
> The very sight o' Moodie's face
>   To's ain het hame had sent him,
>   Wi' fright that day.
>
> " Hear how he clears the points o' faith
>   Wi' rattlin' and wi' thumpin' !

> Now meekly calm, now wild in wrath,
>   He's stampin' and he's jumpin'!
> His lengthened chin, his turned-up snout,
>   His eildritch squeal and gestures,
> Oh, how they fire the heart devout,
>   Like cantharidian plasters,
>   On sic a day."

In the vicinity of Moodie's grave are the burying-places of the Cuninghames of Caprington and the Campbells of Treesbank, and many curiously-carved headstones which will repay attention; but, with the exception of an eccentric miser who died in East Shaw Street, Kilmarnock, on the 17th July, 1817, and who is interred in an out-of-the way corner near the gate, the unkept sward does not cover any other very celebrated individual. William Stevenson—as this character was named—was a native of Dunlop, and at one time filled a respectable position in society; but, owing to some unexplained cause, he became a professional beggar, and lived wholly upon charity. In the "Book of Days" the following curious account of his death and burial may be found:—

"About the year 1787 he and his wife separated, making the strange agreement that whichever of them was the first to propose reunion should forfeit one hundred pounds to the other. It is supposed that they never met afterwards. In 1815, when about eighty-five years old, Stevenson was seized with an incurable disease, and was confined to his bed. A few days before his death, feeling his end to be near, he sent for a baker, and ordered twelve dozen burial cakes, a large quantity of sugar biscuits, and a good supply of wine and spirits. He next sent for a joiner, and instructed him to make a good, sound, dry, roomy coffin; after which he sent for the Riccarton gravedigger, and requested him to select a favourable spot in a dry and comfortable corner of the village churchyard, and there dig for him a roomy grave, assuring him that he would be paid for his trouble. This done he ordered an old woman who attended him to go to a certain nook and there bring out nine pounds to pay all these preliminary expenses, telling her not to grieve for him for he had remembered her in his will. Shortly after this he died. A neighbour came in to search for his wealth, which had been shrouded in much mystery. In one bag was found large silver pieces, such as dollars and half-dollars, crowns and half-crowns, and in a heap of musty rags a collection of guineas and seven-shilling pieces; while in a box were found bonds of various amounts, including one for three hundred pounds, giving altogether a sum of about nine hundred pounds. A will was also found bequeathing twenty pounds to the old woman who attended him, and most of the remainder to distant relations, setting aside sufficient to give a feast to all the beggars in Ayrshire who chose to come and see his body lie in state. The influx was immense, and after the funeral, which was attended by a motley group of gaberlunzies, all retired to a barn that had been fitted up for the occasion, and there indulged in revelries but little in accordance with the solemn season of death."

When "the decent church which tops the neighbouring hill" was erected, the quaint, weather-worn structure which stood in the centre of the churchyard was demolished, and more the pity, for it was of great antiquity, being in existence, according to Chalmers, so early as 1229. "The chapel of Ricardtoun," he states, "was afterwards established as a parish church, which belonged to the monks of Paisley; and it remained as such till the Reformation. The monks, meantime, received the tithes and revenues, while the church was served by a chaplain who was appointed by them. In a rental of Paisley Abbey, which was given up to Government in 1562, it was stated that the monks derived from the church of Richardtoun 17 chalders, 6 bolls, and 1 firlot of meal yearly."

Upon resuming the journey I held along the wall of the manse garden and turned into Craigie Road, and after a brisk walk reached Knowehead, an eminence from which an excellent view of the surrounding district is obtained. Strolling onward, I passed through the toll-bar of Shortlees, and soon gained a shady portion of the road near to the entrance gate of Treesbank estate. Here a nameless burnie gurgles through a small plantation and gladdens the heart of the wayfarer with its music as it steals from beneath a small bridge by the roadside. Its tone was seductive, but despite it and the picturesque scene, I commenced the ascent of Scargie brae, and soon gained the row of humble thatch-covered cots which present their gables to the highway.

There is nothing about the buildings worthy of note, except perhaps the fact that John Burtt, author of "Horæ Poeticæ" and "Transient Murmurs of a Solitary Lyre," spent his early years in one of them may be of interest. Burtt was for some considerable time a schoolmaster in Kilmarnock, and afterwards a clergyman in America; but he is best known on this side of the Atlantic as the author of several lyrics, and more especially of the following, which is often mistakenly ascribed to Robert Burns, being supposed to have been written by the bard after the death of Highland Mary :—

"O'ER THE MIST-SHROUDED CLIFFS.

" O'er the mist-shrouded cliffs of the lone mountain straying,
    Where the wild winds of winter incessantly rave,
What woes wring my heart while intently surveying
    The storm's gloomy path on the breast of the wave.
Ye foam-crested billows, allow me to wail,
    Ere ye toss me afar from my loved native shore,
Where the flower that bloomed sweetest in Coila's green vale,
    The pride of my bosom—my Mary's no more.

No more by the banks of the streamlet we'll wander,
    And smile at the moon's rimpled face in the wave;
No more shall my arms cling with fondness around her]
    For the dew-drops of morning fall cold on her grave.
No more shall the soft thrill of love warm my breast;
    I haste with the storm to a far distant shore,
Where unknown, unlamented, my ashes shall rest,
    And joy shall revisit my bosom no more."

Leaving Scargie behind, a pleasant walk along the undulating, hedge-bordered highway brought me to Knockmarloch and the little plantation which all but conceals the shattered remnant of its manor house, and ultimately to the base of Craigie Hill, as a rugged upheaval forming the terminus of a rocky range of eminences rising to a height of some 550 feet above the level of the sea is termed. The view from the summit of this locally-famous height is very fine, comprising as it does the Firth of Clyde, the Coast of Ireland, the Mull of Kintyre, the Paps of Jura, the heights of Arran, Ben Lomond, and the Grampians. Landward, Loudoun Hill is also distinctly seen, and on the plain the town of Kilmarnock, with its surroundings, is witnessed to great advantage—indeed a better bird's-eye view of the Land of Burns cannot well be had, and the pedestrian will do well to avail himself of it. Entering a rude path or cart-track leading past the lime mines of Howcommon, I followed the rugged way until it merged into a substantial parish road, and afterwards steered my course to a farm-house with the intention of making certain doubly sure by inquiring the way to Lochlea. "Doon, ye deevil, doon!" cried the stripling addressed, as with a well-aimed kick he drove away a frolicsome whelp that nearly upset me in a mud-hole with its great paws while endeavouring to lick my face. "Lochlea! my certie ye're a braw bit frae it; but it's a fine day, and you'll manage brawly. Ye'll be lookin' for calves, nae doubt?" "Yes; two legged ones," said I, with a significant glance, and without the least suspicion that the joke would penetrate his dull pate and recoil upon myself. "Then," said he, with roguish glee, "ye'll be hard to please gin ye judge ithers by yoursel'." He laughed, and I laughed, and the whelp barked, and from that moment we were friends; and when I left, I did so perfectly satisfied that if I lost my way the fault would be his, so thoroughly bewildered had I become with his instructions, and the intricate windings of the route he counselled me to follow.

Trusting to perseverance I returned to the road, and soon gained the extremity of the heath-covered heights behind which the remote but picturesque village of Craigie nestles. For a long way the scene was cheerless and barren, and nought was heard save the cry of the peesweep and the song of the lark; but gradually the country opened, and a rich agricultural district met the gaze. Arriving at a very conspicuous farm-house, according to instructions received I rounded a small pond on the wayside and turned into a hedge-bordered road on the right, and held onward, for the sun was in its glory, and the whin and the broom-clad banks and the fields and the green pasture lands looked luxuriant in the exhilirating rays. At the termination of this road I found myself in that running between Mauchline and Ayr, but turning to the left I took the first on the right and held onward. It proved one of the old sort—steep and rugged—but following its undulating windings, a two mile walk brought me to the farmstead of Lochlea, and the fields which Burns furrowed with his plough and reaped with his sickle at harvest time.

The fields pertaining to the farm slope gently to the road,

which at this point verges on a low-lying track of mossy looking land. This at one time formed the bed of the loch from which the place takes its name. In 1839, when the speculative proprietor had the water drained off, two canoes of rude manufacture were discovered near a mound whose summit had formed a kind of island, but they attracted little attention, and in course of time the circumstance was all but forgotten. Towards the close of 1878 the marshy nature of the soil rendered its re-drainage absolutely necessary, and it was subjected to the operation. When cutting a portion of the mound referred to, the workmen came upon what they considered to be the remains of a house which had rested upon piles systematically driven into the ground. The discovery coming under the notice of Mr. James Brown of Tarbolton, a most intelligent and discriminating gentleman, he at once wrote to Mr. J. Anderson, keeper of the Museum of the Society of Antiquaries of Scotland, who communicated with R. W. Cochran-Patrick of Woodside, the respected secretary of the Archæological Society for the counties of Ayr and Wigtown, and he proceeded to the scene of operations and at once recognised in the remains the remnant of a crannog or lake dwelling. In presence of Mr Cochran-Patrick, Mr Turner (factor for the Duke of Portland), Mr Anderson, and other gentlemen, a series of systematic excavations were begun, which in course of time disclosed rows of rude oaken piles driven firmly into what had been the bed of the loch, and secured by horizontal beams, planks of oak, and young trees, all of which were in an excellent state of preservation, and marked by the indentations of some cutting instruments. The area which the piles enclosed was some 60 feet in diameter. Within it were discovered four pavements of stone, which upon investigation were found to rest upon layers of clay, boulders, and logs of oak firmly imbedded and interspersed with charred wood, burnt bones, and ashes.

From this peculiar structure three rows of closely-set wooden piles, which had evidently supported a gangway extending to what had been the shore of the loch, were also laid bare; but the most curious circumstance connected with the discovery was the enormous quantity of bones which the excavators met with. They were strewn about in all directions, and in sufficient quantities to have filled several carts, and when the writer visited the spot every turn of the spade disclosed others which were interspersed with brushwood and small boulders. These bones were evidently the remains of animals which had been used for food by the occupants of the peculiarly situated structure which occupied the spot, but who or what they were can only be conjectured. That they were the primeval inhabitants of the district, and lived in a rude, barbarous age, however, is evident from the numerous articles which the explorers brought to light—such as stone hammers, bone chisels, querns, boars' tusks, and rudely formed instruments made of deers' horns, bone, and wood; and also a canoe formed out of a solid log; a knife of metal, with a yellow ferrule adhering to the remains of the haft; and a variety of iron and flint implements. Dr Munro of Kilmarnock took a deep interest in the excavations, the success of which was greatly owing to his personal exertions, and to his able and elaborate account of the discovery, which is illustrated with plans, sections, and drawings of the crannog, I must refer the reader.

The whole of the articles discovered being found on the ground of the Duke of Portland, were the property of His Grace; but through the intervention of Mr Turner, he generously presented them to the town of Kilmarnock, so that they might form the nucleus of a Museum and be open to the inspection of the curious.

Upon entering the farm-yard of Lochlea, a glance was sufficient to show that the hand of improvement had wholly changed its aspect, the buildings surrounding it being modern, substantial, and slated. In the poet's time the steading consisted of a one-storied thatched dwelling house, with a barn on the one side and a stable and byre on the other. The old dwelling is now converted into a stable, and a comfortable residence has been erected in its stead; and the barn, which the poet is said to have roofed with his own hands, has given place to a more modern and shapely erection, which, thanks to the Duke of Portland's factor, Mr Turner, contains at least one stone of the old fabric. It bears the following inscription :—

"The Lintel of the Poet's Barn.

Re-built 1870."

While surveying the old dwelling-house strange thoughts passed through my mind. At Whitsunday, 1777, the flitting from Mount Oliphant drew up before its door and the Burns family entered, and for seven years they valiantly strove to avert the crisis that had its beginning at the farm they had left. Robert was in the nineteenth year of his age then, and to him "life was young and love was new," but the tender passion had no sooner animated his bosom than he burst into song and celebrated his amours in verse. Authorship with him may be said to have had its beginning at Lochlea. Within the old dwelling he penned many of his early effusions, and, in the language of Dr Currie, "while the ploughshare under his guidance passed through the sward, or the grass fell under the sweep of his scythe, he was humming the songs of his country, musing on deeds of ancient valour, or wrapt in the illusions of fancy as her enchantments rose on his view." Within the old dwelling, also, the poet's father closed his eyes in death. Mrs Begg remembered the event, and affirmed that he had a presentiment of Robert's future career, and more than feared that Robert would wander into paths from which he had preserved his own footsteps. On the day of his death the old man said that there was one of his family for whose future conduct he feared. "Oh, father! is it me you mean?" said Robert. Upon learning that it was, he turned to the window, and, with smothered sobs and scalding tears, acknowledged the reproof; but why he did so is more than I can understand, for his brother Gilbert assured Dr Currie that his temperance and frugality were everything that could be wished during his residence at Lochlea.

John Murdoch, a young man who at one time acted as tutor to the poet and his brothers, tells us that William Burness was an excellent husband and a tender and affectionate father, taking a pleasure in leading his children in the path of virtue—"not in driving them, as some parents do, to the performance of duties to which they themselves are averse. He took care to find fault but very seldom, and therefore, when he did rebuke, he was listened to with a kind of reverential awe; a look of disapprobation was felt, a reproof was severely so, and a stripe with the taws, even on the skirt of the coat, gave heart-felt pain, produced a loud lamentation, and brought forth a flood of tears. He had," we are told, "the art of gaining the esteem and good-will of those that were labourers under him." In fact, " he practised every known duty, and avoided everything that was criminal; or, in the Apostle's words, 'Herein did he exercise himself in living a life void of offence towards God and towards men.'" His sons are no less earnest in their expressions of admiration for their father. Gilbert says :—" My father was for some time almost the only companion we had. He conversed familiarly on all subjects with us as if we had been men, and was at great pains, while we accompanied him in the labours of the farm, to lead the conversation to such subjects as might tend to increase our knowledge, or confirm us in virtuous habits." Robert, again, writing in February, 1784, says :—" On the 13th curt. I lost the best of fathers. Though, to be sure, we have had long warning of the impending stroke, still the feelings of nature claim their part, and I cannot recollect the tender endearments and parental lessons of the best of friends and ablest of instructors without feeling what perhaps the calmer dictates of reason would partly condemn."

The present guidman of Lochlea is William Spiers, Esq., late of Shortlees, in the parish of Riccarton, a jolly good-natured farmer, who is at all times glad to see visitors. I found him affable, jocular, and hospitable, and will not readily forget the pleasant hour spent with him in his spacious kitchen, nor the courtesy of his amiable daughter,

" A dancin' sweet, young, handsome queen,
  O' guileless heart."

With a lingering look at the walls of the old dwelling wherein Burns spent some of the happiest days of his life, I returned to the road and resumed my journey, having determined to enter Tarbolton by way of Coilsfield—a round-about approach certainly, but nevertheless best suited to my purpose, because it winds through scenery immortalised by our Poet, and past places associated with the most pathetic passage in the history of his life. Passing up the road, which is somewhat steep and skirted for some distance by a plantation of young firs, I arrived in the highway between Mauchline and Tarbolton, near to the toll-bar of Mossbog. The country here is unattractive, being composed

of undulating uplands which rise from the bank of the river
Ayr, and slope downwards in the direction of Lochlea.
After indulging in a little gossip with the toll-wife, as she
sat knitting a stocking by the door of her cot, I turned down
a road on the right, and, according to her instructions, held
"straught on." The way proved long, hilly, and thoroughly
rustic, being skirted on the left for a considerable distance
with a long strip of pleasant woodland, through which the
sunshine glinted as if toying with the bramble bushes in its
shade. The knolls by the wayside were decked with tufts
of fragrant broom and whin, and spangled with many a
"bonnie gem" which the summer sun had called from dust
to splendour. Dear wild flowers—

> "Like orphan children silent, lone,
>   I've met you spread o'er wild and moor,
> Where wand'ring ye have cheer'd me on
>   And sooth'd me, ramble-toil'd and poor.
>
> "I've seen you when the matin ray
>   First dawn'd upon the purpling east,
> Your petals ope, and noiseless pray,
>   More eloquent than cassock'd priest.
>
> "Sweet teachers, you from green hillside
>   Breathe fragrance forth to sooth and cheer
> The heart of those whose tread of pride
>   Has made thy beauties disappear."

At the termination of this really pleasant walk I found
myself in the highway between Mauchline and Ayr, and in
the immediate vicinity of Coilsfield. Passing through the
toll-bar of Woodhead the scene suddenly changed from the
commonplace to that of the most romantic description, for
down in a gorge by the wayside,

> "Ayr gurgling kissed its pebbled shore
>   O'erhung with wildwoods thick'ning green,"

and dashed its waters into foam against fragments of rock as
it rolled on its way. The scene was enchanting, and to
enjoy it more fully I descended to the water edge and sat
down on a mossy bank to rest and gaze on the beautiful
scene. How long I remained it is unnecessary to say, but
when the journey was resumed it was with a more elastic
step and happier frame of mind, for

> "The saddest heart might pleasure take
> To see a scene so fair."

Reaching Failford—a cluster of neat cottages at the mouth of the rivulet from which the place takes its name—a pleasant walk along a beautiful wood-fringed road brought me to the entrance gate of the grounds which surround Coilsfield House, one of the most romantically situated mansions in the county—but it will be as well to reserve the account of it and King Coil's grave for next chapter.

CHAPTER XI.

THE ENTRANCE TO THE DOMAIN OF COILSFIELD—COILSFIELD MAINS—KING COIL'S GRAVE AND WHAT WAS FOUND IN AND NEAR IT—THE CASTLE O' MONTGOMERY—"HIGHLAND MARY"—"HIGHLAND MARY'S THORN" AND ASSOCIATIONS—FROM COILSFIELD TO TARBOLTON—THE VILLAGE—BURNS—AN OLD INN—THE DEBATING CLUB AND DANCING SCHOOL—THE OLD HALL, ETC.

"The banks and braes and streams around
    The Castle o' Montgomery"

are of the most romantic description, and replete with poetical associations—in fact, the foliage-draped road in which the chief entrance to the estate is situated is sylvan in the extreme, and irresistibly fascinating in the eyes of those who feel that they
                ———"tread
    Where Coila's Bard harmonic sung,
    And mark with awe around them spread
    Those scenes which once inspired his tongue."

Admiration for the genius of Burns, and a love of everything associated with his name, caused me to pause and ultimately tap at the door of a circular thatch-covered cot which stands in a shady nook by the wayside, as if guarding the gate of the drive which winds through the domain of Coilsfield and terminates near the village of Tarbolton. The summons was unheeded, for the goodwife had "thrawn the key in the door" while doing an errand, but a passing country-girl, whose face beamed with health and good humour, came to my assistance and answered my queries in a very amusing and coquettish manner. "Heelan' Mary's Thorn—div I ken it? O aye! brawly that! It's yont the big house there, an' an auld stump it is an' no worth gaun aff yer gait to see, but I suppose ye'll be keen to get a glower at it?" "I should like very much." "Weel, weel, then—gang through the gate an' haud straught on till ye come to the big hoose an' ye'll see it on yer richt hand a wee bit ayont it. The family's frae hame, an' gin ye're no seen, naebody 'ill sae ocht to you." Not very likely, thought I. "King Coil's grave? O aye! it's in the park at the back o' Coilsfield Mains—the farmhouse 'mang the trees owre yonder; but there's nocht to see aboot it either but a pickle trees an' a wheen auld stanes, but gin ye ha'e a notion o' gaun to it, yer best plan 'll be to gang alang the road an' up to the farm, an' when ye've seen the grave gang through the slap an' doon the brae to the thorn. It's no ill to fin'." After some further conversation, I held along the really beautiful road for a short distance and turned up the avenue to Coilsfield Mains, fairly charmed with the scene and the music of the woods.

"Ye sweet birds of summer that sing from the brakes;
Ye larks that the blue vaulting skim,
How the bound of the heart to your melody wakes;
'Twas your sires that gave rapture to him."

Passing the farm-steading I entered a grass park and directed my steps to a cluster of trees that a stripling pointed to, and found in their midst a mound surmounted by three large pieces of rock intersected with moderately-sized boulders. And this is the grave of "Old King Coil, the merry old soul," of nursery celebrity, said I, sitting down on the top of the tumulus. Well, it does not amount to much after all, and if it ever contained the remains of a monarch, then it is true indeed that

"The glories of our birth and state
Are shadows, not substantial things;
There is no armour against fate;
Death lays his icy hand on kings—
Sceptre and crown
Must tumble down
And in the dust be equal made
With the poor crooked scythe and spade."

Unvarying tradition points to this spot as the resting-place of one Coil, or Coilus, a king of the Britons, who is said to have fallen in a bloody battle which he fought with Fergus I., King of Scots, in a field in the vicinity which bears the name of "The Dead Men's Holm," and in which pieces of ancient armour and fragments of bones have from time to time been unearthed by the plough. This, and the fact that a brooklet close to it is named the "bloody burn," and that the district of Kyle, as antiquaries affirm, derives its name from him, in a measure proves that the tradition has some foundation, or at least that an important battle was at some period of our country's history fought near the place indicated. Buchanan, the historian, who wrote about 1570, affirms that Coilus lived three hundred and twenty-five years before the Christian era, and in Bleau's "Atlas"—a work published in the middle of the seventeenth century—the battle is mentioned at some length; but, on the other hand, Chalmers, the antiquary, scouts the whole story, and modern historians look upon the monarch as a fictitious personage, for the reason that the date assigned him is anterior to the period of genuine history.

The accuracy of the tradition will ever remain a matter of dispute; but that it is not wholly a myth is evident from the following interesting narrative which appeared in the *Ayr Observer:*—"On the evening of the 29th May, 1837, in presence of several gentlemen, the two large stones were removed. The centre of the mound was found to be occupied by boulder stones, some of them of considerable size. When the excavators had reached the depth of about four feet, they came on a flag-stone of a circular form, about three feet in diameter. The light had now failed, and rain began to fall in torrents; but the interest excited was too intense to admit of delay; candles were procured, all earth and rubbish cleared away, and the circular stone carefully lifted up. The seclusion of the spot, the beauty of the surrounding lawn and trees, the eager countenances of the spectators, and above all, the light and voices rising from the grave, in which there had been darkness and silence (as supposed) for upwards of two thousand years, rendered the scene which at this time presented itself at Coil's tomb a very remarkable one. Under the circular stone was first a quantity of dry, yellow-coloured, sandy clay; then a small flag-stone laid horizontally, covering the mouth of an urn, filled with white-coloured burnt bones. In removing the dry clay by which the urn was surrounded, it was discovered that a second urn, less indurated in its texture, so frail as to fall to pieces when touched, had been placed close to the principal urn. Next day the examination

H

of the mound was resumed, and two more urns filled with
bones were found. Of these urns, one crumbled into dust as
soon as the air was admitted; the other was raised in a frac-
tured state. Under flat stones, several small heaps of bones
were observed, not contained in urns, but carefully surrounded
by the yellow coloured clay mentioned above. The urns, in
shape, resemble flower pots. They are composed of clay, and
have been hardened by fire. The principal urn is $7\frac{1}{8}$ inches
in height, $7\frac{7}{8}$ inches in diameter, $\frac{3}{8}$ of an inch thick. It has
none of those markings supposed to have been made by the
thumb nail so often to be observed on sepulchral urns, and it
has nothing of ornament except an edging or projecting part
about half an inch from the top. No coins, armour, or implements of any description could be found. The discovery
of these urns renders it evident that at a very remote period,
and while the practice of burning the dead still prevailed—
that is to say, before the introduction of Christianity—some
person or persons of distinction had been deposited there.
The fact of sepulchral urns having been found in the very
spot where, according to an uninterrupted tradition and the
statements of several historians, King Coil had been laid,
appears to give to the traditionary evidence, and to the statements of the early Scottish historians (except with respect to
the date), a degree of probability higher than they formerly
possessed."

"In 1796, while some of the labourers about Coilsfield
were digging a marl pit in the vicinity of the grave, they
came upon a curiously carved stone, a drawing of which
Colonel Montgomerie (afterwards Earl of Eglinton) caused to
be sent to the museum of the Society of Antiquaries, Edinburgh, where it still remains. Professor Wilson, in his 'Prehistoric Period,' written chiefly from the remains of antiquity
contained in the museum of the society, gives an etching of
this stone. . . . . . . It is worthy of remark that
the symbolic slab was not found in the tumulus, but in a
marl pit at some distance, where an urn was at the same time
dug up, a drawing of a portion of which was also sent by
Colonel Montgomerie to the Society of Antiquaries. If the
battle happened between the Britons, Scots, and Picts, as
Buchanan tells us, the symbolic cist slab may have covered
the remains of some Pictish or Scottish chief, though more

probably Pictish, as these stones are chiefly to be found in the Pictish division of the country, or where colonies of the Picts are known once to have existed."*

Musing on

"Names once famed, now dubious or forgot,
And buried 'midst the wreck of things which were,"

I strolled across the field to the fence which separates it from the grounds surrounding Coilsfield House—or "the Castle o' Montgomery," as it is poetically termed by Burns—and in the absence of convenient entrance, vaulted across the barrier and threaded a narrow path along a grassy sward which leads to the gravelled walk in front of the mansion. The verdant carpeting was thickly strewn with wild flowers, and above was a delightful canopy formed of the interlaced branches of trees through which the screened sunlight softly fell.

The mansion is an elegant modern building with a portico at the front entrance, but on the whole gloomy and deserted in appearance. It is delightfully situated on a high embankment of the Fail, a rivulet whose music joins in chorus with the song of the birds singing you know not where, but everywhere, in the bosky woods in which it is embosomed.

The lands of Coilsfield were purchased from the Eglinton family by the present proprietor, William Orr, Esq., "who changed his name to *Paterson*, in compliance with the will of a relative, which name only he now bears. By the same will he was bound to call the estate, purchased with Mr. Paterson's funds, Montgomerie, which is accordingly now the name of Coilsfield."†

Ninety-four years ago Coilsfield House was the residence of Colonel Hugh Montgomery—not a very remarkable fact certainly, but then in this gentleman's service, in the capacity of dairymaid, was a Highland girl, named Mary Campbell, who won the affections of Burns, and who has been vouchsafed an immortality which rivals that of any other heroine of song, for the verses in her praise are justly ranked among the most finished efforts of her lover's muse. This

---

* "History of the County of Ayr."
† Ibid.

attachment has been described as the purest and most elevated ever formed by Burns, and its object as " a sweet, sprightly, blue-eyed creature, of a firmer modesty and self-respect than too many of the other maidens he had addressed." This may be, but tradition (which is seldom wholly incorrect) has it that she was neither graceful nor feminine, but was a coarse-featured, ungainly country lass, which may possibly be conformable to truth, for his brother Gilbert tells us that he was somewhat of an amorist, and that "when he selected any one out of the sovereignty of his good pleasure to whom he should pay his particular attention, she was instantly invested with a sufficient stock of charms out of the plentiful stores of his own imagination; and there was often a great dissimilitude between his fair captivator as she appeared to others and as she seemed when invested with the attributes he gave her."

The history of "Highland Mary"—as she is poetically termed—is wrapt in considerable mystery, but thanks to Robert Chambers and others, a few facts have been rescued from oblivion. She appears to have been the daughter of a sailor in a revenue cutter, who had his residence at Campbeltown, and to have spent her early years in the family of the Rev. David Campbell of Loch Ranza (a relative of her mother), in the island of Arran. In early womanhood she was induced to come to Ayrshire and take a situation as a domestic servant, but her movements on her arrival could never be traced. However, it is almost a certainty that she was serving in the family of Burns' friend, Gavin Hamilton, writer, Mauchline, in 1784, and removed to Coilsfield in 1785.

About fifty yards from Coilsfield House I paused before an aged but shattered and decayed thorn which grows by the side of the drive leading to the Tarbolton entrance of the domain. The stately trees by which it is guarded overlook a steep bank clothed with verdure and dense masses of shrubs which screen the rippling Fail as it gurgles on to mingle its water with winding Ayr. There is nothing remarkable about the appearance of the thorn, nothing to attract attention, yet curiously enough its rotten moss-grown trunk is chipped and hacked, and its remaining limb disfigured with rude initials and gashes which wanton relic-hunters have inflicted with pocket knives. What is the cause of all this? and why is the grass round about it trampled and bare? Well, tradition states that it is the identical tree beneath which Robert Burns took the last farewell of his sweet Highland Mary.

> "How sweetly bloomed the gay green birk,
>   How rich the hawthorn's blossom,
> As underneath the fragrant shade,
>   I clasped her to my bosom!
> The golden hours, on angel wings,
>   Flew o'er me and my dearie:
> For dear to me as light and life,
>   Was my sweet Highland Mary.
>
> "Wi' mony a vow, and lock'd embrace,
>   Our parting was fu' tender;
> And, pledging aft to meet again,
>   We tore ourselves asunder;
> But, oh! fell death's untimely frost,
>   That nipt my flower sae early!
> Now green's the sod, and cauld's the clay,
>   That wraps my Highland Mary!"

In all likelihood the tradition is correct, for the position of the thorn and its nearness to the mansion makes it more than probable that the parting took place beneath its shade—in fact, Burns was by far too great a gallant to part from his mistress at any great distance from her home.

The parting took place on the evening of "the second Sunday of May," 1786. In a note to "the Highland lassie," Burns gives us a little insight into this episode. He says— "My Highland lassie was a warm-hearted, charming young creature as ever blest a man with generous love. After a pretty long tract of the most ardent reciprocal attachment, we met by appointment on the second Sunday of May in a sequestered spot on the banks of the Ayr, where we spent the day in taking a farewell before she should embark for the West Highlands to arrange matters among her friends for our projected change of life. At the close of autumn she crossed the sea to meet me at Greenock, where she had scarce landed when she was seized with a malignant fever before I could even hear of her illness."

Mr. Cromek tells that "their adieu was performed with those simple and striking ceremonials which rustic sentiment has devised to prolong tender emotions and to impose awe. The lovers stood on each side of a purling brook—they laved their hands in the limpid stream—and holding a Bible between them pronounced their vows to be faithful to each other." As already stated, they exchanged Bibles, but what became of that which Burns received was never known; the half-Bibles presented to Mary are, as the reader will remember, preserved in the monument on the banks of Doon. Mary appears to have left Ayrshire about Whitsunday, 1786, and to have spent the summer at her father's house in Campbeltown, but whether she made arrangements for the "projected change in life" Burns speaks of there is no evidence to show. Robert Chambers thinks that she had agreed to accept a situation in Glasgow in the family of a Colonel M'Ivor, and that she was proceeding thither when she sickened and died. He also mentions as a tradition that her friends believed her illness to be caused by the cast of an evil eye, and at their suggestion her father went to a spot where two burns meet, selected seven smooth stones, boiled them in milk, and gave it her to drink. She was buried in the West Kirkyard of Greenock. Her resting-place is marked by a handsome monument, the cost of which (£100) was raised by subscription.

In a little work entitled "Much about Kilmalcolm," by Alexander S. Gibb, there is an interesting traditional narrative, entitled "A Story of Greenock," which may interest the reader. It was originally told many years ago by a worthy soul named Johnnie Blair, and refers to Highland Mary. Of course, it may be taken for what it is worth. He says :—
"While I was looking at the country side, the river, and Greenock down the water's edge, and hearkening to the whirr o' the moor fowl as they settled in a black flock on the farmer's stooks, I saw a braw buxom lass coming down the Kilmalcolm Road. She was a well-faur'd dame, wi' cheeks like roses. She had on a tartan shawl, and was carrying some things wi' her. I offered to help her to carry them, which she gladly assented to, for she was tired wi' a long journey. She had come frae Ayrshire, she said, and got a drive to Kilmalcolm, and was gaun first to Jamie Macpherson, the shipwright's, whase wife was her cousin, and syne to Argyle, where her folk belanged. I kent Jamie as weel's I ken you, Davie ; we were gude cronies and gude neebors. Twa or three days after this I chanced to forgather wi' Jamie.

' Man, John,' says he to me, ' ye're aye speaking about books and poetry ; ye'll come doun by the nicht an' I'll let you see some richt poems.' I gaed doun by accordingly, an' got a sicht o' the book he spak o'. It was a volume o' poems by Robert Burns, printed at Kilmarnock. ' It was Mary Campbell, Jean's cousin,' Jean explained, ' wha brought the book wi' her frae Ayr; it's juist new out, you see. She's awa to Argyle to see her friends, and she's coming back in a week or twa to be married. And wha do you think till ?' I said I couldna guess. ' Well, it's juist to the chiel wha made that book. She said he had been fechtin' wi' the ministers, and was thinking o' gaun awa to the West Indies; but she didna care, she was willing to gang wi' him.' Jamie read a lot o' the poems ower, and we held at them till twal o'clock. Jamie said he didna a'thegither like the way the chiel spak o' the kirks, but he thocht ' the lassie micht help to haud him straught; and he sudna be the man to mak' strife amang sweethearts.' He let's see a wee sang the lass had brocht wi' her, beginning—

    ' Will ye gang to the Indies, my Mary,
      And leave auld Scotland's shore?'

which Mary had shown as a great secret to his wife, and which was written upon herself. Mary returned across the Firth the week after. It was a cold, rainy, muggy day that she had got to cross and she had gotten a dreadful chill. The fever was then raging in Greenock, for ye ken wi' our houses a' hauled thegither, an' the ill water we had then, and the foul air that hangs about our wynds and closes, we never hardly want fever. Puir Mary onyway took it; whether it was the chill she had gotten, or the foul air of Minch Callop Close, baith thegither that brocht it on I canna say, but Mary sickened and grew worse day by day. Jamie Macpherson's wife nursed her like a sister; a doctor was called in, but nothing wad do. Her time was come. Jamie's wife tell'd me a' aboot it. She lay in a wee room aff the kitchen; there was a chest o' drawers an' a clock in't; three or four stuffed birds, and a picture of a naval battle between French and British; also, twa models of ships. There was a wee window that neither opened up nor down; but the air outside was that foul wi' vapours that it was maybe better it didna. Nae doubt, to her coming out o' the country, the close air that the dwellers' lungs had got used to wad no be beneficial. Man, I whiles think that thae fevers are juist brocht on by the air a'thegither. Whiles the poor sufferer was a wee raivell'd; whiles she repeated verses out o' the Bible, ane in particular—'Thou shalt not forswear thyself, but shall perform unto the Lord thine oaths;' and ance she cried out, 'O for a drink o' caller water!' but it was thocht at the time that water was ill for fevers. But afore she died she was quite sensible, an' said to her cousin Jean, 'If it had been God's will I wad hae liked to be Robert Burns' wife; but I ken I'm deein' an' I'm quite willing.' 'Dinna speak that way, Mary,' said Jean, 'or ye'll break my heart; ye'll get better yet, lassie, for a' this.' But she did not get better; an' the night following her spirit took its flicht from this world of sin and misery, to the great sorrow of all her friends, and, was kent some years after, to that of her admirer, Robert Burns. Ye ken his sang 'Highland Mary' was written about her, and ither sangs o' his, gin I could mind them."

With a lingering look at "the Castle o' Montgomery" and the old thorn tree, I passed down the drive and began to walk briskly in the direction of Tarbolton. On my left was a beautiful lawn studded here and there with fine specimens of natural wood, and on my right a highly romantic scene, through which the Fail glided

"Wi' bickering, dancing dazzle,"

as if anxious to escape from the shade of the trees on its banks and gain the open glade in the distance. Passing through a dilapidated gateway I entered a shady avenue, and in the course of twenty minutes arrived at the ancient village, which stands on some rising ground, and occupies a place in the heart of one of the sweetest localities in the west of Scotland. It is a quaint little place, chiefly consisting of one long street, from which short thoroughfares branch, but, with the exception of weaving and the manufacture of fancy woodwork, no trades are carried on save what are incidental to all rural settlements. The population last census was 829, but it has considerably diminished, very many individuals, and in some instances whole families, having been compelled to remove to the large centres of industry to procure employment. Tarbolton contains three places of worship, a Mechanics' Institute, and a handsome school, which is more than adequate to the requirements of the community. It is governed by two bailies and twelve councillors, who are elected annually, and was created a burgh of barony by Charles II. in 1671.

Although Tarbolton is an ancient village, there is nothing of historical interest connected with it, and it is only on account of it having been a favourite resort of our poet when residing in the farm of Lochlea that it has become famous. It was the scene of several of his early amours, and in it he spent some of the happiest hours of his brief life. Thirty years ago the sojourner experienced little difficulty in meeting and conversing with people in this village who had known the bard; but now they are all gone, and with his associates and boon companions rest from their labours in the churchyard. However, it is gratifying to note the pride some middle-aged people take in telling that their grand-fathers " kenned Rabbie weel, an' ran wi' him i' their young days." They appear gratified to identify their "forebeers" with his name, and have it in their power to relate anecdotes of him and them. The following extract from David Sillar's account of the poet when he frequented the village will be of interest :—" His social disposition easily procured him acquaintances; but a certain satirical seasoning, with which he and all poetical genius are in some degree influenced, while it set the rustic circle in a roar, was not unaccompanied by its kindred attendant, suspicious fear. . . . . He wore the only tied hair in the parish; and in church his plaid, which was of a particular colour, I think fillemot, he wrapped in a particular manner round his shoulders. . . . . After the commencement of my acquaintance with the bard we frequently met upon Sundays at church, when, between sermons, instead of going with our friends or lasses to the inn, we often took a walk in the fields. In these walks I have frequently been struck by his facility in addressing the fair sex : many times when I have been bashfully anxious how to express myself, he would have entered into conversation with them with the greatest ease and freedom ; and it was generally a deathblow to our conversation, however agreeable, to meet a female acquaintance. Some of the few opportunities of a noontide walk that a country life affords her laborious sons, he spent on the banks of the river, or in the woods, in the neighbourhood of Stair, a situation peculiarly adapted to the genius of a rural bard. Some book he always carried and read when not otherwise employed."

The main artery of the village possesses a very rural appearance, being lined on either side with unassuming dwellings, most of which are of one storey and thatch-roofed. At the Cross—a rather confined place of the kind—there is an old-fashioned two-storied house that to all appearance has seen better days. The signboard above its door intimates that James M'Connachie retails spirits, porter, and ales in the interior; but there is something of a deeper interest associated with it. It was the principal inn in the village when our Poet resided in the farm of Lochlea, and was kept by John Richard, who was an intimate friend of the bard. In a hall attached to this house Burns often "presided o'er the sons of light," and "spent the festive night" with the "brethren of the mystic tie." In it he took his tearful farewell of the fraternity, and bade them "a heart-warm fond adieu" when about to proceed to Jamaica. When Robert Chambers visited Tarbolton he conversed with a shoemaker named John Lees, who recollected the parting. "Burns," he said, "came in buckskin breeks, out of which he would always pull the other shilling for the other bowl, till it was five in the morning. An awfu' night that."

The debating club and dancing school in which Burns took an active part were also held in this house. In the "History of the rise, proceedings, and regulations" of the club, I find that the first meeting was held in the house of John Richard, upon the evening of the 11th of November, 1780, commonly called Hallowe'en, and that Robert Burns was chosen president for the night. The club met every fourth Monday night to debate questions raised by the members; and as no one was allowed to spend more than threepence at one sitting, the potations must have been scant indeed. The poet and his brother Gilbert continued members till they left the parish.

When attending the dancing school, Burns made sad havoc among "the Tarbolton lasses," or rather they made sad havoc of him. To one reigning predominant in his affections at the time, he addressed the beautiful song of "Mary Morison."

> "Yestreen when to the trembling string
>   The dance gaed through the lighted ha',
> To thee my fancy took its wing—
>   I sat, but neither heard nor saw.
> Though this was fair, and that was braw,
>   And yon the toast of a' the town,
> I sighed, and said amang them a'
>   Ye are na Mary Morison."

Mrs Begg, the poet's sister, had a vivid recollection of the dancing school. Robert Chambers says: "There could not well be any objection on his father's part to his acquiring this accomplishment (dancing), for Gilbert and the two eldest sisters, Agnes and Annabella, besides their ploughman, Willie Miller, all attended likewise. . . . . On a practising ball occurring, Burns paid Willie's expenses, that he might have Janet Brown as a partner, so as to enable the bard to have as *his* partner some other lass who was then reigning in his affections."

Being anxious to see the interior of this humble hostel, I entered, and was cordially received by the landlady, a lively little Irishwoman, but learned nothing beyond the fact that she had heard that Burns frequented the house "in oulden times," and that he attended the Lodge St. James when it met in a room up stairs. The information was meagre indeed, but I felt gratified to be in a place where *he* had been, and perhaps this caused me to linger longer in the little low-roofed apartment into which I was shown than I otherwise would have done.

Upon leaving the hostel, I sought the back of the premises, ascended an outside stair, and tapped gently at a porched door. It was opened by a neatly dressed woman, who invited me in, with all the frankness of an old acquaintance, the instant the name of a Kilmarnock friend was mentioned. "So this is the old dancing hall," said I, by way of introduction. "'Deed is't, and but little altered since Rabbie danced in't," said she; "but to make it habitable, a partition was run through it, as you see, an' noo it serves for baith room an' kitchen." "And a comfortable one, too, to all appearance," I rejoined; "but what proof have you that Burns danced on this floor and presided over the sons of light within these walls?" "Plenty o' proof," she replied, smiling—" my great grandfather, John Richard, kept the inn in the front there, in the time of Burns, an' was weel acquaint wi' him. Besides, my grandfather, William Dick, ran wi' Rabbie, and the only wonder is that he's no mentioned in ony o' his poems, for he blackfitted him to Highland Mary an' a lass in the Bennels ca'd Leezie Paton, who had a wean to him, and to whom he addressed the sang beginning—

> 'From thee, Eliza, I must go,
> And from my native shore;
> The cruel fates between us throw
> A boundless ocean's roar.'"

"Really!" I replied, "but the heroine of that song is supposed to have borne the name of Betty Miller—she figured as one of the Mauchline belles." "That may be," she sharply answered, "but her name *was* Paton." And Paton my friend stuck to, and perhaps she is right after all, for, according to Motherwell, some discrepancy of opinion exists as to the heroine of the song. Cunninghame affirms that she was an Elizabeth Black, who early became acquainted with Burns and made no small impression on his heart, and possessed several love epistles he had addressed to her. Despite this, I have more faith in family tradition than in any printed statement. During the time I remained in the old hall, my friend entertained me with many anecdotes of "Rabbie," and showed me a flagstaff which the lodge St. James owned when Burns took an active part in it, and also the Bible of her great grandfather, a curiosity in its way. It bears the following:—"John Richard, his book. God gave him grace to make a good use of it." I spent a pleasant hour in the snug dwelling, and will not readily forget the hospitality and kindness of the good lady.

CHAPTER XII.

HOODSHILL—AN ANCIENT CUSTOM—THE SCENE OF "DEATH AND DR. HORNBOOK"—"WILLIE'S MILL"—GRANNIE HAY'S RECOLLECTIONS OF BURNS AND THE MILLER'S WIFE—A SOUVENIR OF THEIR FRIENDSHIP—TARBOLTON CHURCH AND CHURCHYARD—THE VILLAGE SMITHY—A WALK TO TORRCROSS AND ITS OBJECT—"BROTHER BURNS"—FAIL CASTLE—THE FRIARS—THE WARLOCK LAIRD AND HIS CANTRIPS—ADAM HILL—HOME AGAIN.

FEW streets are more intimately associated with the memory of Robert Burns than that which branches off Tarbolton Cross. It very appropriately bears his name, and was often traversed by him when residing at Lochlea and Mossgiel. In fact, it was and still is the direct line of communication between these farms and the clachan, which, as we have seen, was a favourite resort of his when residing in the neighbourhood. Being aware that the poet toddled down it when returning from the Masonic meeting at which he had the famous dispute with the village pedagogue that provoked the satire of "Death and Dr. Hornbook," I did the same, and soon arrived at a humble thatched cottage which stands at the right hand corner of its extremity. It is now occupied as a dwelling-house, but it was at one time a portion of a noted inn, and is now memorable as the house wherein the brethren of St. David's lodge of Freemasons held their meetings and initiated the bard into the mysteries of their craft. Mr. Neil Murchy, who is in possession of the chair, toddy ladle, and drinking glass of this the mother lodge of Robert Burns, kindly allowed me to inspect the old minute-book of the society, and from it the following interesting extract is taken:—"Sederunt for July 4th (1781)—Robert Burns, in Lochly, was entered an apprentice.—Signed, Joseph Norman.". "Sederunt, October 1st, 1781.—Robert Burns, in Lochly, was passed and raised, Henry Cowan being master,

James Humphrey being senior warden, and Alexander Smith, junior; and Robert Wodrow, secretary; and F. Manson, treasurer; and John Tannock, James Taylor, and others of the brethren being present.—Joseph Norman, W.M."

At the cot referred to, a road turns abruptly to the right and winds round the base of a lofty green mound from which the village takes its name.* Paterson affirms in his history of the county that it was used as a place of Pagan worship long before the era of Christianity, and goes on to say that it would seem, from the remains of trenches, that it had been used as an encampment, probably by the ancient Britons, or during the Scoto-Irish wars. It is more certain, however, that it was the hill on which the open Courts of Justice, or Justice-aires of the district, were regularly held, and that fire worship was practised on it is probable from the immemorial custom of the annual kindling of bonfires near its summit. "On the evening preceding the Tarbolton June Fair a piece of fuel is demanded [by the boys of the village] at each house, and is invariably given by the poorest inhabitant. The fuel so collected is carried to a particular part of the hill where there is an altar or circular fire-place of turf about three feet in height, and is placed upon the altar. A huge bonfire is kindled, and many of the inhabitants, old and young, men and women, assemble on the hill and remain for hours apparently chiefly occupied with observing a feat performed by the youths who are to be seen leaping with indefatigable zeal upon the altar or turf wall enclosing the ashes of former fires and supporting the present one."† Instead of going "round about the hill," as Burns tells us he did when he had the imaginary interview with Death, I turned into a path fronting a row of unpretentious dwellings and ascended to the top of the mound, for from it an excellent view of Willie's Mill and its surroundings is obtained. This celebrated building stands in a vale on the banks of the Fail and is little more than three hundred yards from the village, but, saving the name, it is wholly changed since the days of the poet, and I suppose no more like the place he frequented than the farm-steading is where he dwelt and composed the

---

* *Tor*, or Thor-Bol-ton, or town, is the Town at Baal's hill, *i.e*, the town at the hill where Baal was worshipped.—*New Statistical Account.*

† Ibid.

verses which have made it so widely known; but nevertheless, although only in a slight degree associated with his name, visitors come from all quarters and gaze with a kind of reverence upon it and the humble thatch-covered cots by its side. From the elevated position, I descended to the main road which sweeps round the base of the hill, and toddled down to Willie's Mill, passing on my way the spot where Burns and Death are supposed to have "cased their shanks" and held the memorable conversation about "Jock Hornbook i' the Clachan," and the means he employed to foil the dread spectre of his prey. The seats are situated about half-way between the hill and the mill, and consist of a portion of rock which juts out from beneath a high hedge by the wayside, but whether it is due to enthusiastic visitors sitting down or the exertions of the boys that mould is prevented from gathering and grass growing on them I am not prepared to say, but I am a little suspicious that it is owing to the latter that they are so well preserved.

At the foot of the brae a small stream of water foamed from beneath the road and surged onward to a waterwheel laboriously revolving behind the mill a short distance off. Passing a byre and a thatch-covered dwelling-house I entered the mill, and found the miller and his man busy among sacks of grain; but in answer to the question, "Have you anything connected with Burns here?" they at once left off their labour and entered into conversation. "We have a barrow that was about the place when the friend of Burns leev'd in't," said a dusty denizen as he produced an old-fashioned two-wheeled hurly, whose moth-eaten spokes and trindles bespoke the tear and wear of former years. "In what way is it connected with Burns?" said I. "Atweel, I dinna ken," was the reply, "but there's little doubt that Burns has often had it in his hand." "O yes," added the miller, "an' a lady frae America wanted to buy it, an' gin I'd selt it she'd taen it hame wi' her." "And what on earth would she have done with it?" I enquired. "O, she said that she would place the poet's portrait in't." "What!" I exclaimed, "place the portrait of the bard in a wheelbarrow!" and I laughed at the absurdity of the proposal. The miller proved racy of speech and very obliging. After pointing out that the mill was not wholly rebuilt as supposed, and showing me the water wheel, he accompanied me to the road and bade me a cordial good-bye.

The parish mill of Tarbolton—or "Willie's Mill," as it is called—was for many years tenanted by Mr. William Muir, an intimate friend of the Burns family. The poet frequented it when residing in the neighbourhood, and on many occasions assisted his friend in the mill, and doubtless often used the barrow referred to in the laborious operation of shifting sacks from place to place. In fact, this is borne out by the interesting gleanings of the Rev. Hately Waddel, for, in referring to his gift of eloquence and story-telling, he says:— "When assisting at the mill at 'hand-sifting' of the meal in trough, all hands got so absorbed in listening, that no sifting could proceed; in consequence of which the machinery in producing overtook the folks in removing, and a general block-up took place."

"The late Mrs. Grannie Hay, aged 94 in 1866," he also states, "was servant at 'Willie's Mill' at the age of 14 to 15. Her sister also followed her in the same place and situation. She remembered Burns distinctly as a tall, swarthy, and at that time rather spare young man, with long black hair on his shoulders, accustomed to ride to Tarbolton from Lochlea or Mossgiel on Freemason lodge nights or other special occasions. He rode booted; he used to stable his horse at the mill; was remarkably kind, pleasant, and affable, and 'straiket her head wi' his hand on the last occasion when she was there.' Her mistress, Mrs. Muir, was a superior woman; could read, write, and cipher easily; and was fit to maintain discourse with Burns on all topics, even on poems occasionally rehearsed by him at the tea-table at the mill: 'aye took his tea when he cam' about four hours.' He 'was a great frequenter o' kirks and preachings, baith at Tarbolton and round about, on which occasions he was often, almost invariably, accompanied by the 'miller himsel',' who had a taste for pulpit oratory, and was 'an unco judge o' doctrine.' 'Burns would speir in for him as he gaed by, and the twa gaed awa thegither.' On one special occasion Grannie Hay remembered well that Burns complained to the mistress of not being able to finish some song that had occurred to him on a Sabbath morning, in consequence of which he was afraid he could not attend church that day—' it wouldna be richt; he couldna hearken when he was fashed.' In despair, he rambled out by some dykeside, where he strolled alone 'till he got the sang a' right,' when he repaired to church as usual with the cheerfulness of relief and of a good conscience. This difficulty and deliverance, it appears, he related in Mrs. Hay's hearing with the simplicity of a boy 'that very mornin' at the mill afore they gaed up to the kirk!' One would give much to know what very song that was. His conversation then and always was cheerful, entertaining, and correctly pure."

When the result of Jean Armour's second intimacy with the poet was discovered, she was driven from the dwelling of her incensed parents, and was left in a manner friendless and destitute. Finding her, says Burns in a letter to Mrs. Dunlop, "literally and truly cast out to the mercy of the naked elements," he took her under his charge, and, according to the writer from whom the above is quoted, secretly conveyed her to Tarbolton Mill, where she gave birth to twins under the superintendence and care of his friend and admirer, the miller's wife. She was a kind, motherly woman; and when Jean's marriage was made public went to Ellisland to "brew the first peck o' maut" for the family and celebrate the home-coming. Grannie Hay had a vivid recollection of the circumstance, and informed the writer quoted above that "the visit was protracted for a fortnight, and was the cause of much offence to the old miller, who did not know of his wife's departure, and threatened to ding her wi' a stick when she cam hame. Na, he keepit his stick by the chimla-lug for twa or three days on purpose, but when he saw her coming down the road his han' trummilt, and he set by the stick, and didna ken what to do wi' her when she cam ben. But she was angry when he spiered at her afterhin' what way she gaed awa without telling him or asking his leave, and syne mair angry words cam on baith han's, and she wadna speak to him ony mair that night; but she spak' to me, and they war never sic guid friends after.' The miller, in fact, was much older than his wife, and her conduct in undertaking such a visit without his knowledge or permission was decidedly reprehensible. She left the mill, it appears, one afternoon when the old gentleman was asleep on the 'deas,' 'for fear he wad hinder her frae gangin' if he

I

waukenit.' Grannie Hay, who was an accomplice in the mistress's manœuvre, was charged with the responsibility of appeasing his wrath when he awoke, and 'had ill doin' o't'!"

Burns kept up correspondence with Mrs Muir after his settlement in Ellisland, and, in recognition of her kindness to his Jean, presented her with a pair of silver sugar tongs, which she long treasured. On her death-bed, she gave them to Mrs Humphrey of Tarbolton. They afterwards came into the possession of her niece, Miss Ann Humphrey, but for a consideration she was induced to part with them, and they are now the property of Mr J. S. Gregory, Kilmarnock. Having had the pleasure of seeing them and hearing their history narrated, I may add that they are of plain make, and of the ordinary size. Over the bow the Poet's name is engraved in *fac-simile* of his hand-writing, and on each blade the names of the several possessors; and the dates on which the relic changed hands are inscribed in the same manner.

Upon returning to the village, I entered the Crown Inn for the purpose of recruiting my energies and enquiring about the *memorabilia* in possession of the brethren of St James' lodge. Here I was shown the chair Burns occupied when Depute-Master, and also the minute book in which his bold signature repeatedly occurs as such. The jewel, or badge to which he alludes in his "Farewell" to the lodge, was put into my hand, as also another interesting relic in the shape of an autograph letter, dated Edinburgh, August 23rd, 1787. These, with a flag and a mallet, I think constitute the whole of the Burns relics in the possession of this lodge, and the brethren are justly proud of them, as they have every right to be.

After a rest, "a crack" (well, I may as well write it down), and a toothful of good malt liquor, I thanked the brethren in attendance for their courtesy, bade them good-bye, and crossed over to the Churchyard.

Like most places in the locality it has undergone a great change since the days of Burns. The dingy little building in which he worshipped is wholly removed, and a neat modern edifice, with an elegant spire and clock, erected in its stead. In pensive mood I wandered among the grassy hillocks and read semi-obliterated memorials of the now forgotten dead, for many of the tombstones are old and not a few bear curious and interesting devices. One near the church door deserves more than passing notice, because it testifies that Tarbolton, like other districts in Ayrshire, shared in the perils of the Persecution. It bears the following inscription:—

"Here lys William Shillaw who was shot at Woodhead by Lieut. Lauder for his adhereance to the Word of God and Scotland's Covenanted work of Reformation. 1688. Erected 1729. Renewed, 1810, by William Drinning."

Shillaw's name occurs in a list of Lieutenant Lauder's victims in the appendix to "The Cloud of Witnesses," but in no other work to which I have had access is it mentioned, and curious enough, the circumstances of the martyr's death appear to have entirely worn out of the traditional mind.

Upon leaving the churchyard I commenced my homeward journey, but had not proceeded far when the ringing tones of an anvil smote my ear, and brought to mind the well-known lines of the poet—

"When Vulcan gies the bellows breath,
And ploughmen gather wi' their graith."

Being anxious to see if this village blacksmith was aught like the one Wordsworth describes, I looked in at the open door. He lifted his dusky visage, and with several onlookers glanced enquiringly at me. "Is this the smithy where Burns got his plough irons sharpened?" I jocularly enquired. "Deed is't," he replied, "an' he made a poem sittin' on that hearth there, an' wrote it on the slate on which my grandfather marked his jobs." This was an unexpected discovery. "Do you know the name of that poem?" "Deed I dinna, though I should hae a copy o't somewhere; but the way it was, my father was for opening a shop, an' he askit Burns to make him twa or three lines mentioning the things he was gaun to sell, so that he might get them set owre his door— for it was customary in thae days to hae a verse o' poetry on a body's sign—so he sat doon an' wrote him aff a screed in which was named maist everything you could think on." "Aye," broke in a friend of the smith, "an' there's a poet here that's maist as guid as Burns himsel'." "As Burns!" said I, "then I'd go a good way to see that chap—Where is he?" "O, he leeves about a mile up that road; gin ye gang up you'll likely fin' him—he aye carries a pickle o' his poetry i'e his pouch." After some further conversation with the smith about the verses composed on the hearth, I bade him goodbye, and set out to make the acquaintance of the man that promised to be "maist as good's Burns." Having held along the road indicated, in due time I arrived at the farm-steading of Torrcross, and found my man on the top of a stack filling a cart with sheaves of grain. Having accused him of "committing the sin of rhyme," he frankly admitted the charge, and in proof of his guilt handed me a copy of the *Freemasons' Journal* containing one of his pieces, which, I must say, flowed smoothly, but to give the reader an idea of John Campbell's poetic abilities, the following masonic song, which was composed for and sung in the lodge St. James, is subjoined :—

BROTHER BURNS.

" If e'er there was an honoured name
    To Masonry and Scotia dear,'
'Twas *his* who gave our lodge to fame,
    And oft has worn the 'jewel' here.
Then surely 'tis our duty here,
    Whene'er his natal day returns,
To pledge his memory with 'a tear'—
    The memory of Robert Burns.

" On Coila's plains he first drew breath,
    'Twas Coila's maids he loved and sung,
He won the bard's immortal wreath,
    Lone wand'ring Coila's woods among.
And Coila's sons shall honour now—
    For sadly still old Scotland mourns—
The mighty minstrel of the plough,
    The gifted mason, Brother Burns.

" His songs are sung on Ganges' side,
    Zambezi's banks his strains have heard,
Siberian forests wild and wide
    Have echoed strains of Scotia's bard.
The broad St. Lawrence hears his voice—
    Where'er the Scottish wanderer turns,
His name can make the heart rejoice—
    The deathless name of Brother Burns.

" But here within our native vale,
    On every glen and flowery brae,
On classic Ayr and winding Fail
    His fame hath shed a brilliant ray—
And here shall reign his glorious name
    Until the grave its dead unurns,
For every craftsman here can claim
    Reflected fame from Brother Burns.

> "Then brethren of the lodge St. James,
> And sister lodges gathered here,
> One silent round his memory claims—
> The round requested with 'a tear.'
> Let's be upstanding to the call
> Of him, the bard whom Scotia mourns,
> To pledge in solemn silence all—
> The memory of Brother Burns."

Upon taking leave of my poetic friend, I struck through the fields and steered my course to Fail Toll. It is situated on the Kilmarnock road about a mile distant from Tarbolton, at the entrance of a little village—if it may be dignified by that name—and near to the ruins of what is locally termed Fail Castle, but which is nothing more than the remains of the manor-house of Fail monastery—founded and dedicated to Saint Mathurine in 1252. It was inhabited by a tribe of monks, styled "Fathers of Redemption," who wore a white habit with a red and blue cross upon the shoulder, and religiously devoted themselves to the humane task of redeeming captives from slavery; but, notwithstanding their sanctity, they appear to have been a merry lot, who knew what was good for them—that is, if there be any truth in the following traditional rhymes:—

> "The Friars of Fail
> Gat never owre hard eggs, or owre thin kail,
> For they made their eggs thin wi' butter,
> And their kail thick wi' bread;
> An' the Friars of Fail they made good kail
> On Fridays when they fasted,
> An' they never wanted gear enough
> As lang as their neighbours' lasted."

> "The Friars of Fail drank berry-brown ale,
> The best that ever was tasted;
> The Monks of Fail they made gude kail
> On Fridays when they fasted."

However, the jolly fathers have passed away, and no portion of their house now remains save the shattered gable and side-wall of the residence of the prior or chief minister. But a word may be said regarding its last occupant—a notorious warlock laird—who was said to possess an evil eye, and to have the faculty of charming milk from cows, butter from the churn, cheese from the dairy tub; and to be able not only to fortell future events, but to control human actions—spreading disease and death among men and cattle by the simple exercise of his will. One of his acts is made the subject of the following ballad :—

"THE WARLOCK LAIRD OF FAIL.

" As Craigie's knight was a hunting one day
    Along with the Laird of Fail,
They came to a house, wherein the gudewife
    Was brewing the shearers' ale.

" Sir Thomas alighted at the door
    Before the Laird of Fail,
' And will ye gi'e me, goodwife,' quo he,
' A drink of your shearers' ale ?'

" ' I will gi'e thee, Sir Thomas,' quo she,
' A drink of my shearers' ale ;
But gude be here how I sweat and fear
    At sight of the Laird of Fail !'

" ' What sees auld lucky the Laird about
    That may not be seen on me ?
His beard so long, so bushy, and strong,
    Sure need not affrighten thee !'

" ' Tho' all his face were cover'd with hair,
    It never would daunten me ;
But young and old oft have heard it told
    That a warlock knight is he.

" ' He caused the death o' my braw milk cow,
    And did not his blasting e'e
Bewitch my barn, cowp many a kirn,
    And gaur my auld doggie die ?' "

Sir Thomas tells the laird of the goodwife's tremor and asks him to "put in the merry pin." This is agreed to, and the result is somewhat ludicrous.

" He put then a pin aboon the door
    And said some mysterious thing,
And instantly the auld wife she
    Began to dance and sing——

" ' O good Sir Thomas of Craigie tak'
    The warlock laird of Fail
Awa frae me, for he never shall pree
    A drap of our shearers' ale !'

" The Laird he cried on the auld gudeman
    And sought a drink of his beer ;
' Atweel, quo he, ' kind sir you shall be
    Welcome to all that is here.'

> "But just as he passed under the pin,
> He roared out—'Warlock Fail,
> Awa frae me, for you never shall pree
> A drap of our shearers' ale.'"

The laird and the knight watch the sport, and as the reapers drop into dinner, they are asked for a drink of the ale, but they no sooner pass under the merry pin than they take up the strain of the goodwife and join in the dance, and, according to the poet,

> "They would have sung the same till yet
> Had not the Laird of Fail
> Drawn out the pin before he went in
> To drink of the shearers' ale."

The laird does not appear to have been very malicious, for many of his cantrips are of a humorous cast. "One day a man leading an ass laden with crockery ware happened to pass the castle. The laird, who had a friend with him, offered for a wager to make the man break his little stock in pieces. The bet was taken, and immediately the earthenware dealer, stopping and unloading the ass, smashed the whole into fragments. When asked how he had acted so foolishly, he declared he saw the head of a large black dog growling out of each of the dishes ready to devour him. The spot where this is said to have occurred is still called 'Pig's Bush.' On another occasion, the laird looked out of the upper south window of the castle. There was in sight twenty going ploughs. He undertook upon a large wager to make them all stand still. Momentarily eighteen of them—ploughs, ploughmen, horses, and gadmen—stood motionless. Two, however, continued to work. One of them was ploughing the Tarbolton croft. It was found out afterwards that these two ploughs carried each a piece of rowan-tree—mountain ash—proverbial for its anti-warlock properties.

> 'Rowan-tree and red thread
> Keep the devils frae their speed.'

In what year the death of the warlock took place is unknown; but circumstances lead us to believe that it must have been near the close of the seventeenth century. When about to depart, he warned those around him not to remain in the castle after his body was carried out; and it being autumn, he further recommended them not to bury him until the harvest was completed, because on the day of his interment a fearful storm would ensue. He was accordingly kept as long as the state of his remains admitted. Still the harvest was not above half-finished. True as the laird's prediction, the moment the body, on the funeral day, had cleared the doorway, a loud crash was heard—the castle roof had fallen in. The wind rose with unexampled fury, the sheaves of corn were scattered like chaff, and much damage was sustained all over the land.*

Passing Fail Mill I held along the road, and after a long walk reached a spot where two ways meet. The one to the left—as the milestone states—leads to Kilmarnock and the other to Galston. Although anxious enough to reach home, I decided upon a circuitous approach, and held along the Galston highway. The country in this district is almost wholly under cultivation, and the pedestrian as he trudges onwards finds little to engage his attention beyond the chirping birdies that flit in the hedges and the wild flowers whose fragrance is wafted on the wings of the wind. After a mile of weary thoughtful plodding, I reached the avenue leading to the farmhouse of Adamhill, which occupies a rather romantic situation, being planted near to a stripe of woodland and close to a row of stately trees, whose arms, in all probability, have often shaded Robert Burns when he came to visit the "rough, rude, ready-witted Rankine" of poetic memory, who had his residence here. According to Chambers, "he was a prince of boon companions and mingled a good deal in the society of the neighbouring gentry, but was too free a liver to be on good terms with the stricter order of the clergy. Burns and he had taken to each other no doubt in consequence of their community of feeling and thinking on many points. The youngest daughter of Rankine had a recollection of the poet's first visit to their house at Adamhill, and related that on his coming into the parlour he made a circuit to avoid a small carpet in the centre, having probably at that time no acquaintance with carpets, and too great a veneration for them to tread upon them with his ploughman's shoes." The farmhouse is well built, and the present occupant, Mr. A. G. Parker, is well known for his genial hospitality.

---

* This ballad and some very interesting information regarding the monastery and the Warlock Laird will be found in "Songs and ballads of Ayrshire." From this excellent but scarce work the above anecdotes are taken.

A little beyond Adamhill, I entered a pleasant byeroad which winds over hill and dale, and terminates near the village of Craigie, but before it was traversed

> "The sun was out o' sight,
> And darker gloamin' brought the night."

Nevertheless, "my heart rejoiced in Nature's joy" as I trudged along enjoying the solitude and watching "the glimmering landscape" fading on the sight. Having passed Craigie Manse, the snug residence of the Rev. David Stirling, the respected parish minister, I soon reached the summit of the rocky ridge over which the highway passes and beheld the lights of Kilmarnock gleaming in the distance. The reader may rest assured that their appearance was most cheering, and that I stepped out with renewed vigour. After a brisk but lonely walk, I arrived in Riccarton, and shortly thereafter received a hearty welcome from my bits o' bairns. Laying aside my hat and stick, I sat down by the ingleside a tired but better man from having visited scenes rendered famous by the poet Burns.

CHAPTER XIII.

KILMARNOCK—A GLANCE AT ITS HISTORY, PROGRESS, AND APPEARANCE—KILMARNOCK HOUSE—THE LADY'S WALK—BURNS IN KILMARNOCK—FRIENDS, AND PLACES ASSOCIATED WITH HIS NAME—THE TOWN OF HIS DAY—THE LAIGH KIRK—THE CHURCHYARD—THE HIGH CHURCH—"BLACK JOCK RUSSELL" AND BURNS—THE SOULIS MONUMENT—"WEE JOHNIE"—THE KAY PARK—THE BURNS MONUMENT.

AT this stage it will be as well to pause and say a word about Kilmarnock, for it is not only as intimately associated with the Poet's name as any spot visited, but the centre from which these Rambles are taken. The town is beautifully situated in a valley through which the rivers Marnock and Irvine flow, and is, as Chambers' describes it, "the largest and most elegant town in Ayrshire." Two centuries ago it was a mere hamlet under the jurisdiction of a baronial lord who dwelt in Dean Castle, a now ruinous stronghold in its vicinity. In 1591 it was created a burgh of barony, and in 1672 a second charter was conferred upon it which endowed it with further privileges. In 1700, the Magistrates received a grant of the whole Common Good and Customs of the burgh from the superior, and from the date of that transaction its prosperity has been marked beyond all precedent. For a long period it was celebrated by the manufacture of the broad, flat worsted bonnets and striped cowls at one time universally worn throughout Scotland; and also for tanning, shoemaking, weaving, calico-printing, and the manufacture of carpets—but now the snort of the steam engine, and the roar of machinery in numerous workshops and factories, proclaim a new era in its history, and announce that these crafts are superseded by engineering and other mechanical industries. With an increase of trade came the remodelling and extension of the town. Old streets were reconstructed or swept away altogether—in fact, as its historian (Archibald M'Kay) states, "so numerous are the additions which have been made to Kilmarnock since about the year 1816, that it may now be considered an entirely new town when compared with what it was at that period." True, and it may be added that it now exhibits a series of broad modern streets little inferior to those of Glasgow and other cities, and that its 24,000 of a population are noted for industry and thrift. To facilitate the various businesses carried on, it has seven banking establishments; and, consistent with its old character, it abounds with "the means of grace," there being no fewer than nineteen churches within a short distance of each other. Verily, the words of Burns are as applicable as ever—

> "Now, auld Kilmarnock, cock thy tail,
>   And toss thy horns fu' canty;
> Nae mair thou'lt rowt out owre the dale,
>   Because thy pasture's scanty;
> For lapfu's large o' gospel kail
>   Shall fill thy crib in plenty,
> An' runts o' grace, the pick and wale,
>   No gi'en by way o' dainty,
>   But ilka day."

The modern buildings throughout the town are of a superior order, but those which may be termed "public" are few, and contain little to interest the stranger. The Corn Exchange, however, is a most imposing structure, and in an antiquarian point of view Kilmarnock House is worth attention. It is situated in what is now St. Marnock Street, and is easily distinguished by its quaint old-fashioned appearance; but before the town encroached on its privacy it was surrounded by extensive well wooded policies, and was the residence of the Boyds, Earls of Kilmarnock, after the destruction of Dean Castle by fire. The fourth and last Earl crossed its threshold one blustry December morning to join the standard of Prince Charlie, but never returned to the quietude of its baronial shade. He fought at the battle of Falkirk, and materially assisted the Prince in gaining the victory, but at the disastrous battle of Culloden his brief career of adventure was brought to an abrupt close. When the army of the Prince had been defeated, and was seeking safety in flight, "the Earl of Kilmarnock, being half blinded with smoke and snow, mistook a party of Dragoons for the Pretender's horse, and was accordingly taken. He was soon after led along the lines of the British Infantry, in which his son, then a young man, held the commission of ensign. The Earl had lost his hat in the strife, and his long hair was flying in disorder around his head and over his face. The soldiers stood mute in their lines, beholding the unfortunate nobleman. Among the rest stood Lord Kilmarnock, compelled by his situation to witness, without the power of alleviating, the humiliation of his father. When the Earl came past the place where his son stood, the youth, unable to bear any longer that his father's head should be exposed to the storm, stepped out of the ranks, without regard to discipline, and taking off his hat, placed it over his father's disordered and wind-beaten locks. He then returned to his place without having uttered a word, while scarcely an eye that saw his filial affection but confessed its merits by a tear."* It is only necessary to add that he was convicted of high treason, and was beheaded on Tower Hill, London, on the 18th August, 1746. A portion of a shady avenue, known as "The Lady's Walk," may still be seen in the vicinity of this sad memento of the fallen house of Boyd, which is said to have been a favourite resort of Lady Kilmarnock after the tragic and melancholy end of her lord. There she is said to have wandered and given vent to the grief which ultimately broke her heart. A strolling player, named Ashton Carle, composed the following highly meritorious lines during a visit to the locality :—

"THE LADY'S WALK

" A wild, wierd look has the 'Lady's Walk,'
  And the trees are stripp'd and old;
They solemn bend in mute-like talk,
  In the twilight grey and cold.

" Each gaunt and rugged sinewy root
  Starts up along the way—
Memento sad of the lady's foot
  That erst did mournful stray.

" Ghost-like the boughs loom in the sky,
  And, skeleton-like, they meet;
The very pathway, white and dry,
  Curves like a winding-sheet.

" The rustling leaves that Autumn weaves
  In wither'd hillocks lie,

---

* Chambers's "History of the Rebellion."

And the chilly wind soughs just behind
  Like the lady's tearful sigh.

' Heavily rolls the evening mist,
  And the rising night-winds throb
By root and shoot, just where they list,
  Till they sound like the lady's sob.

" And the nightly shadows come and go,
  And the gaunt trees bow and wave,
Like weeping mourners, to and fro
  Over a dear one's grave.

" Then this is the far-famed ' Lady's Walk,'
  And walketh she there to-night ?
Holdeth her spirit silent talk
  With that moon so sickly white ?

" I hear no sound but the rushing bound
  Of the swell'd and foaming river,
That seems to say : I cannot stay,
  But must on for ever and ever."

So much for the famous town of Kilmarnock. Famous did I write ? Yes. Well, it is famous for many things, but more especially for being the poetical birthplace of Robert Burns. When residing at Mossgiel he was often to be seen standing in its Cross on market-days, and from the shop of John Wilson, the only printer and publisher in the town at the time, the unpretentious first edition of his poems was given to the world. In it, too, he was introduced to individuals who were in every way superior to the rustic class amongst whom the circumstances of his birth compelled him to mingle, and it is no exaggeration to state that it was mainly owing to the assistance and encouragement he received from Kilmarnock men when " skulking from covert to covert " in its vicinity, that his poems were printed and himself prevented from bidding " farewell to dear old Scotland, and his ungrateful, ill-advised Jean."

It is stated in an article in the *Contemporaries of Burns*—a now scarce work—that John Goudie, whom Burns styles " terror of the Whigs," had the honour of bringing this about. It appears that he called at Mossgiel during harvest, and that Burns went out with him, and while sitting behind a *stook* read to his visitor several of his poems. " Goudie, delighted with what he heard, threw out hints of a desire to get the poems published and invited the bard to visit him at Kilmarnock. There, it is said, Burns met at Goudie's table a group of the better class of people living in the town—the town clerk Paterson, a Dr. Hamilton, Major Parker (banker), Dr. William Moore, and Mr. Robert Muir (merchant). He appeared amongst these respectables in his simple hodden grey, but doubtless astonished them by his wit and verses. As visitors of Goudie we cannot doubt that they were most of them partisans of the new light. What immediately followed from the visit to Goudie we cannot tell; apparently, any wish that may have been formed either by the arch-heretic himself or any of his friends to get the poems published did not come to any immediate effect." John Goudie lived in the second flat of the building now occupied by the Messrs Stewart, ironmongers, Cross, and was next door neighbour to Bailie Gregory, father of Mr. J. S. Gregory, registrar. Burns was on intimate terms with both families, corrected many of his proofs in the house of the first, took "pot luck" occasionally in that of the second, and delighted to listen to the tones of a piano which Mrs. Gregory occasionally played for his entertainment. This piano was the first instrument of the kind in Kilmarnock, and probably the first Burns ever saw or heard. It is in good preservation, and has found an asylum in the house of her now aged son, who cherishes it as a souvenir of loved ones gone before. Goudie was a man of considerable learning, held advanced ideas, and was the author of several heterodox publications. One of these—*Essays on various important subjects, moral and divine, being an attempt to distinguish true from false religion*—attracted considerable attention, and was designated "Goudie's Bible." " Happening to go into a bookseller's shop one day in Ayr he met a clergyman of his acquaintance at the door. 'What have you been doing here?' jocularly inquired Goudie. 'Just buying a few ballads,' retorted the minister, 'to make psalms to your bible.'" He died in 1809 at an advanced age.

The Kilmarnock friends of Burns were all gentlemen of refined intellectual tastes and social standing. Gilbert Burns says :—" Mr. Robert Muir, merchant in Kilmarnock, was one of those early friends that Robert's poetry procured him, and one who was dear to his heart." Seemingly his affection for this friend was not misplaced, for he subscribed for seventy-two copies of the first edition of his poems, and forty of the second.

Mr. Thomas Samson of elegiac fame was another warm friend of our poet. He carried on the business of nursery and seedsman, was an ardent sportsman, and altogether a jolly good fellow. Burns visited at his house, sat at his table, and was intimate with his family and friends; indeed, the glass out of which he was in the habit of drinking is an heirloom in the family. The worthy sportsman's nephew Mr. Charles Samson, Turnbull the poet, William Parker, and other early friends and patrons of the Ayrshire ploughman in Kilmarnock, might be enumerated to show how his manly worth and poetic ability were appreciated.

On the 26th October, 1786, Burns was honoured by being elected an honorary member of St. John's Masonic Lodge, Kilmarnock, and from the circumstance there is little doubt of his having spent many "festive nights" with the brethren. The following extract from a chapter in Mr. M'Kay's *History of Kilmarnock*, which is entirely devoted to "Burns and his Kilmarnock friends," is quite appropriate:—"The house of Nanse Tinnock, in Mauchline, has been much talked of; and the Edinburgh taverns of Johnnie Dowie and Lucky Pringle, where he (Burns) often met Nichol of the High School and others, have also been noticed by some of his biographers; but nothing has been said, so far as we are aware, respecting the house of Sandy Patrick, in which the poet was wont to spend many merry evenings in *Auld Killie*, with the hero of one of his happiest poems, namely—Tam Samson, and other boon companions. Sandy, who was married to a daughter of Mr. Samson, brewed within his own premises the *cap ale* which the old gentleman used to drink with Burns and other social *cronies* after a day's shooting. Sandy's Public, which consisted of two storeys, and which was famed

'Thro' a' the streets an' neuks o' Killie'

for its superior drink, was situated at the foot of Back Street (at the time one of the principal thoroughfares of the town), and was called 'The Bowling-green House,' from being near the old Bowling-green, which lay immediately behind it, in the direction of the present George Inn. But like Sandy himself, and other jolly mortals who were accustomed to assemble within its walls, the house which the presence of genius had hallowed, and which would have been an object of interest to many at the present day, is now no more, having been taken down about the time that East George Street was formed. In our humble opinion, however, the name of Sandy Patrick is worthy of a place in the biographies of the poet, along with those of Nanse Tinnock, Lucky Pringle, and Johnny Dowe."

When Burns frequented Kilmarnock it had only some 6000 of a population, and its streets were few, narrow, and intricate. Indeed, according to the *History* already quoted, "the town presented a mean and inelegant appearance," and the Cross was "somewhat contracted in form compared with the spacious appearance it now presents." At the widening of the Cross many old buildings were removed, and amongst them the one which contained the shop of John Wilson, the printer of the first edition of the poems of Burns. It is stated in the above work that it stood "where Portland Street now opens into the Cross," and that "the printing-office in which the poems were first put into type was in the attic storey of that land on the left of the Star Inn Close, as entered from Waterloo Street." The writer goes on to say that "the property then belonged to Mr. James Robertson of Tankardha', whose sister, the late Mrs. Buntine, used to tell his informant that, when living in the Star Inn Close, she noticed frequently the visits of Burns to the printing premises when his work was in the press." The premises of Mr. James M'Kie, the enterprising publisher, who has done so much for the literature of Burns, and who lately issued a perfect fac-simile of the unpretentious first edition of the poet's works, are within a few yards of the humble tenement referred to, in which the wooden press of "Wee Johnie," with many a jolt and creak, gave out printed sheets which were destined to make Kilmarnock famous, and waft the name of Burns over the world.

As Mr. M'Kie is an enthusiastic admirer of the Poet and collector of Burnsiana, and as his name is inseparably associated with the Burns Monument movement in Kilmarnock, a brief notice of his career may prove acceptable, seeing that he is in every sense of the word a self-made man, and that the position he has attained is wholly due to indomitable perseverance. On the 7th of October, 1816, he made his appearance on the stage of life, but not having been gifted with the proverbial "silver spoon," he was at the tender age of eleven-and-a-half years apprenticed to Mr. Hugh Crawford, Printer and Bookseller, Kilmarnock, at the munificent sum of one shilling weekly for the first year. At the conclusion of his apprenticeship he set off to Glasgow, and there received a six months' engagement to work at his trade in Elgin. At its fulfilment he removed to Saltcoats to manage a bookselling establishment, and remained there for nine years, during which time he succeeded to his employer's business, and entered into the married state; but like most Kilmarnock men, he sighed for his native town, and upon the old-established business of Messrs Hugh Crawford & Son coming into the market he purchased it and settled in the place of his birth in November, 1844. In October, 1839, Mr. M'Kie commenced a periodical, consisting almost wholly of poetry, entitled the *Ayrshire Inspirer*, and in 1843, a meritorious annual, entitled the *Ayrshire Wreath*. In October, 1856, he started the *Kilmarnock Weekly Post*, and sustained it for several years. In May, 1878, he was entertained to dinner by a large number of friends on the occasion of his having completed the fiftieth year of his active business life, and was highly complimented on its success. Few men have done more to disseminate Burns literature than Mr. M'Kie. He is at all times zealous in everything concerning the memory and fame of the Bard, and may be said to have been the life and soul of the movement so successfully carried out for the erection of a monument to the Poet's memory in Kilmarnock.

The spacious Cross of Kilmarnock is the great point of attraction to strangers and residents. Seven streets branch off it, and in its immediate neighbourhood are the only antiquities and places associated with the name of our poet of which the town can boast.

> "Swith to the Laigh Kirk ane and a',
> And there tak' up your stations;
> Then aff to *Begbie's* in a raw,
> An' pour divine libations
> For joy this day."

"Begbie's" is now the Angel Inn. It is situated in Market Lane, is as attractive as ever, and presided over by as accommodating a host as it was in the days of Burns; but the Laigh Kirk, to which he refers, and in which the "Ordination" which provoked his satire took place, was taken down, and the present edifice somewhat enlarged occupies its site. The massive square tower which belonged to the old church, however, still stands, and bears date 1410. The churchyard is of peculiar interest, and the rambler will find much in it to cause him to linger. At the north-west corner of the church will be found the graves of Mr. Thomas Samson, the Rev. Dr. Mackinlay, and the Rev. John Robinson, *dramatis personæ* of our poet, who curiously enough lie within a few inches of each other, and are mentioned together in the first stanza of the worthy sportsman's elegy.

> " Has auld Kilmarnock seen the Deil?
> Or great M'Kinlay thrawn his heel?
> Or Robinson again grown weel
>   To preach an' read?
> ' Na, waur than a'?' cries ilka chiel,
>   ' Tam Samson's dead.' "

These worthy clergymen rest side by side, and the "weel-worn clay" of Mr. Samson at the head of their graves under a freestone tablet on which the epitaph by Burns is graven. Near to the graves of these contemporaries are the resting places of several local martyrs. A stone behind the church bears the following :—" HERE LIE THE HEADS OF JOHN ROSS AND JOHN SHIELDS, WHO SUFFERED AT EDINBURGH, DEC. 27TH, 1666, AND HAD THEIR HEADS SET UP IN KILMARNOCK."

> " Our persecutors mad with wrath and ire,
> In Edinburgh members some do be, some here;
> Yet instantly united they shall be,
> And witness 'gainst this nation's perjury."

These martyrs were found with arms in their possession, and were executed on suspicion of being in town to watch the movements of the King's troops.

Another stone of like interest, which was renewed by the inhabitants in 1823, is to the memory of John Nisbet, the only martyr executed in the town. The particular spot in the Cross where the gallows stood was for many years marked by the initials of his name, but during the recent repairing of the causeway the white stones which formed the letters were removed and a circular block of granite substituted. It was indented into the causeway by Mr. Charles Reid, road surveyor, a gentleman whose antiquarian taste has prompted him to preserve many old landmarks and nick-nacks at once interesting and curious. It will be found near the kerbstone a little to the east of Waterloo Street. It bears the following :—"JOHN NISBET WAS EXECUTED HERE ON 14TH APRIL, 1683."

The humble memorial to the memory of this martyr bears this inscription :—"HERE LIES JOHN NISBET, WHO WAS TAKEN BY MAJOR BALFOUR'S PARTY, AND SUFFERED AT KILMARNOCK, 14TH APRIL, 1683, FOR ADHERING TO THE WORD OF GOD AND OUR COVENANTS."

> "Come, reader, see, here pleasant Nisbet lies,
> His blood doth pierce the *high* and lofty skies ;
> Kilmarnock did his latter hour perceive,
> And Christ his soul to Heaven did receive.
> Yet bloody Torrence did his body raise,
> And buried him into another place ;
> Saying, 'Shall rebels lie in graves with me?
> We'll bury him where evil doers be.'"

The only other martyrs' stone is close to the former, and in the following simple language tells the mournful tale of those whom it commemorates :—

"SACRED TO THE MEMORY OF THOMAS FINDLAY, JOHN CUTHBERTSON, WILLIAM BROWN, ROBERT AND JAMES ANDERSON (NATIVES OF THIS PARISH), WHO WERE TAKEN PRISONERS AT BOTHWELL, JUNE 22ND, 1679, SENTENCED TO TRANSPORTATION FOR LIFE, AND DROWNED ON THEIR PASSAGE NEAR THE ORKNEY ISLES. ALSO, JOHN FINDLAY, WHO SUFFERED MARTYRDOM 15TH DEC., 1682, IN THE GRASSMARKET, EDINBURGH."

> "Peace to the church! when foes her peace invade,
> Peace to each noble martyr's honoured shade !
> They, with undaunted courage, truth, and zeal,
> Contended for the church and country's weal ;
> We share the fruits, we drop the grateful tear,
> And peaceful altars o'er their ashes rear."

The stones referred to are the most noteworthy, but there are others to the memory of the honoured dead which will also prove interesting.

Tradition has it, and excavation has proved, that this graveyard was of much greater extent, and included part of the ground now forming surrounding streets. Indeed, the writer has seen human bones exhumed in the centres of the now populous thoroughfares on its west and south sides.

In 1731, the Low Church became too small, and a new church or chapel-of-ease was erected to accommodate the increasing population. It is also situated within a short distance of the Cross, and deserves the rambler's attention, as it was the building in which the Rev. John Russell, a well-known Burns' hero who figures in the *The Holy Fair*, *The Twa Herds*, and *The Kirk's Alarm*, officiated.

> "But now the Lord's ain trumpet touts,
>   Till a' the hills are rairin',
> And echoes back return the shouts—
>   BLACK RUSSELL is na sparin':
> His piercing words, like Highland swords,
>   Divide the joints and marrow;
> His talk o' hell, where devils dwell,
>   Our vera sauls does harrow
>   Wi' fricht that day."

And again—

> "He fine a mangy sheep could scrub,
>   Or nobly fling the Gospel club,
> And New-Light herds could nicely drub,
>   Or pay their skin;
> Could shake them o'er the burning dub,
>   Or heave them in."

A correspondent of Robert Chambers wrote—"He was the most tremendous man I ever saw. Black Hugh Macpherson was a beauty in comparison. His voice was like thunder, and his sentiments were such as must have shocked any class of hearers in the least more refined than those whom he usually addressed." It is stated in the *History of Kilmarnock* that "his appearance completely harmonized with his severity of manner, for he was uncouth and robust in person, remarkably dark-complexioned, and stern and gloomy in countenance. On Sabbaths, during the intervals of divine services, he would frequently go through the streets, and even to the outskirts of the town, with a large walking stick in his hand, watching for disorderly boys and other stragglers; and such as he discovered, he would rebuke for their ungodliness. In short, he was such a terror to the inhabitants, especially on the Sabbath, that the moment the sound of his ponderous staff was heard upon the streets the doors that chanced to be opened were instantly closed, and every countenance assumed an air of the deepest sanctity. In theological knowledge few of his companions were more deeply versed; and, in religious controversy, he was not easily driven from his position. Even Burns, beneath whose strokes of satire the clergy of Ayrshire were wont to lie prostrate, was on one occasion defeated, it is said, by his determined mode of arguing. They had met accidentally in a barber's shop in Fore Street, and whether Mr Russell knew the poet and meant to chastise him for his reputed heresy we know not, but they soon became engaged in a warm discussion respecting some particular point of faith; and, according to our informant, who was present, the poet, with all his ingenuity and argumentative powers, was so baffled by his opponent that he became silent, and left the shop in a hurried manner."

The High Church is now a parish church, is beautifully fitted-up internally, and contains handsome stained-glass " memorial " windows, though externally it is a plain-looking edifice. It is surrounded by a neatly kept churchyard, enclosed by a high wall. In a niche in this wall, near the gateway in Soulis Street, there is a fluted pillar surmounted by an urn, which commemorates an English nobleman named Lord Soulis. Tradition states that he was killed by an arrow which one of the Boyds of Dean Castle shot at him from a distance. On the front of the pediment surmounting the niche is the following :—

"To the Memory of Lord Soulis, A.D. 1444.
Erected by Subscription A.D. 1825.
'The days of old to mind I call.'"

The graveyard contains many handsome tombstones; but the most noteworthy is to the memory of John Wilson, the cautious, close-fisted printer of the first edition of the poems of Burns. He was the son of a Kilmarnock bailie, and attained the same civic position himself in the town of Ayr, where he settled and in company with his brother Peter established the *Ayr Advertiser* shortly after giving the

Mossgiel ploughman's poems to the world. The epitaph—

"Whoe'er thou art, oh reader, know
That death has murder'd Johnnie;
And here his body lies fu' low—
For saul he ne'er had ony"—

which Burns hurled at him, and made him print by way of joke, has been considered too severe; but if the statement that the poet " pocketed, all expenses deducted, nearly twenty pounds" from the sale of his Kilmarnock edition be true, and there is no reason to doubt it, it is not a whit. Indeed, when Wilson's account for printing is looked into stronger language would be justifiable. The following fac-simile of this curious document, and the remarks appended to it, are taken from Chambers's excellent edition of the poet's works:

"Mr. Robert Burns.
                                            To John Wilson.   Dr.

Aug. 28, 1786.—Printing 15 sheets at 19s,   ... £14 5 0
              19 Reams 13 quires paper at 17s,   16 4 0
              Carriage of the paper, ...   0 8 9
              Stitching 612 Copies in blue
                 paper at 1¾d, ...   4 9 3
                                                   ─────────
                                                   £35 17 0

Aug. 19.—By Cash, ... £6 3 0
  ,, 28.— ,, ,, ... 14 13 0
              By 70 Copies, ... 10 10 0
                                         ───────── £31 6 0
                                                   ─────────
                                                    £4 11 0
         By 9 Copies, ...   1 7 0
                                                    ─────────
                                                    £3 4 0
Oct. 6th. By cash in full, ...   3 4 0

Kilmarnock.   Settled the above account.

                                           John Wilson.

"It appears that Mr. Wilson had here, by an error in his arithmetic, undercharged the Poet Ten Shillings, the second item in the account being properly £16 14s., instead of £16 4s.

"Six hundred Copies at 3s. each would produce £90; and if there were no more to be deducted from that sum than the expenses of paper, print, and stitching, there would remain upwards of £54 as profit. The Poet, however, speaks of realising only £20 by the speculation."

Wilson died at Ayr on the 6th May, 1821, and by his will left a share in a property in Kilmarnock, to accumulate until there was sufficient funds to build a school in which poor children were to be taught "reading, writing, and arithmetic only."

In the vicinity of the Cross also is the Kay Park—an ornamental piece of ground well adapted for recreation and healthful enjoyment, which was gifted to the town by the late Alexander Kay [born March 1795, died January 1866] —a Kilmarnockonian who amassed a fortune of £70,000 in Glasgow as an insurance broker. Of the £16,000 bequeathed to his native place £6000 was set aside by the trust for the erection and endowment of two schools, and the remainder for the purchase and maintenance of this place of public resort. On a height within these grounds, overlooking the town, stands the handsomest tribute to the poet's memory yet erected. It is built of red sandstone hewn from rock on the banks of the Ayr near to the spot where the poet viewed the bonnie lass of Ballochmyle, and towers to a height of sixty-five feet. It is Gothic in design, and represents a baronial tower of the olden time. At its front, stairs lead up to an alcove fifteen feet in height, in which stands a chaste statue of the poet cut from a block of the finest Sicilian marble by the eminent sculptor, W. G. Stevenson of Edinburgh. The figure—which is eight feet from foot to head—represents the poet, attired in a tight-fitting coat and knee-breeches, leaning against the trunk of a tree, with a book in the one hand and a pencil in the other. The head is turned slightly to the right, which gives the spectator in front of the figure the view of the features as they are shown in the now familiar portrait by Naysmith. Round the base is a walk three feet wide, and in the interior of the building is a room devoted to relics and articles associated with the life and writings of the poet. From the top of the tower—which is reached by a winding stair—a most gorgeous and extensive view of the land of Burns is witnessed. At the spectator's feet is the town of Kilmarnock, hemmed in as it were by verdant slopes and distant rugged hills, which rigorously preclude a glimpse of

"Auld Ayr, wham ne'er a toun surpasses
For honest men and bonnie lasses."

To the north is the ruin of Dean Castle—a sad memento of the fallen house of Boyd—nestling in a beautiful vale through which the Marnock glides; and beyond it the moors of Fenwick and Eaglesham, famed lurking places of the Covenanters during the era of the Persecution. To the east there is a fine far-stretching view backed by Loudoun Hill, "Loudoun's bonnie woods and braes," and the moors of Galston, on which the poet witnessed the glorious light of the rising sun on the morning of "The Holy Fair"—a pleasing reminiscence; but they also recall a sad passage in his history, for when traversing them on a bleak blustry afternoon he measured the last song he ever expected to measure in Caledonia. A little to the southward the position of the farm of Mossgiel can be indicated with considerable distinctness, as also other places which the poet loved and celebrated in song. There is also, when the weather is clear, a magnificent prospect of Arran and the Frith of Clyde. On the whole, the view is one of great natural beauty; but no word picture can convey an adequate idea of the hills, woods, plains, and fells which lie around in panoramic magnificence.

It was long considered a blemish on the reputation of Kilmarnock that it contained no memorial of the poet. Although a statue to his memory was long talked of by the town's people, no practical step for its erection was taken until the movement received an impetus by the unveiling of a statue to the poet's memory on the 25th of January, 1877, in Glasgow. "On the evening of the day following a public demonstration was held in the George Inn Hall, Kilmarnock —Provost Sturrock in the chair, and Mr Andrew Turnbull (president of the Burns Club), croupier—at which it was proposed, and unanimously agreed to, that a statue be erected in some suitable place in Kilmarnock in honour of the poet. The following were appointed a committee to carry out the proposal:—Provost Sturrock, Bailie Craig, Bailie Muir, Bailie Wilson, Dean of Guild Andrews; Messrs John Baird, John Gilmour, Thomas M'Culloch, George Humphrey, James Stirling, John A. Mather, Alexander Walker, William Mitchell, John G. Hamilton, James Robertson, Hugh Shaw, David Phillips, Andrew Christie, James Arbuckle, Ninian Anderson, Dr M'Alister, Andrew Turnbull, James M'Kie, and James Rose—Andrew Turnbull, convener; Hugh Shaw, treasurer; James Rose and James M'Kie, joint-secretaries. At a meeting of the committee on February 23rd, 1877, the Convener, Treasurer, and Secretaries, with Messrs John Baird, Ninian Anderson, Thomas M'Culloch, and James Arbuckle were appointed a sub-committee to carry out the details of the movement, and it was intimated that the sum of six hundred and fourteen pounds (£614) had already been subscribed. At a meeting of the general committee on April 6th, 1877, a report from the sub-committee recommending open competition by sculptors was agreed to—two premiums, one of £50 and one of £25, being offered for the best and second best models. The amount of subscriptions at this date was twelve hundred and eighty-two pounds (£1282). On June 7th, 1877, it was suggested at a meeting of the general committee that, as the subscriptions had far exceeded expectations, an ornamental building and a marble statue of the poet in it should be erected. At a general meeting of the subscribers held in the Town Hall on September 8th, 1877, the sub-committee recommended that a marble statue to cost eight hundred pounds (£800), and an ornamental building estimated at fifteen hundred pounds (£1500), should be erected in the Public Park—a site for the building having been granted by the Kay Trustees. This was agreed to, and the sub-committee instructed to carry out the decision. At a meeting of sub-committee on October 9th, 1877, Mr Robert S. Ingram, architect, on behalf of Messrs J. & R. S. Ingram, submitted amended design of ornamental building, which was accepted, and he was instructed to prepare drawings and specifications of the same. On December 6th and 7th, 1877, the competing models, 21 in all, were publicly exhibited in the George Inn Hall, and on December 14th the committee awarded the commission for the statue to Mr W. G. Stevenson, 2 Castle Terrace, Edinburgh; the premium of fifty pounds (£50) to Mr D. W. Stevenson, 2 Castle Terrace, Edinburgh; and the premium of twenty-five pounds (£25) to Mr Chas. M'Bride, 7 Hope Street, Edinburgh. On the Burns Anniversary, Jan. 25th, 1878, a Burns Concert was held in the Corn Exchange Hall, which was crowded to overflowing. On March 29th, 1878, the contract between the sub-committee and Mr. W. G. Stevenson, Edinburgh, for the marble statue was duly signed. In the months of March, April, and May the sub-committee got working plans and estimates for the erection of the ornamental building in the Kay Park. These, after modifications, were finally agreed to, and at a meeting of June 4th, 1878, Mr Ingram, architect, intimated that Mr. Andrew Calderwood had signed contract for the erection of the building, the entire cost of which was estimated at fourteen hundred and fifty pounds (£1450)."*

When the building was partly constructed it was agreed that the Memorial Stone should be laid with full Masonic honours by R. W. Cochran-Patrick, Esq. of Woodside, Depute Provincial Grand Master for Ayrshire, and on the 14th of September, 1878, about fifteen thousand people of all classes and conditions of life assembled to do honour to the Poet's memory. Kilmarnock was moved to its depths, and excitement ran high as a highly imposing procession moved along the streets to the scene of operations in the following order :—Body of Police, the Burns Monument Sub-Committee, Carters, Town Council and County Gentlemen, Burns Monument General Committee and Burns Club, 5th Battery Ayrshire Artillery Volunteers, 1st Ayrshire Rifle Volunteers, Iron Trades, Good Templars, Oddfellows, Tailors, Free Gardeners, Foresters, Joiners and other Wood Workers, Operative Masons, Chimney Sweeps, Operative Gardeners, and one hundred Masonic Lodges.

The following account of the procession is taken from the report of the proceedings in the *Kilmarnock Standard* of September 21, 1878 :—"The procession was exceedingly well organised and presented a most imposing appearance. Immediately behind the pioneers, as usual, came the carters, who undoubtedly formed the most note-worthy feature of the display. They numbered no less than 106—the largest turn-out of the kind ever seen in Kilmarnock—and were mounted on strong, well-built, and gaily-decorated horses. Each man wore a Kilmarnock bonnet, decked with blue ribbons, and also a blue rosette on the breast of his coat. The calvacade as it passed along the streets attracted great attention, and the hearty cheers which greeted the men showed how favourable was the impression they created. Another noted group was the Foresters. Each lodge was preceded by three mounted men dressed in the picturesque

---

* From "Short Sketch of the Monument Movement," deposited in the Memorial Stone of the Monument.

garb of the craft, having the bow slung over the shoulder with the quiver by the side. The Free Gardeners also appeared in a very pleasing costume. Foremost among the trades by rightful position, though the order of them had been determined by the accident of the ballot, marched the iron trades, which now form the chief element of our local industry. . . . . They carried some beautifully finished models, including a locomotive, two carriages and a van, forming a railway train with every appliance complete. The joiners excited the interest of the crowd by appearing with a lorry which had been fitted up with a double bench, at which two men in white aprons carefully planed away at a piece of wood, and seemed to be so intent on their work as to be altogether ignorant of the panorama of which they formed a part, or of the thousands of eager eyes under whose gaze they were passing. The Oddfellows as usual presented a highly respectable appearance, and the Good Templars also turned out well, among them being a goodly sprinkling of females. Almost hid in the general mass was a small band of chimney-sweeps, whose presence would have passed unnoticed had it not been for the banner which they carried and on which was inscribed in large letters, 'By dirt we live.' Their appearance did not bear out the motto, as for once, at least, they had cleaned all the dirt away from themselves, and come out in presentable fashion like the others to honour the Ayrshire bard. It is impossible to notice in detail all the component parts of the procession, but it may not be out of place to refer to the presence among the Freemasons of the Lodge 133—St. David's of Tarbolton. This is the mother lodge of the poet, which from some cause lay dormant for 42 years, and was only resuscitated by the Mauchline brethren in January of last year in order that it might take a part in the Burns demonstration in Glasgow. Alongside of this lodge was 135—the St. James Kilwinning of Tarbolton—which the poet joined on his leaving the St. David, and in which he occupied the second highest post. It is estimated that about 4000 people took part in the procession."

When the procession was marshalled round the monument, the ceremony of laying the Memorial stone was proceeded with amid a dead impressive silence. The following account of the ceremony is taken from the newspaper report already quoted :—" The Rev. Mr Inglis of Kilmaurs, Provincial Grand Chaplain, offered up a brief, appropriate and impressive prayer, after which the Depute Provincial Grand Master having directed the Provincial Grand Secretary (Bro. Wylie) deposited in the cavity of the stone a glass bottle, hermetically sealed, containing :—Short sketch of the monument movement. Alphabetical list of subscribers showing subscriptions to the extent of two thousand two hundred and fifty pounds. Copy of Burns' poems (Mr M'Kie's fac-simile edition.) Copy of the *Kilmarnock Standard*, the *Glasgow Herald*, *N.B. Daily Mail*, *Glasgow News*, *Scotsman*, *Review*, Ayr and Ardrossan newspapers; all of date, September 14th, 1878. Registration statistics of the parish of Kilmarnock for 1858; digest of census of 1871 for the parish, with registration statistics; vital statistics from the registers of the parish, for 1876 and 1877, by Mr James Smith Gregory, registrar. The current coins of the realm from a farthing to a sovereign. Standard measure of one foot and standard weight of 1 lb. Monograph on a new genus of rugose corals from the carboniferous lime-stone of Scotland by James Thomson, F.G.S. The Provincial Grand Secretary then read the inscription on the brass plate placed over the glass bottle. The inscription is as follows :—' BY THE FAVOUR OF ALMIGHTY GOD, ON THE 14TH DAY OF SEPTEMBER, ANNO DOMINI EIGHTEEN HUNDRED AND SEVENTY-EIGHT, AND THE ERA OF MASONRY 5878. AND IN THE FORTY-SECOND YEAR OF THE REIGN OF OUR BELOVED SOVEREIGN, VICTORIA FIRST, THE MEMORIAL STONE OF THIS MONUMENT, ERECTED BY PUBLIC SUBSCRIPTION IN HONOUR OF THE GENIUS OF ROBERT BURNS, SCOTLAND'S NATIONAL POET, WAS LAID BY R. WM. COCHRAN-PATRICK, ESQ. OF WOODSIDE, BEITH, RIGHT WORSHIPFUL DEPUTE PROVINCIAL GRAND MASTER FOR AYRSHIRE (ATTENDED BY NUMEROUS MASONIC LODGES), ACCORDING TO THE ANCIENT USAGES OF MASONRY.' After the Kilmarnock Brass Band had played ' Old Hundred,' the necessary workmen were then brought forward, and these having completed the operative part of the ceremony, the Depute Provincial Grand Master spread the mortar in a most workman-like fashion with the silver trowel, and the stone was lowered. The acting Provincial Grand Wardens, under orders from the Provincial Grand Master, severally applied the level and the plummet.

The Substitute Provincial Grand Master, under like orders, applied the square, and the Depute Grand Master then said : 'Having, my Right Worshipful Brethren, full confidence in your skill in our Royal Art, it remains with me now to finish this work,' whereupon he gave the stone three knocks, saying : 'May the Almighty Architect of the Universe look down with benignity upon our present undertaking, and on the happy completion of the work of which we have now laid the memorial stone, and may this monument be long preserved from peril and decay.' The band then played the Masons' Anthem. On the music ceasing, the Substitute Provincial Grand Master then delivered to the Depute Grand Master a cornucopia, and to the acting senior and junior Provincial Grand Masters, silver vases with wine and oil. The Depute Provincial Grand Master then spread corn on the stone, and poured thereon wine and oil, conformably to ancient custom, saying : " Praise be to the Lord, immortal and eternal, who formed the Heavens, laid the foundations of the earth, and extended the waters beyond it : Who supports the pillars of the nations, and maintains in order and harmony surrounding worlds. We implore thy aid : and may the Almighty Ruler of events deign to direct the hand of our gracious Sovereign, so that she may pour down blessings upon her people : and may that people, living under sage laws in a free Government, ever feel grateful for the blessings they enjoy.' Three hearty cheers on the part of the crowd, and 'Rule Britannia' by the band, completed the Masonic part of the ceremony."

After an eloquent address had been delivered by Mr. Cochran-Patrick, and a few remarks made by Provost Sturrock, the procession re-formed and marched back to town, where it dispersed. In the evening a public dinner was held in the George Inn Hall, at which Provost Sturrock presided. It was numerously attended, and amongst those present were several distinguished personages and local celebrities.

More need not be said regarding the quiet town of Kilmarnock, so I will conclude this chapter by reiterating the wish of George Campbell, a local poet, who flourished about 1787 :—

> "O! happy Marnock, lasting be thy peace!
> May trading flourish and thy wealth increase!
> Still may the loaded axle press the sand,
> And commerce waft thy wares to ev'ry land!
> Happy returns fill every heart with joy,
> And poor industrious never want employ!"

CHAPTER XIV.

FROM KILMARNOCK TO MOSSGIEL—NOTES BY THE WAY—MOSSGIEL—
A NOISY RECEPTION—THE DWELLING-HOUSE—THE SPENCE—AN
INTERESTING RELIC—THE "MOUSE" AND "DAISY"—JOHN
BLANE'S RECOLLECTIONS—THE OLD DWELLING-HOUSE—THE
POET'S STUDY—THE SCENE OF "THE VISION"—THE POET'S
PERSONAL APPEARANCE AND MISFORTUNES WHEN IN THE FARM.

HAVING roved by bonnie Doon and winding Ayr, and sketched the town of Kilmarnock, I would now, courteous reader, ask you to accompany me in a ramble to Mossgiel and the places of interest in its vicinity, which are inseparably associated with the poet's name, for he removed there in May, 1784, and with his brother Gilbert began life anew with the little the family had been able to wrench from the avaricious grasp of the Lochlea landlord.

The day set apart for the journey being favourable, I left Kilmarnock at an early hour, and after a pleasant walk reached Crookedholm, an unpretentious hamlet chiefly occupied by miners, who find employment in numerous coalpits in its vicinity. Unimportant as it now is, it was at one time a place of some note, and, according to a work lately published,* possessed a "flour mill, a cloth factory, and a place of worship near the beginning of the eighteenth century." Beyond it I passed two handsome Churches, crossed a substantial stone bridge, and entered Hurlford, another mining settlement which has assumed the proportions of a town within the memory of persons still living. This transition is owing to the presence of rich seams of coal in the vicinity, to the opening of the Portland Ironworks, and to its connection with a line of railway which bears away the produce, and brings the village into direct communication with the large centres of industry. The village possesses the churches referred to, a mechanics' institute, a Post and Telegraph Office, a flourish-

---

* "Hurlford Sixty Years Ago," &c., by M. Wilson.

ing co-operative store, a commodious police station, and a fair sprinkling of public houses and places of business. According to the work already quoted, " the inhabitants are a very mixed race, and a large proportion of them are either Irish or descendants of Irish. Of the exotic element of the population, a portion are Catholics, while those who are Protestants are Orangemen. Hence frequent quarrels leading to breaches of the peace arise between these two irreconcilable sections of Irishmen." From this it may be inferred that renewals of the obsolete sports of Donnybrook Fair are of common occurrence on pay nights, and that " a party man " need have no anxiety about turning blue-moulded for want of a sound thrashing.

The road to Mauchline branches off what may be termed Hurlford Cross. It was the way Burns came to and returned from Kilmarnock when residing at Mossgiel. Allan Cunningham states that John Wilson suggested the propriety of placing a piece of a grave nature at the beginning of the poems he printed, and that acting on the hint the bard composed or completed " The Twa Dogs" when walking home to Mossgiel. The local work quoted states that " the first wayside inn was kept by James Aiton ; it was on the western side of the Mauchline Road, and he occupied it at the time Burns was in Mossgiel, and was having his poems printed by Wilson in Kilmarnock. He was acquainted with Burns, and being—like many Scotchmen of that era—an inveterate snuffer, was presented by the bard with a snuff-box. This box Aiton long retained, but after Burns had grown famous, he was often asked by his visitors for a pinch of snuff from the poet's box, and at last it was stolen from him." This is a very pleasing reminiscence, but the following is more so : An old man named Andrew Howat who "had wrought a good deal about coal-pits, which were then being worked at Norris Bank, about two miles on the road to Mauchline and about four miles from Mossgiel, remembered Burns, and related that most of the farmers in the district were known to him as coming to the *heugh* for coals. Burns, he said, came frequently and generally carried a book with him which he read by the way." How characteristic ! " Some book he always carried and read," says David Sillars, and another writer records that he wore out two copies of

"The Man of Feeling" by carrying them about in his pocket —he walked like a thoughtful man and was always meditative when alone.

A short walk along Mauchline Road brought me to a bridge which spans the Cessnock—a streamlet celebrated by our poet in an early love song. It takes its rise at Auchmannoch Moor in the parish of Sorn, and forms some fantastic windings in which it serves as the boundary line between the parishes of Mauchline, Galston, and Riccarton, and empties itself into the Irvine a mile or so above Hurlford. Ellison Begbie, the heroine of the song referred to, was the daughter of a small farmer in the parish of Galston, but was a servant in a family on the banks of the Cessnock when Burns made her acquaintance. This attachment is spoken of as one of the purest he ever engaged in, and he declared in mature years, after he had visited Edinburgh, that of all the women he had ever seriously addressed, she was the one most likely to have formed an agreeable companion for life. He addressed a series of letters to her, and employs a song of thirteen stanzas to describe her personal charms, which tradition states were few in the eyes of her neighbours. Although his passion was not reciprocated, the poet maintained his suit with considerable warmth, and in addition to that dangerous mode of courtship—letter-writing—visited the fair one at her home, and "beneath the moon's unclouded light" poured in her ear the language of love. Mrs Begg had a distinct recollection of this attachment, and related that her brother went frequently in the evenings to pay his addresses to the damsel, and generally returned home at a late hour; and Chambers tells us that "the old man resolved to administer to his son the practical rebuke of sitting up to let him in, and also to give him a few words of gentle admonition. When Robert returned that night the father was there to administer the intended correction, but the young bard defeated his plan. On being asked what had detained him so long, he began a whimsical narration of what he had met with and seen of the natural and supernatural on his way home, concluding with the particulars afterwards wrought up in the well-known verses in his 'Address to the Deil':—

'Ae dreary, windy, wintry night,
The stars shot down wi' sklentin light,

> Wi' you mysel' I got a fright,
>   Ayont the lough;
> Ye like a rash bush stood in sight,
>   Wi' waving sough.
>
> The cudgel in my nieve did shake,
> Each bristled hair stood like a stake,
> When wi' an eldrich, stoor quaick—quaick—
>   Amang the springs,
> Awa' ye squattered like a drake
>   On whistling wings!'

The old man was in spite of himself so much interested and amused by this recital as to forget the intended scolding, and the affair ended in his sitting up for an hour or two by the kitchen fire enjoying the conversation of his gifted son."

Beyond the bridge referred to a long stretch of road, which winds through an agreeably diversified landscape of gently rising grounds, lay before me. The walk proved lengthy and lonely, but the glorious sights and sounds of nature ministered delightfully to my eye and ear. I entered into conversation with a countryman driving a horse and cart in the direction I was pursuing. He was well acquainted with the district, and entertained the highest veneration of the Poet's memory, and seemed to dwell with fondness upon every little trait and anecdote associated with his name. When we came to Cross hands, where there is a school and a smith's shop, he said— "Robin was often here about, and in a corner o' a park abent that wood there a horse o' his lies buried that dee'd wi' him when ploughin'; but haud on an' ye'll see Mossgiel in a wee." The "wee" soon passed, and from the brow of a brae over which the road passes he pointed with his whip to a farm-steading on the summit of a swelling piece of ground, and in a self-satisfied manner added—"There it is. The parks are the same, but the hoose is a' changed. Yonder's the ane he turned up the mousie's nest in; but haud on a wee an' I'll set you doun at the yett o' the ane whaur he ploughed down the daisy. Haud alang the side o't—it's the nearest way into the farm." Upon arriving at the yett I took leave of my rough good-natured friend and entered the field. A number of cows were browsing in it, and myriads of daisies spangled its surface. As I pensively gazed on the scene the following from the pen of William Scott Douglas, of Edinburgh, came to mind:—

K

> "The warblers around me seem proud to repeat
> The wild notes that gave rapture to him;
> And the daisies that spangle the ground at my feet
> Have their birth from the *one* of his theme;
> There's a boast from yon belfry-tower borne on the breeze
> That it caught Robin's ear every day;
> And the murmuring waters and whispering trees
> Can but sigh that their minstrel's away!"

My arrival in Mossgiel farm-yard was announced by a demonstrative collie dog, whose "bow-wows" not only startled but caused me to think seriously about taking to my heels. Finding, however, that it kept at a respectful distance, I ventured forward, and as unconcernedly as possible addressed a sturdy servant girl and enquired for her master. "Just bide ye a wee, sir," said she, when she had left off scolding the guardian of the steading for kicking up such a row, "and I'll find him for you." Off she went on her mission, and left me to watch the dog and the dog to watch me, but he proved a good-natured brute and offered no further molestation. The dwelling-house is a substantial two-storeyed slated building, and bears no resemblance whatever to "the auld clay biggin'" which rises before the mind's eye when perusing "The Vision," while the offices which form an angle round the paved court are all modern and roofed in the same manner. The master soon made his appearance, and, in answer to my request, led the way into the house and began to show the little about the place which is associated with the poet's name. "This," said he, as he opened the door of a neatly-furnished room, "is 'the spence,' but the roof, as you will observe, is heightened, and the set-in beds which occupied the apartment when the Poet lived here are torn out." Yes, torn out and the place spoiled, thought I, but nevertheless I felt gratified to stand within the walls which had sheltered the most wonderful peasant that ever lived. On the walls the original copy of "The Lass o' Ballochmyle," and the letter which accompanied it, hang in separate frames, having been kindly placed there by the late Boyd Alexander, Esq. of Ballochmyle, for the inspection of visitors. The documents are somewhat faded and aged looking, but the bold vigorous writing of the poet is still legible, and almost as clear as it was when it left his pen. On the table lay a bulky visitors' book, which I was informed might have been filled over and over again had a tithe of the pilgrims recorded their names. The first entry is dated "August 30, 1872," and is as follows:—"W. H. Glen, Melbourne, Australia, and Mrs W. H. Glen, Melbourne, Australia--both delighted with Mossgiel and country round." Not a few are those of persons of distinction, and very many names belong to individuals who have travelled long distances to visit the lone farm steading. After a pleasant chat my cicerone next led me to the front of the house and pointed out a tall neatly-cut hedge, which the poet had planted with his own hands, and afterwards the fields wherein he turned up the "wee sleekit, cow'rin', timorous beastie's" nest, and turned down the "modest crimson-tipped flower" with the plough. These fields adjoin each other, and are in much the same condition as they were when the poet traversed them. An old man named John Blane, who had served in Mossgiel when a boy, told Robert Chambers that he had a distinct recollection of the mouse's nest. "Burns was holding the plough, with Blane for his driver, when the little creature was observed running off across the field. Blane, having the *pettle*, or plough-cleaning utensil, in his hand at the moment, was thoughtlessly running after it to kill it, when Burns checked him, but not angrily, asking what ill the poor mouse had ever done him. The poet then seemed to his driver to turn very thoughtful, and during the remainder of the afternoon he spoke not. In the night-time he awoke Blane, who slept with him, and reading the poem which had in the meantime been composed, asked what he thought of the mouse now."

The incident was trivial, but it formed the groundwork of a beautiful and interesting poem, and evidenced his tenderness of heart: he saw in the smallest of all quadrupeds an "earth-born companion and fellow-mortal," and felt equally for a pet ewe, an auld mare, and a wounded limping hare.

The lines to "The Daisy" were composed while the poet was ploughing, but I am not aware of any anecdote associated with the incident. "These two poems," says a celebrated writer, "derive additional interest from the attitude in which the poet is himself presented to our view. We behold him engaged in the labours of the field, and moving in his humble sphere with all the dignity of honest independence and conscious genius."

The view from the height on which the farm-steading

stands is well described by William Wordsworth in the following sonnet :—

> "'There,' said a stripling, pointing with much pride,
> Towards a low roof, with green trees half-concealed,
> 'Is Mossgiel farm ; and that's the very field
> Where Burns plough'd up the daisy !' Far and wide
> A plain below stretched seaward, while, descried
> Above sea clouds, the peaks of Arran rose ;
> And by that simple notice, the repose
> Of earth, sky, sea, and air was vivified.
> Beneath the random bield of clod or stone,
> Myriads of daisies have shown forth in flower
> Near the lark's nest, and in their natural hour
> Have passed away ; less happy than the one
> That, by the unwilling ploughshare, died to prove
> The tender charm of poetry and love."

Mossgiel possesses very many interesting associations, but the only thing pertaining to the original steading is the walls. When they were heightened and repaired, every scrap of wood about the roof and floor was purchased by a boxmaking firm in Mauchline and converted into fancy ornaments, "warranted from the farm of Mossgiel." When the Burns family dwelt in it, it was a simple thatched cottage of one storey, which afforded the limited accommodation of a room and kitchen and a small garret which was reached by a trap stair. It contained a bed and a small table, which stood under a sloping window in the roof, and there Burns committed to paper the verses he composed during the day. John Blane, the gaudsman or driver already referred to, shared the bed with the poet, and in after years told of his services to him in amorous nocturnal visits to farm steadings, and how he was often roused from sleep to listen to newly-composed poems. These effusions were stored in a little drawer, and Chambers relates that the poet's young sister often stole up after he had gone out to his afternoon labour to search it for verses he had just written off.

"When my father's affairs grew near a crisis," says the stolid, worldly-wise Gilbert in his memoir of the Poet, "Robert and I took the farm of Mossgiel, consisting of 118 acres, at the rent of £90 per annum (the farm on which I live at present), from Mr Gavin Hamilton, as an asylum for the family in case of the worst. It was stocked by the property and individual savings of the whole family, and was a joint concern amongst us. Every member of the family was allowed ordinary wages for the labour he performed on the farm. My brother's allowance and mine was seven pounds per annum each, and during the whole time this family concern lasted, which was four years, as well as during the preceding period at Lochlea, his expenses never in any one year exceeded his slender income. As I was entrusted with the keeping of the family accounts, it is not possible that there can be any fallacy in this statement in my brother's favour. His temperance and frugality were everything that could be wished." Really! and so they might, for whatever charges may be brought against the poet, his bitterest traducer cannot add that of extravagance to the list. Seven pounds a year! Egad, the sum is barely sufficient now-a-days to keep some of our young men in pipes and tobacco.

The room, or "spence" as it was termed, was the scene of "The Vision." To its seclusion the bard often withdrew of an evening when tired with "the thresher's weary flingin-tree."

" Ben i' the spence right pensivelie,
 I gaed to rest."

"There, lanely, by the ingle cheek
I sat, and e'ed the spewin' reek,
That filled, wi' hoast-provoking smeek,
 The auld clay biggin';
And heard the restless rattons squeak
 About the riggin'.

"A' in this motty, misty clime,
I backward mused on wasted time;
How I had spent my youthful prime,
 And done nae thing,
But stringing blethers up in rhyme,
 For fools to sing.

 .   .   .   .   .

"When, click! the string the sneck did draw,
And jee! the door gaed to the wa',
And by my ingle-lowe I saw,
 Now bleezing bright,
A tight, outlandish hizzie, braw,
 Come full in sight.

 .   .   .   .   .

" With musing deep, astonished stare,
I viewed the heavenly-seeming fair,

> A whispering throb did witness bear
>   Of kindred sweet,
> When, with an elder sister's air,
>   She did me greet.
>
> "'All hail! my own inspired bard,
> In me thy native muse regard!
> Nor longer mourn thy fate as hard,
>   Thus poorly low!
> I come to give thee such reward
>   As we bestow.
>
> . . . .
>
> "'And wear thou this,' she solemn said,
> And bound the holly round my head;
> The polished leaves and berries red
>   Did rustling play,
> And, like a passing thought, she fled
>   In light away."

His father's death and parting words seem to have made a deep impression on the poet's heart. When he entered Mossgiel he did so with the determination of becoming wise. He read farming books, calculated crops, attended markets, and believed that "in spite of the world, the flesh, and the devil" he would succeed; but alas! the first year he purchased bad seed and the second lost half his crops by inclement weather and a late harvest. Things were trying enough, but when they were at their worst he solaced himself with song, and laid the foundation of his fame by composing the very cream of his poetry.

The four years the bard spent on this farm may be considered the most eventful of his chequered career. What agony of mind, what cares, troubles, and disappointments he experienced in the brief period, and what scenes of social enjoyments and literary triumphs he passed through! From obscurity he rose to fame, and from abject poverty to comparative affluence—an affluence, however, of short duration.

After lingering about the celebrated and now classic spot, and gazing upon some stately plane trees beneath which the poet loved to recline, I took leave of my cicerone, and in passing the front of the house plucked a sprig from off the thorn hedge and carried it away as a keepsake. It lies on my desk withered and dry, but serves as a memento of a visit to the farm wherein Burns composed his keenest satires and most beautiful poems and songs. Passing along a narrow unfenced road, I soon reached the highway, and after a walk of something like a mile entered Mauchline—a place to which Burns was often decoyed on " a nicht at e'en " to " pree the clachan yill " or perchance " the mou' o' some bonnie lass "— but more of him and it in next Chapter.

CHAPTER XV.

MAUCHLINE—THE RISE AND PROGRESS OF THE BOX-MAKING TRADE—NANSE TANNOCK'S HOUSE—THE HOUSE IN WHICH BURNS LIVED AFTER HIS MARRIAGE—GAVIN HAMILTON'S HOUSE—THE PARISH CHURCH—THE KIRK-YARD—THE HOLY FAIR—JOHN DOO AND POOSIE NANSIE—THE PUBLIC GREEN AND MARTYRS' STONE: A WORD ABOUT THEM—AN ANECDOTE OF BURNS AND JEAN ARMOUR—THE AULD MANSE AND WHO WAS SEEN IN ITS HAUNTED ROOM—THE HAGGIS.

MAUCHLINE is situated in a beautiful district, and although somewhat scattered and irregularly built is a town of neat appearance and considerable bustle. Like many places in the shire it owes its origin to its church and priory, of which the tower behind the burying ground is the only remnant. "In 1510 a charter, erecting Mauchline into a free burgh of barony, was granted by James IV.; and by the act of 1606 it will be observed that Mauchline was again constituted a free burgh of barony. The charters, however, are said to have been destroyed at the burning of the Register Office in Edinburgh, upwards of a hundred years ago, and they have never been renewed."* Otherwise, there is nothing of historical interest connected with the place. The weaving of cotton goods at one time formed the chief support of the inhabitants, but, alas! that trade has received an irreparable shock, and the sound of the shuttle is no longer heard in the streets. The staple industry at present is the manufacture of fancy ornaments, snuff boxes, card cases, &c. It is curious how this industry originated, and still more so how it has developed itself, and made Mauchline known throughout Great Britain, America, and the Continent of Europe. A French gentleman, on a visit to Sir Alexander Boswell at Auchinleck House, having the misfortune to break a handsome curiously-hinged snuff-box, sent it to the late Mr Wyllie, the village

---

* 'History of the County of Ayr.'

watch-maker, to be repaired. During the process, the workman into whose hands it was given inadvertently allowed some solder to run into the joint, and consequently rendered it useless. To remedy the mishap he taxed his ingenuity, and tried every possible means to remove the obstruction, but without success. Latterly he succeeded in making an instrument that answered the purpose so well that the difficulty was overcome, and the hinge put in working order. Being pleased with his success in repairing, the workman—a Mr Crawford—next conceived the idea of making a *fac simile* of the Frenchman's box and presenting it to Sir Alexander. The magical or secret hinge taxed his mechanical skill, but by the aid of the instrument he had made he succeeded in imitating it, and that so well that orders flowed in, and the manufacture of such boxes became his sole occupation. To monopolise the trade, both master and man kept the formation of the hinge a secret, and that for twelve years; but a misunderstanding arising between them, they separated, and each carried on the box-making business on his own account. Crawford settled in Cumnock, and introduced the trade there; but, having employed a watchmaker to make a hinge-forming instrument like unto what he made himself, its use was suspected, and the secret in a short time ceased to be private: one firm after another sprang up in neighbouring towns until the industry assumed considerable proportions. On this hinge—of which a bed-ridden Laurencekirk cripple named Steven is said to have been the inventor—the fancy wood trade in Mauchline is founded; but the honour of its introduction belongs to the late Andrew Smith, a genius who, though bred a stone-mason, raised himself by energy, self-culture, and perseverance to a very respectable position. Having, like others, discovered the secret of the snuff-box hinge, he put it to practical use, and opened a small manufactory in the village, in which he employed three men as box-makers. This venture proving a success, Andrew took his brother William into partnership, and his business habits, combined with his own creative genius, did much to make the industry the staple of the place. It is now fully sixty years since this species of manufacture was introduced into Mauchline, but during that period it has undergone many changes, and snuff-boxes are now the least of its products—

beautifully-fashioned articles of ornament and use being turned out in great variety. The trade is so far developed by the application of steam and mechanical science that an article can now be purchased for a couple of shillings which at one time would have cost as many pounds. There are at present three factories in the place, and close on 400 people find constant employment in them.

When residing in Mossgiel, Burns found many attractions in Mauchline, not the least of which were the lasses, the Masonic Lodge, the debating society, and the delusive pleasures of the ale-house. But at this stage it will be as well to resume the narrative and call attention to what is deemed worthy of regard.

The walk from Mossgiel to Mauchline proved pleasant and enjoyable. Upon entering the town I passed up a long street of clean, comfortable dwelling-houses, and in a very short time arrived in what may be appropriately termed the Cross, but not without being honoured with many a "glower" from chatty village belles, gossiping wives, and garrulous dames of one description and another who idled at doors in the seemingly earnest discussion of some all-important subject. Many of the houses in the vicinity of the local centre are modern; but one old-fashioned thoroughfare which branches off it and steals between two rows of venerable thatched cottages is of peculiar interest, being associated with the Poet's name. Accosting a middle-aged man, he kindly, and in a somewhat self-satisfied manner, pointed to an old house on the left, in which there is at present a tinsmith's shop, and said, "This was Nanse Tannock's place, and that two-storeyed red-stone building on the other side is the one in which Burns began housekeeping with his Jean; that is the auld kirkyard in which the 'Holy Fair' was held, and yonder is the house in which Gavin Hamilton lived, and the window of the office in which Burns and Jean were married." What was at one time the howf of Nanse Tannock is a rickety thatched building of two stories, with a wooden stair going up from the street door to the upper apartments—which, by the bye, have an entrance into a small yard adjoining the burying-ground, which was at one time unenclosed. Nothing remains to indicate this judicious ale wifie's residence but the nails which secured her signboard above the door, and these are pointed to as objects of curiosity by the residents—a circumstance certainly which indicates that the most is made of everything pertaining to the poet.

It is pretty evident that Burns frequented Nanse Tannock's change-house, and that its walls have often rung with the laughter which followed his sallies of wit. In it he promised to drink the health ("nine times a week") of those M.P.'s who would devise some scheme to remove the "curst restriction on aqua vitae;" but when Nanse heard of it she is reported to have said "that he might be a very clever lad, but he certainly was *regardless*, as, to the best of her belief, he had never taken three half-mutchkins in her house in all his life." This may be, but facts are very much against her. The Rev. P. Hately Waddell says—"Mrs Nelly Martin or Miller, who died December 22, 1858, aged 92, and was originally sweetheart to the Poet's brother William, was intimately acquainted also with the Poet himself, and confirmed in the most earnest and emphatic manner, as if living over again in his society the scenes of her youth, the rumours of the extraordinary gift of eloquence with which he was even then endowed. According to her account, to escape from his tongue, if once entangled by it, was almost an impossibility. 'He was unco, by-ordinar engagin' in his talk.' For which reason he was an invaluable visitor at the change-house, where Nanse Tannock had a jesuitical device of her own for detaining him. Nanse carried a huge leather pouch at her side, slung from her waist (as old Scotch landladies used to do), filled with keys, pence, 'change,' and *et ceteras*. When application for Burns was made at her door— as was often the case, 'for atweel he was uncolie in demand'— by personal friends of his or rivals of her own—'Is Rab here?' or 'Is Mossgiel here?'—Nanse would thrust her hand into her capacious leather pouch, and, jingling ostentatiously among keys and coppers, would solemnly and fraudulently declare 'that he wasna *there* (in her pouch) that night!' —Rab, in reality, being most probably engaged at the very moment in rehearsing his last poetical effusion, 'The Holy Fair' or 'The Twa Herds,' to an ecstatic audience in the parlour." The same writer goes on to say that it was in Nanse Tannock's parlour that "the first reading of 'The Holy Fair' took place, when there were present Robert and his sweetheart, Jean Armour; William and his sweetheart, Nelly Miller; and 'anither lad or twa and their sweethearts. Robin himsel' was in unco glee. He kneelit ontil a chair in the middle o' the room, wi' his elbows on the back o't, and read owre "The Holy Fair" frae a paper i' his han'—and sic laughin'! we could hardly steer for laughin'; an' I never saw himsel' in sic glee.' It must be observed, however, that both the quantity and the quality of 'refreshment' on this, as on other similar occasions, were very moderate indeed— 'three ha'penny yill, twa or three bottles for the company' being the average reckoning, with a glass or two of whisky at most. . . . . Miss Brown, Mauchline, states that her father well remembered Robert Burns, and has seen him frequently at Nanse Tannock's after his marriage, carrying his eldest son aloft on his hand, balancing and tossing the child in paternal pride towards the kitchen ceiling. Very beautiful indeed is this homely picture; and Jean herself undoubtedly would be there."

The house in which Burns resided is nearly opposite that of Nanse Tannock. It is a substantial two-storied thatched building containing several apartments. The one up stairs on the left is that in which the Poet and his darling Jean spent their honeymoon—a fact which induces many visitors to call and stare with a kind of reverence at the walls of the room and at the set-in-bed in which the happy pair slept; indeed some strangers—but more especially American— are so enthusiastic that they beg pieces of the wood, and several, I was informed, were so foolish as to get into it altogether.

Holding along a path which skirts the churchyard wall, and winds round the back of what was the residence of Gavin Hamilton, the early friend and patron of the poet, I crossed a rude bridge which spans a trickling narrow stream at the base of the hoary remnant of the priory already mentioned, and after some little difficulty entered a shady lane. This brought me to the gate of the newly laid out grounds which front the now celebrated and almost classic abode which is quaint and old-fashioned in appearance and highly picturesque from its situation.

Gavin Hamilton was a legal practitioner of high respectability, and is described as having been a "man of spirit and intelligence—generous, affable, and enlightened." Gilbert Burns says—"The farm of Mossgiel, at the time of our coming to it, was the property of the Earl of Loudoun, but was held in tack by Mr. Gavin Hamilton, writer in Mauchline, from whom we had our bargain ; who had thus an opportunity of knowing and showing a sincere regard for my brother before he knew that he was a poet. The Poet's estimation of him, and the strong outlines of his character, may be collected from the dedication to this gentleman. When the publication was begun, Mr. H. entered very warmly into its interests and promoted the subscription very extensively." It is almost unnecessary to add that he and Burns were on the most intimate terms, and that he had the poet's warmest sympathy when subjected to the petty annoyances of the kirk-session for digging a few potatoes in his garden on a Sabbath morning. In his office—which is still shown — Burns was married to Jean Armour, not in a ceremonial way, but according to the law of the land and as surely as if the contract had received the sanction of a benchful of bishops. It appears from the session record that the ceremony was performed on the 3rd August, 1788, and also that the poet generously gave a guinea to the poor of the parish on being told that it was customary for the bridegroom to pay a small fine when an irregular marriage was contracted. This room is also memorable as that in which "The Calf" was committed to paper. Burns called on his friend one day when going to church, and finding him suffering from gout, jocularly promised to return and give him the text. He did so, and the humorous satire was the result.

Upon leaving what is commonly termed "Gavin Hamilton's house," I found my way to the gate of the churchyard, which is close by, and luckily found it open. The church is a handsome edifice in the Gothic style, with a turreted square tower ninety feet in height. It occupies the site of the old barn-looking building in which "Daddy Auld" held forth. Hew Ainslie describes it in his *Pilgrimage to the Land of Burns* as having been as ugly an old lump of consecrated stone as ever cumbered the earth. "It seems," he says, ("if one might judge by the arched lintels that attempted to peep through the rough plaster), to have been set up by Gothic hands ; and if so, Presbyterianism has really been tolerably successful in beating it into its favourite model—a barn. The interior is, if possible, more dismal. Cold, damp, dark, and dirty, looking dissolution, and smelling decay, and a fitter place one could hardly imagine for crying 'tidings of damnation' in. Besides the ground floor it contains two wonderful looking things called lofts. One stretches from the east gable down into the body of the kirk; the other sticks out from the wall opposite the pulpit, supported by two wooden pegs, which gives it quite the dangerous look of that cunning engine, the mouse trap. Beneath this queer canopy, Jasper pointed out the 'cutty stool' where Burns sat when 'Mess John, beyond expression, fell foul o' him;' ' But,' said the bellman, ' tho' that's the bit whar he sat, it's no the seat. It's been made into a twa-armed chair, for behoof o' a society here wha haud his birthday.'"

It is stated in Spottiswood's Church History that George Wishart, the celebrated martyr of the Scottish Reformation, was invited to preach in Mauchline Church in 1554. " On his arriving at the place it was found that the Sheriff of Ayr, an enemy to the new faith, had placed a guard of soldiers in the church to keep him out. Some of the country people offered to force an entrance for him, but he would not suffer them, saying : ' It is the word of peace I preach unto you ; the blood of no man shall be shed for it this day ; Christ is as mighty in the fields as in the church ; and he himself, when in the flesh, preached oftener in the desert and upon the sea shore than in the temple of Jerusalem.' Then walking along to the edge of the moor, on the south side of Mauchline, he preached for three hours and upwards to the multitude that flocked about him."

At one time " tent preachings " and common fairs were held in the churchyard of Mauchline, but it has undergone an alteration for the better, and is now enclosed by a high wall, and compares favourably with the best kept village burying-grounds in the shire. After inspecting the church, I began to stray among the grass-covered graves, and conjure up the scene so graphically described by the poet—a by no means difficult task when one is acquainted with the incidents of *The Holy Fair* and remaining landmarks. The back of Gavin Hamilton's house forms part of the boundary. A little further along, the upper portion of Nanse Tannock's house, and two or three old rickets, serve the same purpose; but the first has the accommodation of a back door which, in the good dame's time, opened into the churchyard, and through which droves of drouthy saints poured,

> "To gie the jars and barrels
> A lift that day."

In front, the Cowgate retains a streak or two of its original appearance, for the house which Poosie Nansie occupied is but little changed, and that in which Jean Armour's father lived has undergone no very great alteration. The same, however, cannot be said of "the holy spot," for it is thickly studded with modern tombstones, and very few specimens of ancient sculpture are to be met with. Despite this it is interesting to ramble among the hillocks and scan the memorials of individuals who were associates of the bard or themes of his muse. Entering a gravelled walk that winds round the church, I turned to the left, and at a short distance from the tower paused before a plain upright stone which bears the following inscription:—"IN MEMORY OF A. D. J. JOHN MORRISON, OF THE 104TH REGIMENT, WHO DIED AT MAUCHLINE, 16TH APRIL, 1804, IN THE 80TH YEAR OF HIS AGE. ALSO, HIS DAUGHTER, MARY, THE POET'S BONNIE MARY MORRISON, WHO DIED 29TH JUNE, 1791, AGED 20; AND HIS SECOND SPOUSE, ANN THOMLIESON, WHO DIED SEPTEMBER, 1831, AGED 76." So this is the resting place of the amiable girl who made such an impression on the youthful poet's heart when attending the dancing school at Tarbolton, thought I, and yet she is pronounced unknown. The song in Mary's honour was a juvenile production, but notwithstanding it is considered to be the most pathetic of the poet's love effusions.

> "Oh Mary, at thy window be,
>   It is the wished, the trysted hour!
> Those smiles and glances let me see,
>   That make the miser's treasure poor.
> How blithely wad I bide the stoure,
>   A weary slave frae sun to sun,
> Could I the rich reward secure,
>   The lovely Mary Morison."

A little to the south of the church "Holy Willie's weel-worn clay" has "ta'en up its last abode." Nothing marks the spot, but the best and most enduring memorial of this individual is his well-known prayer; it will survive the wreck of many things, and keep his memory green when obliteration has wiped the inscription off every stone in the yard. The holy man was no better than the poet said he was: that he was an arrant hypocrite the events of his life testify. After being convicted of pilfering money from the church offerings, his morals did not improve, and he ultimately ended his days in a roadside ditch, having been jolted out of a cart which was conveying him and other inebriates home from a country fair. The carter—who appears not to have been altogether *compos mentis* himself—never missed Willie, or knew of the accident, until the dead body of the unfortunate man was discovered next morning. So ended the life of a practical dissembler; but, unfortunately, specimens of his class are not rare, for individuals are still to be found who

"—— display to congregations wide,
Devotion's every grace, except the heart."

A short distance from Willie's narrow bed the remains of Nanse Tannock and Racer Jess are stowed away under the sward. The first died in comfortable circumstances, and, like a judicious browster wife, maintained to the last that Burns never drank twa half-mutchkins in her house in a' his life, and that what he stated in his poems was just a wheen " leein' blethers." Perhaps she was right after all, for it is evident—at least to the writer—that he exercised the poetic license in the matter of dram-drinking. Jess, poor lass, closed her mortal race somewhat suddenly on the 15th February, 1813. She was the daughter of Poosie Nansie, a dame of whom something will be presently said, and was remarkable for her pedestrian powers and the running of errands: hence her cognomen.

In an out-of-the-way corner of the churchyard, which appears to be a repository for rubbish, I stumbled across a massive stone tablet. Having my attention attracted by the name Auld, I set to work and cleared the moss and dirt from the inscription, and made out the following:—"THE REVEREND MR. WILLIAM AULD, MINISTER OF THE GOSPEL AT MAUCHLINE, DIED 12TH DECEMBER, 1791, IN THE 50TH YEAR OF HIS MINISTRY, AND THE 81ST OF HIS AGE." Little need be said regarding Daddy Auld. That Burns satirised him, and that he rebuked Burns before the congregation for a certain moral lapse, is well known. He was a good man, but somewhat over zealous, and doubtless too severe on Gavin Hamilton for digging a few potatoes on the Sabbath; but what else could he be when hounded on by men like Holy Willie? Holding along the back of the church, I came to the burying-place of the Armour family. At its head there is a very handsome tombstone, and over the grave a common flag, much worn and scratched, which bears the following faded inscription:—"ELIZABETH RIDDLE, DAUGHTER OF ROBERT BURNS AND JEAN ARMOUR, BORN AT DUMFRIES 21ST NOVEMBER, 1793, DIED AT MAUCHLINE IN THE AUTUMN OF 1795." A short distance from this burying-place there is a humble tombstone to the memory of an obscure Covenanter, which states that "HERE LIES INTERRED THE CORPSE OF JAMES SMITH, WHO WAS WOUNDED BY CAPTAIN INGLIS AND HIS DRAGOONS AT THE BURN OF ANN IN KYLE, AND THEREAFTER DIED OF HIS WOUNDS IN MAUCHLINE PRISON, FOR HIS ADHERENCE TO THE WORD OF GOD AND SCOTLAND'S COVENANTED WORK OF REFORMATION.— A.D. 1682."

Every reader is, or at least should be, aware that Mauchline Churchyard is the scene of *The Holy Fair*. On it the poet met Fun, his cronie dear, and in "fine remarkin'" put an effectual stop to practices which where a disgrace to Scotland. "Holy Fairs" have happily passed away, but Robert Burns, by his "priest-skelping turns," and the scathing, withering sarcasm of the poem referred to, caused their expulsion, and worked a much needed reformation in the ecclesiastical affairs of Mauchline parish. In his day, the time appointed for the dispensation of the Lord's Supper was looked forward to by the peasantry as a kind of festival, and farm servants, when taking "a fee," were in the habit of making an agreement that they would be allowed to "gang to the preaching" on such an occasion during their period of service. All this wanted reforming, and it was only a satirist like our poet who could apply the lash and make the victim writhe under every stroke. This he did; but, to the eternal honour of his name, he never ridicules the ordinance itself, nor utters a sneer at the "worship of God in spirit and in truth." No. Although often

L

"Misled by Fancy's meteor ray,"

he had a sincere regard for religion, and believed—in fact, he states in a letter to Mrs Dunlop that

> " 'Tis *this* that streaks our morning bright,
> 'Tis *this* that gilds the horror of our night.
> When wealth forsakes us, and when friends are few,
> When friends are faithless, or when foes pursue,
> 'Tis this that wards the blow or stills the smart,
> Disarms affliction or repels his dart,
> Within the breast bids purest raptures rise,
> Bids smiling conscience spread her cloudless skies."

Mauchline Holy Fair was an event of no small importance in the district. People came long distances to be present at it, and while it lasted the public houses did a thriving business.

> " Now but and ben the change-house fills
> Wi' yill-caup commentators,
> Here's crying out for bakes and gills,
> And there the pint-stoup clatters ;
> While thick and thrang, and loud and lang,
> Wi' logic and wi' Scripture,
> They raise a din that in the end
> Is like to breed a rupture
> O' wrath that day."

The Communion was celebrated in the church, but the churchyard, in which there was a rostrum or moveable pulpit and "a shed to fend the showers and screen the country gentry," presented an animated appearance. The scene is graphically described by the Poet, but a still more racy picture is given in a pamphlet bearing date 1759, which purports to be *A Letter from a Blacksmith to the Ministers and Elders of the Church of Scotland, in which the manner of public worship in that church is considered, its inconveniences and defects pointed out, and methods for removing them humbly proposed.* "At the time of the administration of the Lord's Supper upon the Thursday, Saturday, and Monday," says the writer, "we have preaching in the fields near the church. At first you find a great number of men and women lying together upon the grass ; here they are sleeping and snoring, some with their faces towards heaven, others with faces turned downwards, or covered with their bonnets; there you find a knot of young fellows and girls making assignations to go home together in the evening or meet in some alehouse ; in another place you see a pious circle sitting round an ale-barrel, many of which stand ready upon carts for the refreshment of the saints. The heat of the summer season, the fatigue of travelling, and the greatness of the crowd naturally dispose them to drink, which inclines some of them to sleep, works up the enthuiasm of others, and contributes not a little to produce those miraculous conversions that sometimes happen at these occasions—in a word, in this sacred assembly there is an odd mixture of religion, sleep, drinking, courtship, and a confusion of sexes, ages, and characters. When you get a little nearer the speaker, so as to be within reach of the sound though not the sense of the words—for that can only reach a small circle —you will find some weeping and others laughing, some pressing to get nearer the tent or tub in which the parson is sweating, bawling, jumping, and beating the desk ; others fainting with the stifling heat, or wrestling to extricate themselves from the crowd ; one seems very devout and serious, and the next moment is scolding or cursing his neighbour for squeezing or treading on him ; in an instant after his countenance is composed to the religious gloom, and he is groaning, sighing, and weeping for his sins—in a word, there is such an absurd mixture of the serious and comic that were we convened for any other purpose than that of worshipping the God and Governor of Nature the scene would exceed all power *of face.*" How like the poet's description ! From this we know he did not exaggerate, but drew his picture from the life, and poured out the phials of his indignation against the cant and hypocritical humbug of his time.

"Here sits a raw of tittling jades
   Wi' heaving breasts and bare neck,
And there a batch o' wabster lads
   Blackguarding frae Kilmarnock,
      For fun this day.

"Here some are thinking on their sins,
   And some upon their claes ;
Ane curses feet that fyl'd his shins,
   Anither sighs and prays ;
On this hand sits a chosen swatch
   Wi' screwed-up, grace-proud faces :
On that a set o' chaps at watch,
   Thrang winking on the lasses
      To chairs that day.

> "O happy is that man and blest!
>   (Nae wonder that it pride him!)
> Wha's ain dear lass that he likes best
>   Comes clinkin' doun beside him!
> Wi' arm repos'd on the chair back,
>   He sweetly does compose him;
> Which, by degrees, slips round her neck,
>   An's loof upon her bosom,
>   Unkenned that day.
>
> "Now a' the congregation o'er
>   Is silent expectation:
> For Moodie speels the holy door
>   Wi' tidings o' d———tion.
> Should Hornie, as in ancient days,
>   'Mang sons o' God present him,
> The vera sight o' Moodie's face
>   To's ain het hame had sent him
>   Wi' fright that day.
>
> "Hear how he clears the points o' faith
>   Wi' rattlin' an' wi' thumpin'!
> Now meekly calm, now wild in wrath,
>   He's stampin' an' he's jumpin'!
> His lengthen'd chin, his turn'd-up snout,
>   His eldritch squeal and gestures,
> Oh, how they fire the heart devout,
>   Like cantharidian plasters,
>   On sic a day!"

Opposite the churchyard gate is the street along which "Common Sense took the road" on a certain minister making his appearance at *The Holy Fair.* At one corner is the house in which "Poosie Nansie" resided, and the entry at which "Racer Jess," and two or three ladies of questionable virtue, stood "blinking," while the people were gathering to celebrate "the Fair," and at the other a substantial building with the following inscribed on its front chimney:—

> "This is the house, though built anew,
>   Where Burns came weary frae the plough,
> To ha'e a crack wi' Johnny Doo
>   On nicht at e en,
> Or whiles to taste his mountain dew
>   Wi' bonnie Jean."

Why a house can be the same after being rebuilt is difficult to understand, but I suppose the poet must be awarded the usual license. The building, however, which occupied the site when Burns walked the streets of Mauchline, was an inn, and if tradition is to be trusted, it was a favourite resort of his. On the back window of an upper room he scribbled the following amusing epitaph on John Dow, the landlord, which was doubtless more truthful than pleasing to that worthy:—

"Here lies Johnny Pidgeon;
What was his religion?
Whae'er desires to ken,
To some ither warl'
Maun follow the carl,
For here Johnny Pidgeon had nane.

"Strong ale was ablution,
Small beer persecution,
A dram was *mementi mori;*
But a full flowing bowl
Was the joy of his soul,
And port was celestial glory."

The gable of Jean Armour's father's house adjoined the back of the premises, and Burns, it is said, often sat at the window referred to and conversed with her in the language of the eyes—a language, by the by, which lovers aptly understand and appreciate.

The house in which Jean's parents resided is a lowly thatched cottage, but from the fact that it sheltered *her* and *them*, it possesses peculiar interest.

Observing that the house celebrated by the residence of "Poosie Nansie" is "licensed to retail spirits, porter, and ales," I entered for the double purpose of weetin' my whistle and seeing the relics in possession of the occupants. I was shown a caup *supposed* to have been used by the "randie gangrel bodies" who

"held the splore
To drink their orra duddies,"

and also an old engraving representing the merry crew in the midst of their festivities.

Poosie Nansie was a Mrs. Gibson, who lodged vagrants and other questionable characters. The halt, the blind, and the lame found shelter beneath her roof, and her kitchen was not unfrequently the scene of frantic mirth and bouts of drunkenness. Here Burns studied humanity in its lowest forms, and his "Jolly Beggars" is supposed to have been founded on a scene which he witnessed in the establishment. Chambers says—" In company with his friends, John Richmond and James Smith, he dropped accidentally at a late hour into the humble hostelry of Mrs. Gibson. . . . . After witnessing much jollity among a company who by day appeared abroad as miserable beggars, the three young men came away, Burns professing to have been greatly amused with the scenes, but particularly with the gleesome behaviour of an old maimed soldier. In the course of a few days he recited a part of the poem to Richmond, who informed me that, to the best of his recollection, it contained, in its original complete form, songs by a sweep and a sailor which did not afterwards appear."

Having strolled to the Cross, I turned up a lane which terminates at the public green—a triangular piece of ground on which the *seven* annual fairs of the district are held. It is memorable on account of the five martyrs " who suffered for Christ and their adherence to the Covenanted work of Reformation " buried in it, and also for being the spot where Burns had his second interview with Jean Armour. " There was a race at the end of April," says Robert Chambers, "and there it was customary for the young men, with little ceremony, to invite such girls as they liked off the street into a humble dancing hall, where a fiddler had taken up his station to give them music. The payment of a penny for a dance was held by the minstrel as guerdon sufficient. Burns and Jean happened to be in the same dance, but not as partners, when some confusion and a little merriment was excited by his dog tracking his footsteps through the room. He playfully remarked to his partner that ' he wished he could get any of the lasses to like him as well as his dog did.' A short while after, he passed through Mauchline washing green, where Jean, who had overheard the remark, was bleaching clothes. His dog running over the clothes, the young maiden desired him to call it off, and this led them into conversation. Archly referring to what had passed at the dance, she asked ' if he had yet got any of the lasses to like him as well as his dog did ?' From that time their intimacy commenced." Of course, Jean was one of the " Mauchline belles," and according to the poet's notion was " the flower o' them a'." After he was married to her, he very sensibly and justly said, that he could easily *fancy* a more agreeable companion in his journey through life, but had never *seen* the individual instance.

From the public green I strolled down an avenue and paused before the old manse. It is a quaint, curiously formed building, and was the residence of the celebrated Daddy Auld. Daddy's wife was supposed to be a witch, and according to tradition kept queer company—indeed, it is handed down that a servant girl saw the devil warming his hoofs at a fire in one of the rooms. The old gentleman sat with his tail twisted over his knee, but the moment the maid screamed and let fall the shovelfull of fuel she carried, he vanished. Perhaps it was wrong, but I went up and saw "the haunted room," and the spot where his devilship enjoyed a short respite from

"Spairgin about the brunstane cootie
To scaud poor wretches,"

but beheld nothing remarkable, and came away somewhat disappointed, for instead of it being clad with cobwebs and dust, like the haunted chambers we read about, it was scrupulously clean, and wore an air of quiet comfort.

From the old manse, a short walk brought me to Ballochmyle road, and ultimately to the upper end of the Cowgate. Here I again paused, and while thinking on the flight of "Common Sense" from the "Holy Fair," looked upon a snug thatched cottage with a porched doorway, which stands near some mean buildings a little way down the celebrated thoroughfare. It is pointed to as the house in which Burns composed his exquisite address to "a Haggis," and on this account possesses a peculiar interest in the eyes of those who see a charm in everything associated with the poet's name. It was at one time occupied by a Mr. Robert Morrison, a great crony of the poet when he resided at Mossgiel, and it is said that he was in the habit of spending the interval between the church services on the Sabbath-day at this gentleman's fireside. On one of these occasions, Mrs. Morrison invited the bard to partake of a haggis "whose hurdies like a distant hill" almost concealed "the groaning trencher." Having done so to his evident delight and inward satisfaction, he wrote the "address," and well he might, for a proper haggis is worthy of a "grace as lang's my arm" at any time.

From Mauchline I pushed on to Ballochmyle, but what was seen and heard there and at Barskimming will be reserved for next chapter.

CHAPTER XVI.

BALLOCHMYLE—THE BRAES—THE LASS O' BALLOCHMYLE—HER ACCOUNT OF MEETING THE POET—BURNS' SEAT—THE POET'S LETTER TO MISS ALEXANDER—APOLOGIES FOR HER SILENCE—THE BOWER—CAUGHT BY THE GAMEKEEPER—CATRINE—AN EXCURSION PARTY—THE RIVER AYR—BALLOCHMYLE BRIDGE—HAUGH—BARSKIMMING BRIG—"MAN WAS MADE TO MOURN"—THE RAILWAY STATION—BACK TO KILMARNOCK.

BALLOCHMYLE, the seat of Colonel Claud Alexander, M.P. for South Ayrshire, is situated on the Catrine Road, some mile and a half from Mauchline. Although the scenery through which the road winds cannot be termed enchanting, it is at least pleasing, and I enjoyed it and the fragrance of the hay and flowers which the breeze bore from the uplands and wafted across the fields as I strolled on my way. Groups of happy, brown-faced, bare-legged children, who seemingly were returning from school, were gathering posies of daisies and golden dandelions here and there along the wayside in the vicinity of the town, and it made my heart glad to watch them and listen to their innocent laughter as it waked the echoes and mingled with the music of the birds. When I reached the entrance to the estate I found the gate fast, and it was not until I gave a few authoritative raps with my stick that a maiden issued from an antique flower-embowered cot, which nestles beautifully beneath some old trees, to admit me With many thanks for her courtesy, I passed along the fine drive which winds through dense masses of wood and shrubbery, and in due time arrived in front of the mansion. All was quiet, and save the birds that flitted and chirruped in the trees or sought food on the lawn, no sign of life was to be witnessed. Although surrounded by a scene of bewildering beauty, a sense of loneliness weighed me down, for as yet I was an unauthorised visitor. To remedy this I set off in quest of my friend the keeper, and in my explorations stumbled into a secluded path in the shrubbery which leads down to the river Ayr. The solitude was peculiarly impressive. There was a cloudless sunshine, but nothing was heard save the murmuring of the current as it made its way among stones and pieces of rock impeding its progress. Steep banks and precipices, draped in most luxuriant natural wood, rose from the water edge in majestic loveliness, and cast long shadows on the ripples and smooth glassy spaces of the stream. Here the grass and herbage extended close to the brink, and trees bent over and laved the tips of their boughs in the current; there a wall of rock rose from the bed, which looked as if it had been hewn by rough, careless workmen, who in their haste had left many a shelf protruding. On these, and in the intervening spaces, ferns and shrubs grew, and far up on the top of all, on the very brink of the chasm, trees clung to crag and tightly grasped pieces of rock with their knotty fingers. It is a never-to-be-forgotten scene, and I am not at all surprised that the poetic fancy of Burns was roused by witnessing it. Following the path, I entered the thicket, and in its intricate windings over the braes was soon lost among confused stems, bushes, branches, and clustering green leaves which had succeeded those which lay withered and dead on the verge of the rustic footway. Several times I was nearly tripped up by moss-grown tree roots, and more than once startled by rabbits which my unexpected appearance had surprised while basking in gleams of sunshine which fell on the green sward through openings in the trees.

Having threaded this narrow path for some considerable distance, I came to a broader but not less romantic one, for the leafy canopy of interlaced branches continued, and the wild grandeur of the scene, if possible, became more fascinating. Having followed it a short distance, I reached a rustic bower or grotto of ornamental twig work and moss. It was a familiar object, and I at once knew that I had reached the spot where Burns unexpectedly met "The Lass o' Ballochmyle," who, as the reader is probably aware, was a Miss Wilhelmina Alexander, a sister of Mr Claud Alexander, a gentleman who had realized a fortune in India and purchased the estate from Sir John Whiteford, the friend of Burns, and the representative of a once powerful Ayrshire family. The bard sung the departure of the kind gentleman in a set of plaintive verses, in which he makes his daughter Maria take farewell of the lovely braes.

> "Through faded groves Maria sang,
>   Hersel' in beauty's bloom the while,
> And aye the wildwood echoes rang,
>   Fareweel the braes o' Ballochmyle."

Those lovely braes were a favourite resort of the poet when residing in the farm of Mossgiel. One July evening, when walking on them, he somewhat suddenly met Miss Alexander. The lady's account of the interview—if interview it can be called—is that she encountered the poet, whom she describes as "a plain-looking man," musing with his shoulder against one of the trees, and that the evening being far advanced and the grounds forbidden to strangers, she was startled, but recovering herself, passed on and thought no more of the matter. Burns, however, was impressed with the glimpse he got of the beauty, and according to the tradition of the district, remained and composed the song in which her charms are celebrated. The place where he is said to have sat and strung the lovely lyric is only a few paces from the grotto. It is situated at the extreme end of a narrow neck of land, jutting out into the ravine through which the river flows, and is in every way a lovely situation for poet or painter to muse in. A few old trees cluster together, and by their interlaced branches form a kind of bower over "the seat," while down below the river joins in chorus with the song of the birds. When I stood there, I did so with a deep sense of enjoyment to the soft buzzings of the insects around and of the myriads of blue-bells which dyed the dell as they kept nodding in the balmy breeze that swayed their fragile stems. All around was life—fresh, delightful, enjoyable life —and as I stood motionless,

> "The merry, young rabbits came leaping
>   Over the crest of the hill,
> Where the clover and corn lay sleeping
>   Under the sunlight still."

Some months after the incident, Burns wrote the lady, and in a very beautiful letter asked permission to publish the song he had composed in her honour. He says:—"I had roved out, as chance directed, in the favourite haunts of my muse on the banks of the Ayr, to view nature in all the gaiety of the vernal year. The evening sun was flaming over the distant western hills; not a breath stirred the crimson opening blossom, or the verdant spreading leaf. It was a golden moment for a poetic heart. I listened to the feathered warblers pouring their harmony on every hand, with a congenial, kindred regard, and frequently turned out of my path lest I should disturb their little songs, or frighten them to another station. 'Surely,' said I to myself, 'he must be a wretch indeed, who, regardless of your harmonious endeavours to please him, can eye your elusive flights to discover your secret recesses, and to rob you of all the property nature gives you—your dearest comforts, your helpless nestlings.' Even the hoary hawthorn twig that shot across the way, what heart at such a time but must have been interested in its welfare, and wished it preserved from the rudely browsing cattle or the withering eastern blast? Such was the scene, and such was the hour, when, in a corner of my prospect, I spied one of the fairest pieces of nature's workmanship that ever crowned a poetic landscape or met a poet's eye; those visionary bards excepted who hold commerce with aerial beings! Had Calumny and Villainy taken my walk, they had at that moment sworn eternal peace with such an object. What an hour of inspiration for a poet! It would have raised plain, dull, historic prose into metaphor and measure."

To this letter—of which the above is a portion—the bard received no reply. Dr. Currie says:—" Her modesty might prevent her from perceiving that the muse of Tibullus breathed in this nameless poet, and that her beauty was awakening strains destined to immortality on the banks of the Ayr. It may be conceived also that, supposing the verse duly appreciated, delicacy might find it difficult to express its acknowledgments." Chambers, on the other hand, says:—
"The apology now presented by the family for Miss Alexander's conduct is, that she unfortunately fell amongst those who entertained an unfavourable opinion of his character. Feeling it to be necessary to decline yielding to his request, she thought that that resolution would be intimated most delicately towards him, as well as in the manner most agreeable to herself, by simply allowing the letter to remain unanswered. It is easy to enter into the feelings of a sensible

woman of thirty in adopting this course, and even to make some allowance for others not acknowledged, which might cause her to shrink from the acquaintance of a humble tenant of her brother (for Mossgiel now belonged to Mr. Alexander) who, in the exercise of an assumed poetic privilege, dared to imagine her as his mistress. However this might be, Miss Alexander and her kindred learned afterwards to think the woods of Ballochmyle classic, and herself immortal through the genius of Burns. On a question occurring many years after as to the disposal of the original manuscript of the song, Miss Alexander said that there could be no dispute on that point: 'wherever she went it must go.'" Miss Alexander died unmarried in 1843, in the eighty-ninth year of her age.

The rustic bower, erected in commemoration of the abrupt meeting, is a neat circular erection with an open front. It contains a row of seats and an oaken board, on which the following is inscribed in *fac simile* of the poet's handwriting:—

> " 'Twas even, the dewy fields were green,
> On every blade the pearls hang,
> The zephyr wantoned round the bean,
> And bore its fragrant sweets alang:
> In every glen the mavis sang,
> All Nature listening seemed the while,
> Except where greenwood echoes rang
> Amang the braes o' Ballochmyle.
>
> "With careless step I onward strayed,
> My heart rejoiced in Nature's joy,
> When, musing in a lonely glade,
> A maiden fair I chanced to spy:
> Her look was like the morning's eye,
> Her air like Nature's vernal smile;
> Perfection whispered passing by,
> Behold the lass o' Ballochmyle!"

After sitting in the bower listening to the music of the woods and holding communion with my thoughts, I rose to depart, but had not taken many steps when I was confronted by a man with a double-barrelled gun under his arm. "Ho," said he, "what are you doing here?" A glance was sufficient to show that I stood face to face with the vigilant head keeper, and that a prompt answer was absolutely necessary. This I made, and drew his attention to the fact that we had met before. In an instant he was at my service, and proffered to assist me in any way.

Being now an authorised visitor, I took leave of my friend after some pleasant conversation, and commenced the journey to Mauchline railway station. As I moved forward I had an excellent view of the wooded precipitous banks of the Ayr, and of the village of Catrine—a circumstance which brought to mind the fact that it was there that Professor Dugald Stewart, the expositor of the Scottish system of metaphysics, had his residence, and that it was at his table Burns "dinner'd wi' a lord." The professor narrates that the manners of the poet on the occasion were "simple, manly, and independent; strongly expressive of conscious genius and worth, but without anything that indicated forwardness, arrogance, or vanity."

The small but startling incidents of the route added a sort of piquancy to the enjoyment of the scene. At one time I startled a partridge, at another a blackbird, which flew with a sudden flutter and a wild cry from a thicket where its nest was hid. The rustling grass and fern fronds, too, bespoke the sudden flight of rabbits—indeed, numbers of them hurried off in timorous haste at my approach, while almost unconsciously muttering—

> "Tell me, fellow-creatures, why
> At my presence thus you fly?
> Why disturb your social joys,
> Parent, filial, kindred ties?
> Common friend to you and me,
> Nature's gifts to all are free."

A sudden turn in this secluded walk brought me to a neat foot-bridge which spans a broad macadamised road. Here I paused and listened to a party of homeward-bound excursionists who made the wildwood echoes ring, as with stentorian voices they bade a heart-fond adieu to the lovely scenes they were leaving behind. The words of their song were peculiarly appropriate, and, as the sound of their voices became faint by distance, the following snatch smote my ear :—

> "But here, alas! for me nae mair
> Shall birdie charm, or floweret smile;
> Fareweel the bonnie banks of Ayr,
> Fareweel, fareweel! sweet Ballochmyle!"

Upon crossing the bridge I found myself on the verge of

the river and near to a vast wall of red sandstone towering from its channel. The scene is most imposing, but why the stream is thus imbedded I am unable to say—possibly the rock has been rent asunder by some great convulsion, or (though very doubtful) the water has worn a passage for itself. Upon descending some steps cut in the rock, I came upon an angler straying along the brink of the water casting and trailing his line in hopes to catch a trout, but, although he tried every artifice, the finny tribe remained shy, and he disappointed. However, it was not for want of fish, for several rose farther down the stream in a dark, deep pool to snap at unwary flies hovering near the glassy surface.

Keeping in the shade of the massive rocks which rise from the river bed, I soon reached the stupendous erection called Ballochmyle Bridge. It makes a gigantic sweep across the ravine through which the Ayr flows, and rises to a height of 184 feet above its channel. It has an imposing appearance, and eclipses everything of the kind in Great Britain in point of magnitude and elegance. Its foundation stone was laid with Masonic honours on the 10th of September, 1846, and the structure was completed in the month of August, 1848. Near it is the celebrated quarry from which the beautiful red sandstone is procured that makes buildings throughout Ayrshire so conspicuous. The stone is worked to a great depth, but its bottom has not been reached, and the supply appears to be as inexhaustible as it was when operations first began.

Beyond the bridge a beautiful path winds along the foot of the verdant precipices and steep descents which line the river bank. Holding along it, I soon reached "the never-failing brook" which propels the wheel of "the busy mill," and entered Haugh, a very small village consisting of a group of cottages, an agricultural implement maker's shop, a woollen and a curling stone factory.

Finding nothing here worth a sentence, I enquired my way to Barskimming Bridge, and was directed to a small roadway at the end of the village. Out of it, according to instructions, I entered a stile road or beaten track which winds through a couple of fields. Cattle were browsing in them. At my approach they lifted their heads and looked at me with long and wary observation ; but being satisfied that my mission was peace, they again bent their heads and began to crop the pasture.

At the termination of the carpet-like path, I found myself in the highway between Mauchline and Stair, and close at the old bridge of Barskimming, a spacious structure of one arch which spans the Ayr a little below the confluence of the Lugar. Its situation is peculiarly romantic and pleasing. Immediately above it, on the south side of the stream, Barskimming Mill nestles beneath the shade of an immense wall of sandstone, which appears to have been hewn by the hand of man to make room for the diminutive structure. Below, a curve conceals the river from sight, but beyond it, it flows through a perfect chasm of towering rocks which are decked and crowned by the most luxuriant vegetation. Over this wildly romantic gulf, a bridge connects the lands of Barskimming and gives access to the princely mansion which nestles in the beautifully laid off grounds of the estate.

While leaning on the parapet of the bridge enjoying the scenery, I accosted a passing wayfarer, and asked to be shown the holm where Burns composed, "Man was made to Mourn." "Man, it's no here," said he, "its on the Doon." "Na, na, John," said a middle-sized, pleasant-featured old woman who was standing near with a bundle of faggots in her apron, "you are wrong, far wrong, it was no such thing, but it was owre in that holm there, where my kye are, that the poet made 'Man was made to Mourn.' Often have I heard my old father speak about it; he knew Burns and them all, but they are all gone." "And what were the circumstances?" said I, for I must confess that I was somewhat fascinated with her tragic manner and fluent language. "Well, young man," she continued, "I will tell you, for I love to speak about Burns. That is my house at the end of the brig there. Well, in Burns' time, a man lived in it o' the name o' Kemp, wha had a daughter ca'd Kate—Kate Kemp. Well, you know, Burns had an e'e to Kate, and came from Mauchline ae afternoon to see her, but it so happened that the coo was lost and she had gone to look for't. Well, you see, the poet made up his mind to go and look for them baith, but he had gotten no farther than the other side of the brig there when he met the miller. 'Well, Miller, what are you doing here?' said he. 'Deed,' said the miller, 'I was gaun to speer that question at you.'

'Well, then,' said Burns, 'I was doon to see Kate Kemp, but she and the coo's lost.' Weel, ye ken, they cracket awa', but Burns began to get fidgety an' left the miller like a knotless thread, an' gaed awa doon the holm there. But the next time they met he said, 'Miller, I owe you an apology for leaving you so suddenly when we last met.' 'Oh, there's nae need o' that!' said the miller, 'for I suppose something was rinnin' in your head.' 'You are right,' said Burns, 'and here it is;' an' sae wi' that he read 'Man was made to mourn.' Yes, John, that is the Holm where Burns made 'Man was made to mourn,' I can assure you." John heard her statement, intimated his surprise, and moved off, and left the old lady and I to ourselves. She informed me that she had spent the whole of her life in the locality, and entertained me with many reminiscences of her early years. "In the days of Burns," she said, "aye, and in my day to," she added with a sigh, "all round by the holm there was covered with beautiful trees in which the craws biggit their nests, but they are all down; and a beautiful oak that stood 'yont the road a bit, which was admired by everybody, and was drawn by many an artist, is down too. My heart bled to see the noble monarch lying low—but it was not so in the days of Lord Glenlee. No, he would not allow a tree on the estate to be touched, and when one at the big house was blown down, he said 'if a ten pound note will put it up I will gladly pay down the money.'" After enjoying a hearty draught of milk in this intelligent lady's dairy—which, by the by, is cut out of the solid rock—I reluctantly bade her good-bye and pushed on to Mauchline, for train time was nigh, and my step was not so elastic as it was in the morning. The scenery on the road between Barskimming bridge and Mauchline is romantic enough, but it is tame, tame, when compared with the wooded slopes of Ballochmyle. When I reached Mauchline station the train was due. It is needless to add that Kilmarnock was speedily and safely reached.

CHAPTER XVII.

FROM KILMARNOCK TO NEWMILNS—THE AYRSHIRE HERMIT—LOUDOUN KIRKYARD AND RUINED CHURCH—THE QUEIR—LADY FLORA HASTINGS—THE SCOTTISH MILKMAID—GALSTON—LOUDOUN CASTLE—THE OLD CASTLE—LOUDOUN MANSE—DR. LAWRIE AND BURNS—LOUDOUN HILL—NEWMILNS—THE OLD TOWER—THE PARISH CHURCH AND CHURCHYARD.

> " I love not man the less, but Nature more,
> From these our interviews, in which I steal
> From all I may be, or have been before,
> To mingle with the Universe, and feel
> What I can ne'er express, yet cannot all conceal."

It is delightful to stroll along a hedge-bordered country road on a radiant summer day, listening to the hum of the treasure-ladened bee and the song of the lark. It is truly exhilarating, and I never enjoyed Nature's beauties to greater advantage than I did when walking from Kilmarnock to Newmilns. The road I selected is not only secluded, but one of the old sort, winding over heights and through hollows in a manner very pleasing to the pedestrian who has an eye for the picturesque. Any little toil, therefore, which I encountered on the way was amply repaid by the extensive and beautiful prospects obtained from the heights, and especially of that district,

> " Where Loudoun Hill rears high its conic form,
> And bares its rocky bosom to the storm."

After a walk of two miles or so I reached the river Irvine at a point where it sweeps round a curve and rushing along its channel through some beautiful scenery, again emerges and passes triumphantly on its way to the sea. For a short distance the road winds along its bank, but it soon diverges and rises over the brow of a steep hill on which stands a handsome villa. Behind it, in a beautiful holm on the bank of the stream, is an ivy-mantled, ruined cottage, which was at one time the residence of Thomas Raeburn, the Ayrshire hermit—a personage whose eccentric habits and peculiar appearance will not readily be forgotten. His story is as curious as it is brief. It appears that he inherited the house and a few acres of land from his father, but, strange to say, the small property was surrounded by that of other people, and there was no road into it unless one which skirted a field belonging to a neighbour. In course of time the neighbour closed the road, but Raeburn, under the impression that "use and wont" constituted a right, sued him for a restitution of the privilege of passing through his ground, and, as might have been expected, lost the case. The result of the trial preyed upon his mind and made him morose and gloomy. He declared that he had been harshly dealt with, and vowed that he would neither shave his beard, cut his hair, nor renew his clothing until justice was done him, and this vow he solemnly kept until the day of his death. His hair grew long and matted, and his beard, likewise unkempt, hung in tangled masses down his breast. His clothing, too, soon lost its identity, and became so patched and darned that it was ultimately a matter of difficulty to discover an original piece of any garment. His strange appearance naturally attracted many visitors, and in course of time a favourite rural walk with the young people of Kilmarnock was to his residence and back, for he was no recluse, but made all comers welcome. To accommodate such he dealt in lemonade and ginger-beer, and occasionally in a more stimulating beverage, although his infringement of the excise law did not go unpunished. He was parsimonious in his habits, lived sparingly, and drank nothing but water when better cheer could not be procured at the expense of others. He made many attempts at wit in private conversation, of which the following are said to be fair samples:—Upon being asked if his clock was with the town, he replied—"No, it's twa mile and a half aff't." If a visitor asked for a light to his pipe, he was generally told that "There's no as muckle fire i' the house as wad licht a pipe, but ye may licht your tobacco." Upon being asked if he was ever drunk, he replied—"There's naebody wi' a throat big enou' to swallow me." He had a strange influence over animals, and more especially over the songsters of the grove. Often would he go into his garden for the gratification of visitors and call the robins from the trees to perch on his beard and take crumbs from between his lips. He was never married. An old woman kept house for him and managed his dairy, for he had several cows, and was famed for making cheese of excellent quality. He died in June, 1843, in the seventy-fourth year of his age, and the money he so avariciously gathered was divided amongst relatives who speedily put it into circulation, and his plot of ground now belongs to a cattle dealer in Newmilns.

Above the ruined residence of the Ayrshire hermit are Milton Mill, and the miller's house and garden, beautifully situated on the bank of the stream, and beyond them Grougar Row, a collection of miners' dwellings. One obtains occasional glimpses of Galston and the moors beyond it as he plods onward, but there is little else on the landscape to attract attention, and the river is soon lost sight of by a sudden divergence of the road.

The first place of consequence reached is Loudoun Kirkyard, an ancient place of burial surrounded by a wall and a row of sombre-looking trees. It nestles in a picturesque nook by the wayside at a point where a burnie jinks beneath overhanging bushes and steals under a rude bridge with a gurgling sound which seems to say—

"Men may come, and men may go,
But I flow on for ever."

The iron gate being securely chained and padlocked, I sought and gained admittance by a wicket in a cottage garden hard by. The secluded spot is small, unkept, and the memorials of the departed few and scattered. In its centre stands a shattered gable and a portion of the old kirk called the "queir," which is kept in repair on account of it having been the sepulchre of the Loudoun family for nigh four hundred years. It is a venerable square block with a sloping roof, and is embellished with the Loudoun arms and other curious devices, and also has a small barred window through which the coffins of the defunct barons are seen. Here lie the remains of the gifted but unfortunate Lady Flora Hastings, who is said to have died of a broken heart on account of a cruel and unmerited slander which was raised against her by one of the ladies of the bedchamber to H.R.H. the Duchess of Kent.

Had her detractors heeded the advice of Burns—

> "Gently scan your brother man,
> Still gentler sister woman"—

she would not have been "a flower plucked in its bloom." She was an accomplished poetess, and shortly after her death—which occurred at Buckingham Palace in July, 1839—her poems, which are distinguished by much purity of thought, sweetness, and grace, were collected and published. Indeed, as an able reviewer remarked, "such a deep love of the beautiful, the exalted, and the holy reigns through them all that it is impossible to repel the conviction that her actions accorded with her words, and that her words gave but the utterance to the calm and sinless feelings of her heart."

There is a curious old stone at the door of the queir worth attention. It states that it is "IN MEMORY OF MATHO FULTUN, MAISTER MASON—ANE RICHT HONEST MAN WHO DIED IN THE YEAR OF GOD, 1632." According to the semi-obliterated inscription, "Matho" went to his grave as to his bed, with the intention of rising at the Resurrection. Within a few yards of it, and near to the gable of the old kirk, is the grave of the "Scottish Milkmaid," Janet Little, author of a small volume of poetry which never gained any great or lasting popularity, but who is now well known as the poetical correspondent of Robert Burns. The plain slab, which marks the spot, bears the following in yet legible characters:—

"IN MEMORY OF JOHN RICHMOND, WHO DIED AUGUST 10, 1819, AGED 78 YEARS; AND JANET LITTLE, HIS SPOUSE, WHO DIED MARCH, 15, 1818, AGED 54 YEARS; AND FIVE OF THEIR CHILDREN."

Janet belonged to Ecclefechan and came to Ayrshire to serve in the capacity of a domestic servant in the family of Mrs Hendrie, daughter of Mrs Dunlop, the distinguished friend of our poet, when she resided in Loudoun Castle. Having met with a copy of the Kilmarnock edition, she was so captivated by it that she conceived a partiality for Burns, and wrote him a poetical address, of which the subjoined is part:—

> "Fair fa' the honest rustic swain,
>   The pride o' a' oor Scottish plain;
> Thou gi'es us joy to hear thy strain,
>   And notes sae sweet;
> Old Ramsay's shade revived again
>   In thee we greet.

"Lov'd Thalia, that delightfu' muse,
Seem'd long shut up in a recluse;
To all her aid she did refuse
    Since Allan's day;
Till Burns arose, then did she choose
    To grace thy lay.

"To hear thy sang all ranks desire,
Sae weel you strike the dormant lyre;
Apollo with poetic fire
    Thy breast does charm;
An' critics silently admire
    Thy art to charm.

"Cæsar and Luath weel can speak—
'Tis pity e'er their gabs should steek,
But into human nature keek,
    And knots unravel;
To hear their lectures once a week
    Nine miles I'd travel.

"In the latter part of March (1791), Burns had the misfortune to come down with his horse and break his right arm. Janet Little, the poetical milkmaid, had come to see him, and was waiting at Ellisland when the bard returned in the disabled state to which he had been reduced by the accident. She has related in simple verse her own painful alarm when the sad intelligence resounded through his hall, the sympathy with which she regarded the tears of his affectionate Jean, and the double embarrassment she experienced in greeting at such a crisis the illustrious poet whom she had formerly trembled to meet at all."*

Little else regarding Janet is known. The cottage where she resided is within a stone-throw of the kirkyard, and from this it appears that she married and settled in the district after quitting the service of Mrs Hendrie.

Near Janet's grave there is a handsome monument to the memory of the late Rev. James Allan, minister of Loudoun, and a very chaste stone which Mr Robert Mackie has raised to the memory of his sister, Janet, who died at Loudoun Cottage, 24th September, 1872, in the sixty-third year of her age. With the exception of these, and a humble slab commemorating "THOMAS FLEMMING OF LOUDOUN HILL, WHO, FOR HIS APPEARANCE IN ARMS IN HIS OWN DEFENCE, AND IN THE

---

* Contemporaries of Burns.

Defence of the Gospel, according to the Word of God, was shot in an encounter at Drumclog, 1st June, 1679, by Bloody Graham of Claverhouse," there are no stones of special interest, but several may be found decked "with uncouth rhymes and shapeless sculpture," which implore "the passing tribute of a sigh."

Beyond Loudoun Kirk the road is very beautiful and the scenery most sylvan and picturesque. From the height which the road attains before entering the policies of Loudoun Castle, there is an excellent view of Galston, nestling sweetly on the bank of the river Irvine at the foot of a range of uplands studded with farmsteads and patches of woodland, which Burns refers to in the opening stanza of the "Holy Fair." Although it cannot be called flourishing, it is at least a comfortable country town, with some four thousand inhabitants, but there is little in it to stay the feet of a rambler—its antiquities being few, and its buildings lowly. Its chief objects of interest are its church—which stands above the town and is a prominent object for a great distance—and Barr Castle, an old square tower at the top of one of its streets. It also boasts a "boss tree," as the rotten hollow stump of a gigantic willow is termed. The tradition regarding it is that Sir Wm. Wallace concealed himself in its branches when pursued by a detachment of Southern soldiers, a statement which verges on the probable, for from its girth it is of seeming great age. The old tower possesses no history. It is said to have been the residence of a powerful family named Lockhart, and that the reformer, John Knox, addressed the people of Kyle from one of its windows. It was a favourite haunt of John Wright, a gifted but erratic local genius, who made some stir in literary circles in his day. In some verses which he addressed to it, he says:—

"Proud edifice! no annals tell
What thou hast brooked, what thou hast been,
Who reared thee in this lovely dell,
What mighty baron—lord, I ween,
Of hardy Kyle; no bordering tower
Possessed more independent power."

Amongst the many excellent things John wrote is a song entitled "Kiss the goblet and live," which I am almost tempted to reproduce. Unfortunately for him, he kissed it too often and died in the prime of life, and had it not been for the generosity of a few friends would have filled a pauper's grave.

The quaint byroad which we have followed from Kilmarnock terminates at the sylvan avenue leading to Loudoun Castle, the magnificent residence of the Loudoun family. The present Earl succeeded to his mother, the late Countess of Loudoun, who took up the Scotch title at the death of her brother, the Marquis of Hastings.

The grounds are thickly wooded, and contain many beautiful aged trees. Indeed, in the vernal season of the year, the woods and braes around this famed residence are unsurpassed for grandeur, and are in every way worthy of the compliment which the poet Tannahill paid them. To John, fourth Earl of Loudoun, belongs the merit of having made the scenery what it is, for he not only devoted himself to improving the estate in many ways, but planted upwards of one million trees which he brought from various parts of the globe.

Passing up the shady avenue I soon arrived in front of the Castle, which may be described as combining the gracefulness of modern architecture with the massive strength of early times. One battlemented square tower was erected in the twelfth century, and another, which overlooks the entire building, in the fifteenth. To these antiquated structures Sir John Campbell, who was created Lord Chancellor in 1642, made an extensive addition, and in 1811 the whole was augmented by a large and stately portion which gives to the pile quite a palatial appearance. The interior is fitted up with great magnificence, and the walls of several apartments are literally covered with finely-executed portraits of the Loudoun and Rowallan families. Many of these pictures are dimmed with age, and recal to one's mind stirring events of the good old times when plain speaking and hard blows were in fashion, and when the four feet of cold steel which dangled by every gallant's side settled differences and enforced arguments. A picture of Charles I., which is disfigured and patched-looking, is associated with an incident worth relating. It appears that the troops of Oliver Cromwell visited the Castle, and that a company of officers, when straying through its rooms, stopped before the king's picture, and out of contempt for his majesty made thrusts at it with their swords by way of joke.

The library is said to contain over 10,000 volumes, and very many ancient manuscripts and curious documents.

It may be added that few families can boast a more honourable pedigree, or a more lengthened possession of their property, than that of Loudoun. Indeed, the whole line, or rather lines, of the noble house have been distinguished for deeds of patriotism and valour.

A notice of this beautiful domain, be it ever so brief, would be incomplete without some reference to the old yew-tree which grows beside the castle wall. Although ages have fled, and generations of men have passed away since it was planted, it spreads its umbrageous boughs over the lawn, and seems as likely to withstand the blast as any tree on the estate. One of the family charters was subscribed under its deep shade in the reign of William the Lion, and when Scotland and England became united, Lord Hugh Campbell chose the same place to sign the deed. It is also memorable for the trifling incident of James, second Earl of Loudoun, having addressed letters to it, when secretly communicating with his lady during the period of his banishment.

"To the Gudewife at the Aulton,
At the Old Yew Tree,
Loudoun,
Scotland,"

was the manner in which they were inscribed, and there is little doubt that they reached the hand intended.

There are many pleasant rambles to be had amongst "Loudoun's bonnie woods and braes," and not the least of them is from the Castle to Newmilns by the private road. When traversing it I was delighted with the bosky scene. At one part the rustic way passes a stripe of woodland, and is overshadowed by the foliage of stately trees; at another, it merges into the open glade, and winds along a verdant bank, or dips into a dell where some tiny streamlet murmurs among the brackens, and ultimately pursues a zig-zag course until it reaches the brow of an almost perpendicular height overlooking the picturesque hamlet. For a reason which will be apparent, I left the sequestered roadway at a point where it is crossed by the Hag Burn, and turned into a bypath which skirts the stream as it bickers through a beautifully wooded glen. On the one hand a dark wood stretches away towards the Castle, and on the other a steep slope—almost a cliff—which is clad with trees, and tangled masses of briar and bramble rise from the path in wild grandeur. To ascend this cliff is a work of some little difficulty, but it can be managed from several points by planting the foot in ledges or on jutting pieces of rubble and holding tightly to roots which curl and twist in fantastic shapes, or to tufts of long hardy grass which grow here and there within reach.

When the laborious ascent is made, the intrepid rambler will have the gratification of standing on the site of the Old Castle of Loudoun—a building anterior to any portion of the present magnificent structure, but of which nothing remains save shattered fragments of masonry and portions of the foundation, which are partly covered by the mouldering dust of centuries, and clad here and there with ivy. Curiously enough, the history of the ancient stronghold is wrapped in the shadow of night, and all that tradition has preserved regarding it is the simple statement that it was burned by the clan Kennedy. This may have been, for it is an historical fact that a deadly feud existed between the Campbells of Loudoun and the Kennedys of Carrick about the year 1527, and that the Earl of Cassillis was slain during a foray which the former made into the territory of the latter. Also, that in retaliation, and to avenge this nobleman's death, the Kennedys devastated the district of the Campbells, and characterised their raid by deeds of rapine and blood. The stronghold of the hostile chieftain would most probably be attacked, and therefore it is within the range of possibility that this Castle of the Campbells succumbed at that period.

A ballad, which was at one time popular in the district, ascribes the destruction of the Castle to "Adam o' Gordon and his men," but there is nothing to bear out the statement. The following descriptive extract, however, is not without interest:—

"Out then spake Lady Margaret,
 As she stood upon the stair—
The fire was at her goud garters,
 The low was at her hair—

" 'I would gie the black,' says she,
  'And so would I the brown,
For a drink o' yon water
  That rins by Galston town.'

"Out then spake fair Annie,
  She was baith jimp and sma',
'O row me in a pair o' sheets
  And tow me down the wa'.'

" 'O hold thy tongue, fair Annie,
  And let thy talkin' be,
For thou must stay in this fair castle,
  And bear thy death with me.'

" 'I would rather be burnt to ashes sma',
  And be cast on yon sea foam,
Before I'd give up this fair castle,
  And my lord so far from home.

" 'My good lord has an army strong,
  He's now gone to the sea,
He bade me keep this gay castle
  Sae lang's it would keep me.

" 'I've four-and-twenty braw milk kye
  Gangs on yon lily lee,
I'd give them a' for a blast of wind
  To blaw the reek from me.'

"O pittie on yon fair castle,
  That's built o' stone and lime,
But far mair pittie for Lady Loudoun,
  And all her children nine."

The bosky bypath winds along the bank of the wimpling burnie and terminates in the highway at no great distance from the quaint village of Newmilns, and near to "the Hag Brig turn" where the late Rev. Dr. Lawrie "guddled in the burn, and was late for the schule in the morning." Some boys engaged in the same pastime—or possibly in the more questionable one of bird-nesting—made the woods echo with shouts and peals of laughter in such a manner that a pair of jays jabbered round the summit of a tall fir tree, and a flock of crows wheeled about in evident alarm. A blackbird ruffling out his feathers on a rail also uttered a loud cry at the unusual sounds and fled to the security of the thicket, and the warblers drinking from the stream with dainty sips as though its waters were the richest wine followed his example.

The highway which connects Galston with Newmilns—and in which the lane traversed terminates—is draped with hanging boughs, and fringed on the one hand by the grounds of Loudoun Castle, and on the other by stripes of plantation through which the waters of the Irvine gurgling sing a continual farewell to "Loudoun's bonnie woods and braes" as they roll on to the mighty deep.

As one nears the village, and just at a point of the road where a turn brings it into full view, a snug tree-embowered old-fashioned looking house with a lawn in front stands on a height a little to the left. Below the second floor windows is the following hieroglyphical inscription, which may be intelligible to some readers:—"PL. 1768. M.C. JEHOVAH. IJ REH." The place is called St. Margaret's Hill, and the residence is that of the Rev. John Robertson, minister of the parish of Loudoun; but for many years it was that of the Rev. George Lawrie, D.D., the early friend and patron of Robert Burns. Robert Chambers describes him as having been "a remarkably fine specimen of the old moderate clergy of the Scottish establishment—sensible, upright, kind-hearted, and with no mean taste in literature." By what means this worthy clergyman and Burns became acquainted I have been unable to learn, but one thing is certain, no person was received with greater cordiality at St. Margaret's Hill than the poet. "The first time Robert heard the spinnet played upon," says Gilbert Burns, "was at the house of Dr. Lawrie. . . . . . Dr. Lawrie has several daughters; one of them played; the father and mother led down the dance; the rest of the sisters, the brother, the poet, and the other guests, mixed in it. It was a delightful family scene for our poet, then lately introduced to the world. His mind was roused to a poetic enthusiasm, and the following stanzas were left in the room where he slept :—

' O Thou dread Power who reign'st above,
 I know Thou wilt me hear ;
When for this scene of peace and love
 I make my prayer sincere !

' The hoary sire, the mortal stroke,
 Long, long be pleased to spare !
To bless his little filial flock,
 And show what good men are.

> ' She, who her lovely offspring eyes
>   With tender hopes and fears,
>   Oh, bless her with a mother's joys,
>   But spare a mother's tears!
>
> ' Their hope, their stay, their darling youth,
>   In manhood's dawning blush;
>   Bless him, thou God of love and truth,
>   Up to a parent's wish!
>
> ' The beauteous seraph sister-band,
>   With earnest tears I pray,
>   Thou knowest the snares on every hand,
>   Guide Thou their steps alway!
>
> ' When soon or late they reach that coast,
>   O'er life's rough ocean driven,
>   May they rejoice, no wanderer lost,
>   A family in Heaven!'"

It is recorded that Burns was a good dancer, and on this occasion "kept time admirably;" also, that he remarked to the fair musician that she knew the magic way to a poet's heart.

This entertainment took place during the most melancholy period of the poet's history. Being driven to despair by the consequences of his imprudence, he was about to relegate himself from his native land and seek a home in the West Indies, or at least an asylum, in the hope that fortune would smile and enable him to atone for past errors. When he bade this honoured family farewell, he most likely crossed the Irvine at a point opposite their residence, and ascended the slopes of Lanfine, which at the time, and long after, were nothing more than a range of barren, bleak uplands, and steered his course to Mossgiel. "In his way home," says Professor Walker, "he had to cross a wide stretch of solitary moor. His mind was strongly affected by parting for ever with a scene where he had tasted so much elegant and social pleasure, and depressed by the contrasted gloom of his prospects. The aspect of nature harmonised with his feelings. It was a lowering and heavy evening in the end of autumn. The wind was up, and whistled through the rushes and long spear-grass which bent before it. The clouds were driving across the sky; and cold pelting showers at intervals added discomfort of body to cheerlessness of mind." As he plodded onward, doubtless "holding fast his guid blue bonnet," his melancholy thoughts shaped themselves into verse, and despite his ungenial surroundings, he composed what he considered to be "the last song he should ever measure in Caledonia." Here it is :—

"THE GLOOMY NIGHT IS GATHERING FAST.

"*Tune*—'Roslin Castle.'

"The gloomy night is gathering fast,
    Loud roars the wild inconstant blast;
    Yon murky cloud is foul with rain,
    I see it driving o'er the plain;
    The hunter now has left the moor,
    The scattered coveys meet secure;
    While here I wander, pressed with care,
    Along the lonely banks of Ayr.

"The autumn mourns her ripening corn
    By early winter's ravage torn;
    Across her placid azure sky
    She sees the scowling tempest fly:
    Chill runs my blood to hear it rave;
    I think upon the stormy wave,
    Where many a danger I must dare,
    Far from the bonnie banks of Ayr.

"'Tis not the surging billow's roar,
    'Tis not that fatal deadly shore;
    Though death in every shape appear,
    The wretched have no more to fear!
    But round my heart the ties are bound,
    That heart transpierced with many a wound,
    These bleed afresh, those ties I tear,
    To leave the bonnie banks of Ayr.

"Farewell old Coila's hills and dales,
    Her heathy moor and winding vales,
    The scenes where wretched fancy roves,
    Pursuing past, unhappy loves!
    Farewell, my friends! farewell, my foes!
    My peace with these, my love with those,
    The bursting tears my heart declare;
    Farewell the bonnie banks of Ayr!"

Dr. Lawrie was a sincere friend of Burns. He seems to have gently scanned his youthful follies, and to have esteemed him for his talents and the many good qualities which constituted his generous temperament. According to J. G. Lockhart, he gave him "much good counsel, and what comfort he could, at parting; but prudently said nothing of an effort which he had previously made in his behalf. He had sent a copy of the poems (the Kilmarnock edition was then published), with a sketch of the author's history, to his friend, Dr. Thomas Blacklock of Edinburgh, with a request that he would introduce both to the notice of those persons whose opinions were at the time most listened to in regard to literary productions in Scotland, in the hope that, by their intervention, Burns might yet be rescued from the necessity of expatriating himself. Dr. Blacklock's answer reached Dr. Lawrie a day or two after Burns had made his visit, and composed his dirge; and it was not yet too late. Lawrie forwarded it immediately to Mr. Gavin Hamilton, who carried it to Burns." In that letter Dr. Blacklock characterises the perusal of the poems sent him as "one of the finest and perhaps one of the most genuine entertainments of which the human mind is susceptible, and breathes words of approbation and encouragement which must have lighted up the gloomy surroundings of the poet like a gleam of sunshine. Let him describe his circumstances :—

"'Hungry ruin had me in the wind,'"

says he. "I had been for some days skulking from covert to covert, under all the terrors of a jail, as some ill-advised people had uncoupled the merciless pack of the law at my heels. I had taken the last farewell of my few friends; my chest was on the road to Greenock; . . . when a letter from Dr Blacklock to a friend of mine overthrew all my schemes, by opening new prospects to my poetic ambition. The Doctor belonged to a set of critics for whose applause I had not dared to hope. His opinion that I would meet with encouragement in Edinburgh for a second edition fired me so much that away I posted for that city, without a single acquaintance or a single letter of introduction. The baneful star that had so long shed its blasting influence in my zenith for once made a revolution to the nadir." "Blacklock received him," says a celebrated writer, "with all the ardour of affectionate admiration; he eagerly introduced him to the respectable circle of his friends; he consulted his interest; he emblazoned his fame; he lavished upon him all the kindness of a generous and feeling heart, into which nothing selfish or envious ever found admittance."

It is scarce necessary to add that before he was many weeks in Edinburgh his society was courted by the polite and the learned, and sought after by individuals moving in the most elevated circles of society. In short, he became the lion of the season, and had the second edition of his poems published under the most favourable auspices. "The attentions he received during his stay in town from all ranks and descriptions of persons," says Professor Dugald Stewart," "were such as would have turned any head but his own. . . . . He retained the same simplicity of manners and appearance which had struck me so forcibly when I first saw him in the country, nor did he seem to feel any additional self-importance from the number and rank of his new acquaintances." No, his sterling common-sense told him that he had but lately left the stilts of the plough and was fated to return to them again. In replying to a letter which he received from Dr. Lawrie during the meteor-like blaze of reputation which he experienced, he says, "I thank you, sir, with all my soul, for your friendly hints, though I do not need them so much as my friends are apt to imagine. You are dazzled with newspaper accounts and distant reports; but, in reality, I have no great temptation to be intoxicated with the cup of prosperity. Novelty may attract the attention of mankind a while—to it I owe my present eclat—but I see the time not far distant when the popular tide which has come to a height, of which I am perhaps unworthy, shall recede with silent celerity, and leave me a barren waste of sand to descend at my leisure to my former station." He expresses himself in like manner to Mrs Dunlop and others—but there, space is beginning to fail, and so will the reader's patience if I digress at this rate.

A few steps beyond the garden gate of the old and now almost classic manse of Loudoun, the respectable and apparently flourishing village of Newmilns comes into view. It is beautifully situated in a narrow vale through which the river Irvine flows, and from which broad hills ascend on each side. On the right are the wooded slopes of Lanfine, and on the left the green braes of Loudoun; while in the far distance, at the top of the hilly pass in which the village nestles, is Loudoun Hill looming heavily against the sky. The scene is one of extreme beauty, and if transferred to canvas would form a striking picture.

I have no intention of going so far as Loudoun Hill in this ramble, but I can assure the reader who wishes to undertake the journey that he will be amply repaid for the toil and trouble encountered by the extensive and interesting view from its summit, including the scenes of decisive struggles which assisted, in a great measure, to secure Scottish independence. Near its eastern base Sir William Wallace and a handful of co-patriots attacked and routed a troop of English soldiers who were conveying waggon loads of provisions from Carlisle to Ayr, and near the same spot, in May, 1307, Bruce gave the Earl of Pembroke battle, and with six hundred followers is said to have defeated six thousand trained Englishmen. These associations are brimful of interest, but one which remains to be mentioned gives the locality, if possible, still greater interest. On a fair Sabbath morning in June, 1679, a sentinel, in the garb of a peasant, who was stationed on the top of the hill, sprang from the green sward on observing a company of horse men crossing the heights from the direction of Strathaven, and having fired off his carbine, ran towards a group of worshippers on the plain. " We had met," says one of the assembly, " not to fight but to worship the God of our fathers. We were far from the tumult of cities—the long dark heath waved around us, and we disturbed no living creature save the peesweep and the heather cock." When it became known that Claverhouse and a detachment of troopers were approaching, the preacher, who had been telling his hearers

> " How guiltless blood for guilty man was shed;
> How *He*, who bore in Heav'n the second name,
> Had not on earth whereon to lay His head,"

hastily concluded his discourse, and said:—" I have done. You have got the theory—now for the practice. You know your duty. Self-defence is always lawful." The little company being armed, they formed themselves into lines under various leaders, and waited the approach of the foe—first, however, taking the precaution of sending away their women and children. Refusing to lay down their arms and deliver up their ringleaders, Claverhouse cried—" Their blood be upon their own heads," and sounded the attack. The battle

of Drumclog then commenced and waged fiercely for some time. The following wonderfully graphic account of this engagement is taken from a letter penned by Claverhouse:—
"They were not preaching, but had got away all their women and children. In the end they, perceiving that we had the better of them in skirmish, resolved on a general engagement, and immediately advanced with their Foot, the Horse following. They came through the loch: the greatest body of all made up against my troop: we kept our fire until they were within ten paces of us: they received our fire and advanced to the shock: the first they gave us brought down the Cornet, Mr. Crawford, and Captain Beith; besides that with a pitchfork they made such an opening in my roan horse's belly that his guts hung out half an ell, and yet he carried me off a mile, which so discouraged our men that they sustained not the shock, but fell into disorder. Their Horse took the occasion of this, and pursued us so hotly that we had no time to rally. I saved the standards, but lost on the place eight or ten men, besides wounded; but our dragoons lost many more. The town of Stra'von drew up as we were making our retreat, and thought of a pass to cut us off; but we took courage and fell to them, and made them run, leaving a dozen on the place. What these rogues will do yet I know not, but the country is flocking to them from all hands. This may be counted the beginning of the rebellion, in my opinion."

In the words of Hugh Brown, a poetical native of Newmilns, and author of "The Covenanters,"

> "The lover of freedom can never forget
> The glorious peasant band—
> His sires that on Scotia's moorlands met,
> Each name like a seal on the heart is set—
> The pride of his Fatherland."

Newmilns is a very nice rural town. The houses are mostly small and plain, but pleasant looking and free from squalor. Weaving is the staple of the place, and the inhabitants—some 3000—are mostly engaged in it. Male and female take to the loom as naturally as ducks to water, but I cannot help expressing regret with Hew Ainslie "that any bonnie Ayrshire lass should be condemned to make her bread by such thumping and kicking." However, it is only the probationary state with them, for, like their sisters in

Darvel, they generally exchange the "box and bobbins," when married, for a "baby and a blanket."

Possibly Newmilns had its origin from grain mills erected on the bank of the river.* About the centre of its quaint, old-fashioned looking main street a massive square tower may be seen in a courtyard which possesses several interesting associations. It was at one time a residence of the Loudoun family,† and at another the headquarters of Captain Inglis, a notorious scourge of the Covenanters.

The writer of the Loudoun article in the *Statistical Account* in mentioning the tower says—" In one of the expeditions of Inglis's troops in the search of conventicals, eight men who were discovered praying in the Blackwood, near Kilmarnock, were taken prisoners. One of them, it is said, was immediately executed, and the soldiers in mockery kicked his head for a football along the Newmilns public green. Inglis was about to shoot the others when it was suggested to him that it would be prudent to get a written order from Edinburgh for their execution. The seven men in the meantime were confined in the old tower. But while the troop was absent on one of its bloody raids, with the exception of a small guard, a man named Browning, from Lanfine, with others who had been with him at Aird's Moss, got large sledge hammers from the old smithy (still in existence), with which they broke open the prison doors and permitted the Covenanters to escape. John Law (brother-in-law to Captain Nisbet) was shot in this exploit, and is buried close to the wall of the tower. The dragoons soon went in pursuit of the prisoners, but they had reached the heather, and where no cavalry could pursue them. The soldiers, however, having ascertained that John Smith of Croonan had given the runaways food went to Smith's house, and meeting him at his own door shot him dead ! Within a short period his grave was to be seen in the garden of the old farmhouse."

Tradition states that only *one* soldier played football with the martyr's head, and that he shortly afterwards fell from

---

* Sir Hugh Campbell of Loudoun had a charter of the lands of Newmilns, with the mill and granary, dated 4th October, 1533.—*Paterson's Ayrshire Families.*

† The Master of Loudoun died in March, 1612. His latter will was made at " the Newmylnes, the sevint day of Merche." His lady also died the same month and year. Her latter will was made also at " Newmylnes, the penult day of Merche." They seem thus to have resided at the tower of Newmilns.—*Ibid.*

the top of the tower into the court below and broke his neck. There is a tablet in the gable of an old building to the memory of the man shot which bears the following inscription:—

"RENEWED IN 1822. HERE LIES JOHN LAW, WHO WAS SHOT AT NEWMILNS, AT THE RELIEVING OF EIGHT OF CHRIST'S PRISONERS WHO WERE TAKEN AT A MEETING FOR PRAYER AT LITTLE BLACKWOOD IN THE PARISH OF KILMARNOCK, IN APRIL, 1685, BY CAPTAIN INGLIS AND HIS PARTY, FOR THEIR ADHERENCE TO THE WORD OF GOD AND SCOTLAND'S COVENANTED WORK OF REFORMATION.

"Cause I Christ's prisoners relieved
I of my life was soon bereaved,
By cruel enemies with rage,
In that encounter did engage;
The martyr's honour and his crown
Bestowed on me! O high renown!
That I should not only believe,
But for Christ's cause my life should give."

Near the old tower is "The Institute," as a handsome two-storied building is termed which Miss Brown of Lanfine presented to the inhabitants. It contains a library, a reading and a recreation room, and has a very nice bowling green attached. Close by also is the Parish Church, a more handsome edifice than is often met with in country towns. The late Rev. Dr. Norman Macleod preached in it for some time as minister of the parish, and by the side of its pulpit there is a beautiful monumental marble tablet to his memory, which the church officer will be glad to show visitors.

The churchyard is small and unkept, but contains many interesting monuments. When pensively wandering over its uneven sward I stumbled upon the family burying-place of Dr. Lawrie, the friend and patron of the poet Burns. The tablet covering his grave bears a very just estimate of his character. Here is the inscription:—

"UNDER THIS STONE ARE DEPOSITED THE REMAINS OF THE REV GEORGE LAWRIE D.D., LATE MINISTER OF THIS PARISH, WHO DIED 17TH OCTOBER, 1799, IN THE 71ST YEAR OF HIS AGE AND THE 36TH OF HIS MINISTRY.

"*He discharged the duties of his ministerial office with a judgment and firmness of mind which no situation could shake. His piety was exemplary and sincere, devoid of all ostentation. He was an able scholar, and learned divine. His temper cheerful and steady. His heart warm and affectionate. Kind and hospitable to strangers, sincere and hearty in friendship, and fulfilled the duties of husband and parent with the most indulgent and tender affection."*

By his side rests his son and successor, Archibald, a man of great worth. He had twelve children—four sons and eight daughters. One son died in infancy, but the others rose to distinction, and proved themselves worthy of such a parent. The late Rev. Dr. Lawrie became minister of Monkton, and the late James A. Lawrie, M.D., professor of surgery in the University of Glasgow. Francis R. H. Lawrie entered the army in 1822, and retired as Major in 1846.

The churchyard bears ample evidence that the inhabitants of Newmilns shared the struggle for civil and religious liberty. A plain slab bears the following :—

"To the Memory of John Nisbet of Hardhill, who suffered Martyrdom at the Grassmarket, Edinburgh, 4th December, 1685. Animated by a spirit to which genuine religion alone could give birth, the pure flame of civil and religious liberty alone could keep alive, he manfully struggled for a series of years to stem the tide of national degeneracy, and liberate his country from the tyrannical aggressions of the perjured house of Stuart. His conduct in arms at Pentland, Drumclog, and Bothwell Bridge, in opposition to prelatic encroachments and in defence of Scotland's Covenanted Reformation, is recorded in the annals of those oppressive times. His remains lie at Edinburgh, but the inhabitants of his native Parish and friends to the cause for which he fought and died, have caused this stone to be erected."

This martyr was born in Newmilns about the year 1627. When Claverhouse was advancing against the Covenanting army at Drumclog, a message was despatched to Hardhill to apprise him of the fact and induce him to join the little band. Although he had suffered much from prelatic persecution, he mounted a horse at once and rode with all possible speed to the scene of action, merely stopping on his way through Darvel to induce John Morton, the village blacksmith, to accompany him and assist with his brawny arm to discomfit the foe. Both were of immense service to the Covenanters, for they fell into their ranks in time to take part in the successful charge which decided the fate of the battle. In the thick of the fight, the smith encountered a dragoon entangled in the trappings of his wounded horse, and was about to despatch him, but being moved by the man's piteous appeal for mercy, he disarmed him and led him from the field a prisoner. Many of the Covenanters, however, were less humane, and demanded the dragoon's life, but this the smith strongly objected to, and declared that whoever touched a hair of his head would suffer, for having given the man quarter he would defend his life at the risk of his own. None feeling inclined to cross swords with the resolute blacksmith, he was allowed to have his own way, and to this day the dragoon's sword is preserved by his descendants in Darvel.

Besides the above, there are rude memorials of Covenanting times to the memory of John Gebbie, John Morton, and others. Gebbie fought at Drumclog, and was carried off the field mortally wounded, and, like the mighty Nelson, died with the shouts of victory ringing in his ears. Morton was shot by Claverhouse at the same engagement.

After spending a reflective hour in the churchyard, and enjoying a look through the town, I sought out the terminus of the Galston branch of the South-Western Railway. Near it is the scene of Ramsay's popular song, "The Lass o' Patie's Mill." The mill is modern, and occupies the site of the erection which graced the bank of the Irvine in Ramsay's day, but the field wherein the rustic beauty was making hay when she attracted the attention of the Earl of Loudoun is still pointed out, and although one hundred and fifty years have passed since the event the stranger still stops by the brink of the stream and enquires for the song-hallowed scene. The story is well known. It appears that the poet and the Earl were riding along the highway when it occurred to the latter that the comely appearance of the "lass" would form a fit subject for Allan's muse. At the suggestion the bard lagged behind, composed the ditty, and produced it the same afternoon at dinner. The train being due, I bade "Loudoun's bonnie woods and braes" a fond and somewhat reluctant farewell, and in a short time reached Kilmarnock, for a seven mile journey is a mere nothing in these days of railways and telegraphs.

CHAPTER XVIII.

From Kilmarnock to Dumfriesshire—Notes by the Way—Auldgirth and its Scenery—The Hotel—On the Road to Dumfries—Gossip—The Banks of the Nith—Friar's Carse—Friendships of Burns—"The Whistle"—The Hermitage and its Associations.

Having realised £500 by the sale of the Edinburgh edition of his poems, Burns was enabled to live for a time on his means, and to indulge in tours through Berwickshire and the North of England; and also, the Highlands, by Inveraray, Lochlomond, Dunkeld, Castle-Gordon, and Inverness. In the course of these excursions he was received by men of rank and taste, and by the people generally with the most gratifying marks of respect for his brilliant talents, frank manners, and fluent conversation secured him many friends. In referring to his return to Mossgiel, Dr Currie says, "It will easily be conceived with what pleasure and pride he was received by his mother, his brothers, and sisters. He left them poor and comparatively friendless; he returned to them high in public estimation and easy in circumstances. He returned to them unchanged in his ardent affections, and ready to share with them to the uttermost farthing the pittance that fortune had bestowed."

With characteristic generosity of heart he handed his brother Gilbert £180 to relieve him from the embarrassment in which he was involved by the sterile soil of an ungenial farm, and, despite the seductive power of "Clarinda"—a talented lady of fashion whose acquaintance he made in Edinburgh—married his much-loved Jean, and began to look about for the means to earn daily bread. In this world every man is left to work out his own fate, and it depends greatly upon the course he steers what that fate is. Burns at this period of his history was still "without an aim," and still far from the enjoyment of "the glorious privilege of being independent," even although he had amassed a little money and had become famous by dint of his giant intellect. As a means of subsistence he endeavoured to procure a situation in the Excise, but ultimately abandoned the idea for that of returning to his original occupation of farming. After some deliberation, he entered into negotiations with his patron, Mr Patrick Miller of Dalswinton, respecting the farm of Ellisland, and having procured it on favourable terms, set about preparing a home for his young wife on the banks of the Nith. Thither, reader, we will follow him, and while tracing his footsteps in Dumfriesshire, it is to be hoped that my gleaning will prove at once instructive and entertaining.

On the afternoon of a bonnie summer day, I availed myself of a short respite from business, and left Kilmarnock by rail with the intention of wandering at leisure amid the scenery of Nithsdale, and visiting places celebrated by the residence or muse of Robert Burns. As the train glided on the ever-changing scenery had a peculiar charm for me, not only on account of the fact that it was from it the bard drew inspiration, but because its every rood is hallowed by brave men who fought and bled for freedom and Scotland, when might was considered right, and liberty of conscience and action the property of those in power. A short stoppage occurred at Mauchline, and another at the quaint village of Auchinleck, near to which is Auchinleck House, the residence of Lady Boswell. Dr Samuel Johnson made a grumbling, discontented stay at it in the month of November, 1773. The Lugar was then unsung, and the "moors and mosses many" had not been celebrated by the bard of Coila, for he was but in his fifteenth year, and had concluded a grand session of three weeks at the grammar school of Ayr to return to Mount Oliphant to swing the "weary flingin'-tree" in the old barn. The doctor and his biographer have now a very small share of the affection and gratitude of mankind, but the name of the poor boy Robert Burns, who worked hard and fared hard, and received his education by snatches, fame has wafted over the whole world, and his immortal verses are the solace and delight of his countrymen in every land where their lot is cast. The illiterate, the learned, the rich, and the poor admire them, and speak of the poet as of one with whom they were intimate—

in fact, the birch-fringed, amber-flooded streams he has sung appear to murmur more sweetly and rush more proudly to the notes of his lyre—

> " Nor skill'd one flame alone to fan ;
> His country's high-soul'd peasantry
> What patriot pride he taught—how much
> To weigh the inborn worth of man !
> And rustic life and poverty
> Grow beautiful beneath his touch."

Auchinleck House was also the residence of that enthusiastic admirer of Burns, Sir Alexander Boswell, to whose energy the erection of the monument on the banks of the Doon is due. He was a poet of great merit, and it is no small honour to his muse that several of his songs have been mistakenly ascribed to Burns, and have found a place in London editions of his works.

A branch line leads from Auchinleck to Muirkirk, a village famous in Covenanting annals. John Lapraik, author of the song, "When I upon thy bosom lean," resided there when in receipt of poetical epistles from Burns. The poet first heard the song at a *rocking* held in the kitchen of Mossgiel on Fasten e'en, 1785, and was so taken with it that he addressed the author in verse, and in flattering terms solicited his friendship. Lapraik speedily replied, and sent the letter by the hands of his son, who, upon arriving at Mossgiel, found the poet in a field engaged in sowing. "I'm no sure if I ken the hand," said Burns as he took the letter; but no sooner had he glanced at its contents than unconsciously letting go the sheet containing the grain, it was not until he had finished reading that he discovered the loss he had sustained.* Ever afterwards Burns and Lapraik became fast friends, and had frequent and familiar intercourse.

Lapraik was born in 1727. He published a volume of poetry at Kilmarnock in 1788, and died in the eightieth year of his age, on the 7th May, 1807. Robert Chalmers somewhat rashly states in his edition of Burns that he must have stolen the ideas and nearly all the diction of his song from a poem in Ruddiman's *Weekly Magazine*, October, 1773. That Lapraik's song, and the poem referred to, have more than a suspicious similarity is not to be disputed, but whether Lap-

---

* " Contemporaries of Burns," p. 26

raik or the anonymous contributor to that periodical be the plagiarist has yet to be proved.

As the train rushes from the sweet village of Auchinleck it crosses a lofty viaduct which spans the Lugar, a stream celebrated in "My Nannie o'"—a song which is, and ever will be, an universal favourite—and in a short time passes the town of Old Cumnock, beautifully embosomed among the hills. Peden, of Covenanting memory, is buried in its churchyard; and in Breezyhill Cottage—a snug residence in its vicinity—resides Mr Adam B. Todd, author of "Poems, Lectures, and Miscellanies," and other meritorious literary productions. Like Burns he was bred to farm work, and like him also he cultivated literature under many difficulties. The following extract is from one of his tributes to the memory of the ploughman bard:—

> "A chequered lot was thine, O Burns, to bear,
> Though short thy course, thy struggles were severe;
> But now life's thorny path has long been past,
> Weary the way, but sweet the rest at last,
> And thou art not forgotten in the clay—
> Thy fame increaseth with each opening day.
> Seasons may pass as Time sublimely steers
> His onward course, still heaping years on years;
> But while the history of our isle is read,
> Thy name shall rank among the honoured dead."

Beyond New Cumnock—a modest village extending on both sides of the line—the country, if possible, becomes more fascinating. In the distance is Glen Afton and the green swelling braes by which it is enclosed, and also the infant Nith coursing along. It issues from the Black Loch, as a dark sheet of water in the upper part of New Cumnock parish is termed, and traverses twelve miles of Ayrshire soil before entering the county of Dumfries. This loch is also the source of the Glaisnock, and in reference to this fact the writer of the Statistical Account of the parish of Old Cumnock points out the possibility of a trout crossing the mainland. Were it, he supposes, to enter the Ayr at Ayr harbour it might pass into the Lugar at Barskimming, and from thence into the Glaisnock at Old Cumnock, by which it could reach the Black Loch and issue therefrom into the Nith, and eventually drop into the Solway Firth. The Nith has many tributaries in Ayrshire, but the most important is the Afton—a rapid and beautiful stream which traverses Glen Afton and joins it on the east side of the village of New Cumnock. The reader need not be reminded that this stream is celebrated by Burns in the song beginning—

> " Flow gently sweet Afton amang thy green braes,
> Flow gently, I'll sing thee a song in thy praise."

For a long distance beyond New Cumnock the railway skirts the Nith, and as the train dashes along, many a bosky scene, and many a green hillside, which cannot fail to impart pleasure, catches the eye. I just caught a glimpse of Kirkconnel as the train rushed past. It is a nice little village, and likely to be notable in future years as the birth-place of Alexander Anderson, author of " Songs of Labour;" "The Two Angels, and other Poems;" &c. Mr Anderson, although a surfaceman or " common navvy" on the line, has found leisure not only to educate himself and become conversant with the French, German, and Italian languages, but to woo the muses with such success that he is within a stride of being classed in the front rank of Scottish poets. The following homely verses from his pen will be read with interest :—

"CUDDLE DOON."

" The bairnies cuddle doon at nicht,
   Wi' muckle faucht and din ;
O try and sleep ye waukrife rogues,
   Your faither's comin' in.
They never heed a word I speak ;
   I try to gie a froon,
But aye I hap them up and cry,
   ' O, bairnies, cuddle doon.'

" Wee Jamie wi' the curly heid—
   He aye sleeps next the wa'—
Bangs up an' cries, ' I want a piece '—
   The rascal starts them a'.
I rin an' fetch them pieces, drinks,
   They stop awee the soun',
Then draw the blankets up and cry,
   ' Noo, weanies, cuddle doon.'

" But ere five minutes gaug, wee Rab
   Cries oot frae 'neath the claes,
' Mither, mak' Tam gie owre at ance,
   He's kittlin' wi' his taes.'

The mischief's in that Tam for tricks,
  He'd bother half the toon;
But aye I hap them up an' cry,
  'O, bairnies, cuddle doon.'

"At length they hear their faither's fit,
  An' as he steeks the door,
They turn their faces to the wa',
  While Tam pretends to snore.
'Hae a' the weans been guid?' he asks,
  As he pits aff his shoon.
'The bairnies, John, are in their beds,
  An' lang since cuddled doon.'

"An' just afore we bed oursel's,
  We look at oor wee lambs;
Tam has his airm roun' wee Rab's neck,
  An' Rab his airm roun' Tam's.
I lift wee Jamie up the bed,
  An' as I straik each croon,
I whisper, till my heart fills up,
  'O, bairnies, cuddle doon.'

"The bairnies cuddle doon at nicht
  Wi' mirth that's dear to me,
But sune the big warl's cark and care
  Will quaten doon their glee.
Yet, come what will to ilka ane,
  May He who sits aboon,
Aye whisper, though their pows be bauld,
  'O, bairnies, cuddle doon.'"

Beyond Kirkconnell the scenery wears a moorland aspect, but the train speedily tears through it, and in an amazingly short space of time reaches Sanquhar—a compact, neatly built town with which Burns was familiar when journeying between Dumfries and Mauchline. We have an account of one of his visits in a letter to Dr Moore. "In January last, on my road to Ayrshire," says he, "I had to put up at Bailie Wigham's in Sanquhar, the only tolerable inn in the place. The frost was keen, and the grim evening and howling wind were ushering in the night of snow and drift. My horse and I were both much fatigued with the labours of the day, and just as my friend, the Bailie, and I were bidding defiance to the storm over a smoking bowl, in wheels the funeral pageantry of the late great Mrs Oswald; and poor I am forced to brave all the horrors of a tempestuous night, and jade my horse, my favourite horse, whom I had just christened

Pegasus, twelve miles farther on through the wildest moors and hills of Ayrshire, to New Cumnock." Sanquhar also figures in the "Five Carlins," a political ballad by Burns, and is referred to as

> "Black Joan, frae Chrichton Peel,
> O' gipsy kith an' kin."

"Peel" is an old Scotch term for a castle or fortalice, and refers in this instance to the ruined stronghold of the Chrichtons, Lords of Sanquhar, which stands in a field at the end of the town, and is seen to great advantage from the railway. During the War of Independence it passed through many vicissitudes and was the scene of many sanguinary engagements between the English and Scotch. There are many curious traditions connected with it, and one is that Sir William Douglas wrested it from an English garrison in the following ingenious manner:—It appears that he and his men concealed themselves in Crawick Glen, while John Dickson, disguised as a carter, approached it with a load of wood. Having succeeded in disposing of it to the Governor, the portcullis was raised to admit him, but he no sooner entered than he jammed his cart within it, and sounded the onset with might and main. The English being off their guard, Sir William and his men obtained an easy victory. When possessed by the Scotch on one occasion, Robert de Clifford and Sir Henry Percy attempted to reduce it by starvation, and would have succeeded had not the valiant Wallace come to the assistance of the garrison. The besiegers fled at his approach, but they were overtaken near Dalswinton, and in the engagement which followed 500 of them were slain.

Beyond Sanquhar the railway passes through a track of country unsurpassed for picturesque beauty. Having passed Carronbridge and Thornhill—both quiet villages—Closeburn is reached. Streaching away on the east side of the line are Closeburn Hills amid which is the fine waterfall, Crichope Linn, and a cave which tradition states was used by the Covenanters. Sir Walter Scott seems to have been aware of its associations, for in "Old Mortality" he portrays it as the hiding place of Balfour of Burley. Burns was familiar with Closeburn. He used to visit an inn at Brownhill, and made the landlord, whose name was Bacon, the subject of an im promptu effusion. His friend, Kirsty Flint, also resided in Closeburn. She was well acquainted with old music and ballads, and nothing delighted the poet better than to hear her sing his songs—indeed, he generally got her to "lilt" over any new effusion before giving it to the world. A short distance from Closeburn is Auldgirth station. Upon the train drawing up at it, I stepped on to the platform, a pilgrim in the land. However, this added piquancy to the excursion, and was just the thing to gratify my love for adventure and sight-seeing. Following the straggling passengers down a rather steep roadway, I entered the village—if village it can be called, for it only consists of a Gothic-like building called Auldgirth Hotel, and some two or three one-storeyed houses —and beheld a scene of bewitching beauty. In front lay a fine alluvial holm through which the Nith winds like a silver thread, and from which verdant wood-draped, sheep-speckled hills rise in rugged grandeur. Enraptured with the scene I wandered down a broad tree-shaded road, and in an ecstasy of delight listened to the water rippling beneath a stupendous ivy-mantled bridge and to the wild notes of a mavis and a blackbird, which sang an accompaniment in a neighbouring thicket and with other warblers of the grove bade a vocal farewell to departing day. The lowing of cattle and the shouts of a group of rompish children sounded in the distance with a strange captivating solemnity which lured me onward all unmindful of the fact that I had omitted to secure a lodging for the night. Returning to the village, I entered the hotel and was delighted to find that the accommodation, although homely, was good, and completely belied the external appearance of the building. Mr Emeric (for such is the name of the landlord), and his lady proved affable, obliging, and kindly, and I experienced no difficulty in being "put up" for the night; but the hours of the evening wore slowly away, and I was only too happy to be shown to the chamber assigned me. I slept soundly, and when morning returned awoke to find that the sunbeams had entered the apartment and were streaming across the floor. After partaking of a substantial, well-served breakfast, I took leave of mine host and started to visit those scenes in Dumfriesshire which the residence or muse of Robert Burns has rendered famous, but will not readily forget the hospitality of the inmates of Auldgirth Hotel.

I lingered a while at the bridge referred to, to take a farewell look at the lovely scene. A short distance above it is the tree-embosomed mansion-house of Blackwood, the residence of an ancient Dumfriesshire family, who claim descent from Sir John Copland, a Northumbrian knight, who took David II. prisoner at the battle of Neville's Cross in 1346, and knocked out the monarch's front teeth with the haft of his dagger in the struggle. The father of Allan Cunningham, the celebrated Scottish poet, was gardener on this estate, and the house he lived in and in which his illustrious son was born stood under one of the fine yew trees lining the approach to the princely residence. Small wonder it is that the boy imbibed the spirit of poesy in such a retreat, for dull the eye must be that cannot behold the grand, the lofty, poetry of nature in the scenery. The clear pebbly-bottomed stream glistened in the sunshine and purled from among the woods which stud the vale and deck the sides of the steep uplands, rolling on until concealed from view in a cleft of the verdant hills in the distance.

"How lovely, Nith, thy fruitful vales,
 Where spreading hawthorns gaily bloom!
How sweetly wind thy sloping dales,
 Where lambkins wanton through the broom!"

"Birds sang love on ilka spray," and everything was fresh with the dew of the morning, but business and time were pressing and would not permit me to linger long in the locality. Moving slowly along the road I tapped at a cottage door to make sure that the right direction was being pursued. It was opened by a smart girl, who, in answer to a query, called her father, a blythe old shoemaker, with spectacles on brow and a huge leather apron in front of him. He was the real prototype of a village souter, and just the sort of man I was desirous of seeing; therefore, without formality, I made him aware that I was a stranger and anxious to gain information regarding the district, but more especially of the Poet's residence in it. Drawing himself up and pushing the spectacles higher on his forehead he said—"Weel, if it's Burns you're speerin' aboot, there's Friar's Carse, the Hermitage, and Ellisland, doun the river there a bit, but there's naething here about, I'm sorry to say, connected wi' him. Of course he was often here, and gaed alang this road when riding to or frae Mauchline, but that's a'. Auld ruins? Weel, there's nane hereawa' except the tower whaur Lagg, the persecutor o' the Covenanters, leeved; it's amang the hills yonder, but there's nocht to be seen about it. But up in yon wood by the river-side there's the remains o' a Druidical temple; gin ye haud doun the bankin' to the Carse it will be on your way, an' ye should gang an' see it. Antiquarians dispute about it, for you see Glenriddle spoilt it by completing the circle wi' new stane, but I'm inclined to think it genuine, for the basin that received the blood of the victim and let it rin into the earth is aye there. You can get a glint o' the Carse yonder at the bend o' the river, so gin ye haud alang the bankin' you'll come to it, and anybody 'll let you see the Hermitage and Ellisland, for they're a' close thegither—'deed if it hadna been 'Preaching Saturday' I'd gane wi' you mysel', but I canna very weel get awa'." I was sorry for this, for such a companion would have been invaluable. This specimen of the old man's conversation is given that readers who may be inclined to follow my footsteps may have a knowledge of the route to be pursued and a slight idea of the antiquities to be met with. Shoemakers are highly intelligent as a class, but this one, "remote from towns," and who "never changed nor wished to change his place," is exceptionally so. He proved himself conversant with the life and writings of Burns. On no account will he allow the one or the other to be disparagingly spoken of, and woe betide the man who in his presence dares

"To draw his frailties from their dread abode."

In illustration of the Poet's magnanimity and kindness of heart, he told me that his grandmother, who lived in the vicinity of Ellisland, "selt a dram without a license," and carried on a very fair illicit trade. This coming to the ears of the authorities, Burns received notice to call and make a seizure. Before doing so, however, he sent a few hanks of yarn to the old lady with the intimation that she was to wind it speedily, for the gauger would call for it in the afternoon. He went, but all exciseable commodities were removed, and he found nothing to reward the search. This act of course lost a fine to the government but saved the woman. Following the path recommended, I held along the bank of

o

the river until the plantation containing the Druidical remains was reached. It crowns the summit of a high embankment overlooking the stream, and commands a charming prospect of hills, dales, and leafy woods. The place was somewhat "eerie," and the dead leaves rustled strangely beneath my tread, but I had no difficulty in finding the whereabouts of the supposed temple, which consists of a circle of rudely-hewn stones set on end. They are some five feet in height and ten apart, and surround a central one of somewhat larger proportions. Passing through the plantation, greatly to the dismay of its inhabitants, who sounded their notes of alarm as they flew from branch to branch, or bounded away in timorous haste to seek refuge in their burrows, I came to a low stone wall, which I cleared with a bound, and landed in a field. Holding along its edge, I entered a roadway, and after a short walk reached Friars' Carse.

The mansion—a beautiful Gothic building—occupies the site of a monastic house, and is pleasantly situated in a wood-embosomed dell on the banks of the Nith. The present proprietor has made an extensive and tasteful addition to the old residence, improved the grounds in its vicinity, and by the restoration of the Hermitage evinced an appreciation of the poetic genius inseparably associated with the estate.

When Burns tilled the soil of Ellisland, Friars' Carse was the residence and property of Captain Riddle, a gentleman of taste, and an antiquary of some note, whose social disposition won many friends, but none were more welcome to his home than his gifted but less affluent neighbour, the Poet. At his table Burns made the acquaintance of Captain Francis Grose, the antiquary—

> "A fine fat fodgel wight,
> O' stature short, but genius bright"—

and was introduced to Maria Woodley, daughter of a governor of Berbice, and the wife of Glenriddle's young brother, "a lady," says the Rev. Hately Waddell, "of great beauty and spirit, with some fashionable foibles and perhaps follies incident to her sex, but many gifts and accomplishments also —one of the most favoured correspondents and heroines of our author, his friend, his adversary, and his eulogist." She gives a graphic and affecting account of her last interview with the poet, which will be noticed in its proper place. Another lady of culture, whose society was enjoyed by Burns at Friars' Carse, was a Miss Deborah Davis, a relative of Glenriddle, and the heroine of two of the poet's songs. She was of short stature, and from this circumstance was made the subject of the following epigram, which the bard uttered on being asked by a friend why God made her so little and the lady beside her so large—

> "Ask why God made the gem so small,
> And why so huge the granite?
> Because God meant mankind should set
> The higher value on it."

A rather romantic incident in the life of this lady deserves notice. At an early age she fell in love with a Captain Delany, who, to all appearance, reciprocated the passion. "He made himself acceptable to her by sympathising in her pursuits and writing verses on her, calling her his Stella, an ominous name, which might have brought the memory of Swift's unhappy mistress to her mind." Says Allan Cunningham :—"An offer of marriage was made and accepted, but Delany's circumstances were urged as an obstacle; delays ensued; a coldness on the lover's part followed; his regiment was called abroad: he went with it; she heard from him once and no more, and was left to mourn the change of affection—to droop and die. He perished in battle or by a foreign climate soon after the death of the young lady, of whose love he was so unworthy. The following verses on this unfortunate attachment form part of a poem found among her papers at her death. She takes Delany's portrait from her bosom, presses it to her lips, and says—

> ' Next to thyself, 'tis all on earth
> Thy Stella dear doth hold;
> The glass is clouded with my breath,
> And as thy bosom cold—
> That bosom which so oft has glowed
> With love and friendship's name,
> Where you the seed of love first sowed
> That kindled into flame.
>
> ' You there neglected let it burn;
> It seized the vital part,
> And left my bosom as an urn
> To hold a broken heart.

> I once had thought I should have been
> A tender, happy wife,
> And passed my future days serene
> With thee, my James, through life.'"

Beside these and other friendships, the mansion-house of Friars' Carse is celebrated on account of a bacchanalian contest which took place in one of its rooms on the 16th October, 1789. The prize was a little ebony whistle which a Danish champion of Bacchus in the train of Annie of Denmark brought to this country. There was many a contest for its possession, for it appears that he was in the habit of laying it on the table at the commencement of a drinking bout, and whoever outdrank his companions and blew it when they were all under the table carried it off as a trophy. After proving victor on many occasions, this champion of the bottle encountered Sir Robert Lawrie of Maxweltown, and was defeated by him after three days and three nights' hard drinking. The whistle afterwards came into the possession of Captain Riddle, who decided upon having a friendly contest for it at Friars' Carse. For that purpose he challenged Mr. Ferguson of Craigdarroch, and Sir Robert Lawrie of Maxwelton, and invited Burns to witness the fray. The following affidavit graphically describes the proceedings:—

"Closeburn Hall, Dec. 2, 1841.

"I, Wm. Hunter, blacksmith, in Lake-head, parish of Closeburn, was, for three years and a half previous to my being apprenticed to John Kilpatrick, blacksmith in Burnland, parish of Dunscore, servant to Capt. Robt. Riddle, of Friars' Carse, in Dumfriesshire. I remember well the night when the *Whistle* was drunk for at Friars' Carse by the three gentlemen—Sir Robert Lawrie, Mr. Ferguson of Craigdarroch, and Captain Riddle. Burns the poet was present on the occasion. Mrs. Riddle and Mrs. Ferguson of Craigdarroch dined with the above gentlemen. As soon as the cloth was removed the two ladies retired. When the ladies had left the room, Burns withdrew from the dining table, and sat down in the window looking down the river Nith; a small table was before him. During the evening Burns nearly emptied two bottles of spirits—the one of brandy, the other of rum—mixing them in tumblers with warm water, which I often brought to him hot. He had paper, pen, and ink before him and continued the whole evening to write upon the paper. He seemed, while I was in the room, to have little conversation with the three gentlemen at their wine. I think from what I could observe he was composing the 'Whistle' as he sat with his back to the gentlemen, but he occasionally turned towards them. The corks of the wine were all drawn by me, and it was claret the three gentlemen drank. As far as I can recollect, I did not draw more than fifteen bottles of claret. It was about sunrise when the two gentlemen were carried to bed. Craigdarroch never during the course of the night fell from his chair. The other two gentlemen often fell, and had to be helped, with the assistance of Burns and myself, on to their chairs. After Burns, myself, and the other servants now dead, had carried upstairs Sir Robert Lawrie and Captain Riddle, Craigdarroch walked himself upstairs without any help. Craigdarroch then went into one bedroom where Sir Robert Lawrie was and blew stoutly the whistle; next he entered Captain Riddle's bedroom and blew the whistle as stoutly there—Burns being present. Burns, after he had seen and assisted the two above-named gentlemen to bed, walked home to his own farm-house of Ellisland, about a mile from Friars' Carse. He seemed a little the worse of drink, but was quite able to walk and manage himself. Burns often afterwards talked to me of the evening that was passed at Friars' Carse when the whistle was drank for, and he told me again and again that he wrote the whole poem of the 'Whistle' that evening at Friars' Carse. Indeed, he filled that evening, I well recollect, four sheets of paper larger than the present one (large post) with writing, all of which he took home with him. As I was apprentice to Kilpatrick, the blacksmith, who always shod Burns' horses when he was at Ellisland, I often saw Burns while I was shoeing his horses. All the above particulars I am willing to verify on oath.

(Signed)   "WILLIAM HUNTER.

"December 2nd, 1841."

It seems strange at this date that "three jolly good fellows"—one an elder of a church and another an M.P.—could indulge to such excess, but then it was considered no breach of decorum to be "as drunk's a gentleman," or to fall from one's chair overpowered by liquor at the festive board; and there is no apology required for Burns being present at such an orgie.

I would have had a peep at the room in which the contest took place and in which "The Whistle" was composed, but upon learning that the family were from home, I contented myself with a stroll through the grounds, and a right enjoyable one it was.

Accosting a man engaged in mowing grass, I enquired for the Hermitage. Being told that its situation was on the verge of a neighbouring wood, I acted on his advice, and sought out the head gardener. He proved of a cheerful disposition, and so extremely obliging that he proffered to accompany me to the spot and give what information he could regarding it.

After climbing a steep ascent we entered the wood in question, but as we threaded a narrow path among the trees, a colony of crows in the branches over our heads began to caw! caw! caw! and raise a clamour as if indignant at the intrusion of their privacy. I rather liked their din, and stopped now and again to watch their circuitous flight far above our heads, guessing the cause of their alarm to be that some cruelly-disposed person had been making them objects of his murderous aim, for here and there among the grass lay numerous stiffened sable members of the fraternity. Poor things! many had the appearance of having died in great agony, and lay crouched and cramped as they were when mercifully relieved from suffering by death. I lifted a live but disabled one, but not before it seized my finger with its bill, being accustomed to look upon man as a common enemy. I did my utmost to assure it of the kindness of my intentions, but it was no use, and as I could not do anything for it I laid it down saying—

"Seek, mangled wretch, some place of wanted rest,
No more of rest, but now thy dying bed!
The sheltering rushes whistling o'er thy head,
The cold earth with thy bloody bosom pressed."

Crows are certainly thieves, and, despite their black attire and gravity of mien, are not so just and upright as farmers desire, but if the safety of crops demand their partial destruction it should be gone about in a humane and efficient manner.

The Hermitage is situated in an obscure corner of the wood, and looks as sombre as if it had not been visited for months. It is a small modern-looking building of one storey with an inscription over its doorway stating that it was restored in 1874. Previous to its restoration it was in ruins, and it says much for the present proprietor of Friars' Carse that it is in the present tidy condition. The original building measured ten and a-half feet by eight, and was erected by Captain Riddle. When Burns came to Ellisland he delighted to wander by the Nith and through the grounds and woods of Friars' Carse, a circumstance which probably induced the Captain to provide him with a key for the Hermitage, so that he could go in and out when he felt it convenient to do so. He often retired to this retreat, and in its solitude under the character of a bedesman, composed "Verses in Friar's Carse Hermitage." He inscribed the first six lines on the window pane, but this—Robert Chambers informs us—"was removed on a change of proprietors, and being brought to sale at the death of an old lady in 1835 was purchased for five guineas."

When the gate of the railed enclosure of the present retreat is thrown open, the first thing that attracts attention is the rigid form of a monk, with shaven crown, chipped nose, and folded hands, lying on its back at the entrance. Possibly it is a remnant of the "auld nick-nackets" which belonged to honest Glenriddle, and commemorates some holy friar whose name and qualifications are alike forgotten. The little building contains a chair and small table, and is supplied with two windows and a fireplace. The glass of one window bears the following in fac-simile of the poet's handwriting:—

"To Riddle, much lamented man,
  This ivied cot was dear;
Reader, dost value matchless worth?
  This ivied cot revere."

The glass of the other is inscribed in like manner, and bears the following lines:—

"Thou whom chance may hither lead,
Be thou clad in russet weed,
Be thou decked in silken stole,
Grave these counsels on thy soul.
  Life is but a day at most,
Sprung from night, in darkness lost;
Hope not sunshine every hour,
Fear not clouds will always lower.
  Stranger, go! Heaven be thy guide,
Quod the bedesman of Nithside."

Ellisland is a couple of fields distant from the Hermitage, and the instant I took leave of my obliging guide, I hastened towards it by way of the river bank, for it is close by, and accessible by scaling a low stone wall which appears to be as old as the wood it encloses. The Nith winds along its shallow pebbly shore, and the wide swelling verdant uplands which rise from its brink looked so fresh that they appeared like a portion of a newly-created world. Despite a sense of loneliness I felt happy—happy as the bird in the brake, and why? Because Burns traversed the same ground, and enjoyed the same scenery. Holding along a beaten path running through the grass I crossed a purling burnie by a rustic bridge, and passed along the margin of the river. The difficulties of the way were many, but in spite of trailing bramble bushes which seized my legs and laid hold of my clothes, and of branches which brushed my face, I succeeded in reaching a steep tree-shaded path. Ascending it I entered the farmyard of Ellisland, and looked curiously around.

CHAPTER XIX.

ELLISLAND, ITS SITUATION, APPEARANCE, AND ASSOCIATIONS—BURNS AS AN EXCISEMAN—HIS ANTIPATHY TO THE OFFICE—HIS HUMANITY, HOSPITALITY, AND INDUSTRY—THE POET'S FAVOURITE WALK—THE COMPOSITION OF "TAM O' SHANTER"—THE WOUNDED HARE—THE ISLE—HOLYWOOD PAST AND PRESENT—LINCLUDIN ABBEY.

FINDING Ellisland deserted by man and beast, I went up to the open door of the dwelling house and " cannily keekit ben." The apartment was in the utmost confusion, and the scene which met my gaze odd in the extreme. A young woman, with a handkerchief bound round her head, was decorating the walls with indiscriminate dashes of a white-wash brush, while a portly, pleasant-looking woman, whose features were almost hid in the folds of a sun-bonnet, busied herself among the furniture in an endeavour to put matters straight. In the midst of all this sat a man deeply engrossed in the contents of a newspaper; but I am sorry to record that he never lifted his eyes off the page nor in any way recognised the presence of a stranger—a breach of good manners certainly which a previous tenant named Robert Burns would never have been guilty of. The gudewife—for such I understood the dame in question to be—was communicative enough, and although answers drawn from her were generally monosyllabic, yet they were clear and respectful, and made some amends for the reserved demeanour of her lord. Among other things, I learned that the dwelling-house and offices around the courtyard are in the same condition as they were at the time our agricultural Apollo and his bonnie Jean went in and out amongst them. This in itself was something, and, despite the freezing reception experienced, I felt gratified to stand in a door-way through which those near and dear to his heart had often passed, and look upon walls which sheltered him from the blast and upon a floor of stone which echoed the tread of his manly footstep. Having it proven in this particular instance that a conversation cannot be carried on between a less number of persons than two, I withdrew, and commenced an exploration, during which imagination and a previous knowledge of the premises supplied what the occupants declined to communicate. The farmstead of Ellisland is situated on the verge of a high cliff or scaur overlooking the Nith, and commands a prospect which no sordid-minded farmer would care to look upon. The dwelling-house is a humble but commodious one-storied building, and the offices attached to it are of a commonplace description, and appear—with the exception of a barn—to have been erected since the poet's day.

When Burns entered on the farm (Whitsunday, 1788), the dwelling-house was in a ruinous condition—a circumstance which compelled him to leave his Jean in Mauchline until he got one in readiness for her reception. This was built by his brother-in-law, and according to Allan Cunningham, the poet had to "perform the duty of superintending the work; to dig the foundations, collect the stones, seek the sand, cart the lime, and see that all was performed according to the specification," and, I may add, the plan he had drawn out. During the progress of the work he lodged with the outgoing tenant in a hovel which was pervious to every blast that blew and every shower that fell; but more of it by and by.

When Burns fixed on Ellisland, the shrewd factor remarked that he had made a good choice as a poet but a bad one as a farmer. From what I saw of its soil he was correct, for it is perfectly astonishing that he ever thought of devoting his time to its cultivation. He was in the habit of saying that after a shower had fallen a newly-rolled field reminded him of a paved street, but I can assure the reader that one turned over with the plough has a closer resemblance to a macadamized road dug with a pick-axe than anything yet witnessed —in fact, such a mixture of boulders and loam is rarely to be met with beyond the precincts of a dried up water-course. There is nothing under cultivation to equal it in Ayrshire; nevertheless, with the present system of agriculture, excellent crops are grown on it, and the tenant can pay more than four times the rent Burns did when he tilled its acres, and that too with less difficulty.*

---

* Burns paid £50 a year, the present tenant pays £230.

When straying about the steading I entered the barnyard, and leaning on my stick mused. Here, thought I, is the veritable spot where the poet, in an agony of soul, composed the sublime ode " To Mary in Heaven."

> " Thou lingering star, with lessening ray,
>   That lov'st to greet the early morn,
> Again thou usherest in the day
>   My Mary from my soul was torn.
>
> Oh Mary ! dear departed shade !
>   Where is thy place of blissful rest ?
> Seest thou thy lover lowly laid ?
>   Hear'st thou the groans that rend his breast ?
>
> That sacred hour can I forget ?
>   Can I forget the hallowed grove,
> Where by the winding Ayr we met,
>   To live one day of parting love !
>
> Eternity will not efface
>   Those records dear of transports past ;
> Thy image at our last embrace,
>   Ah ! little thought we 'twas our last !"

Although married to his Jean—and all the world knows he loved her—he could not forget Mary Campbell, nor " the golden hours " he spent with her in " the hallowed grove " on the banks of the " gurgling Ayr." No, though " green was the sod and cold the clay " which wrapt her form, he cherished her memory ; and on the third anniversary of her death—a few days after the carnival mentioned in last chapter—" as the twilight deepened he appeared to grow 'very sad about something,' and at length wandered out into the barnyard, to which his wife, in her anxiety for his health, followed him, entreating him in vain to observe that frost had set in, and to return to the fireside. On being again and again requested to do so, he always promised compliance, but still remained where he was, striding up and down slowly and contemplating the sky, which was singularly clear and starry. At last Mrs Burns found him stretched on a mass of straw, with his eyes fixed on a beautiful planet 'that shone like another moon,' and prevailed on him to come in. He immediately, on entering the house, called for his desk, and wrote exactly as they now stand, with all the ease of one copying from memory, the verses ' To Mary in Heaven.' "*

---

* Lockhart's " Life of Burns."

The first year of Burns' occupancy of Ellisland passed pleasantly away. He was frugal and temperate, and paid every attention to his farm, but his seclusion did not obtain privacy. Lockhart states that "his company was courted eagerly, not only by his brother farmers, but by the neighbouring gentry of all classes; and now, too, for the first time, he began to be visited continually in his own house by curious travellers of all sorts, who did not consider, any more than the generous Poet himself, that an extensive practice of hospitality must cost more than he ought to have had, and far more money than he ever had at his disposal." The farm under these circumstances could not pay, and to make matters better he applied to his patron, Mr. Graham of Fintry, to use his interest in procuring him an appointment in the Excise. This was done, and "the golden days of Ellisland," as Dr. Currie calls them, began to wane. "He might indeed still be seen in the spring," says that author, "directing his plough—a labour in which he excelled; or with a white sheet, containing his seed-corn, slung across his shoulder, striding with measured steps along his turned-up furrows, and scattering the grain in the earth; but his farm no longer occupied the principal part of his care or his thoughts. It was not at Ellisland that he was now in general to be found. Mounted on horseback, this high-minded poet was pursuing the defaulters of the revenue among the hills and vales of Nithsdale, his roving eye roving over the charms of nature, muttering his wayward fancies as he moved along." This new occupation brought Burns a paltry £35 a year, but the amount of drudgery it imposed on him overtasked his energies, and did much more to undermine his constitution than the hard drinking his traducers say he indulged in. He had ten parishes to survey, which formed a tract of fifteen miles each way. These had to be continually ridden over. On an average he rode from thirty to forty miles every day, stopping at all the breweries, public-houses, tanneries, and grocery shops on the route to take note of exciseable stock, and enter the same in the memorandum book he carried for the purpose. Burns disliked the unpopular occupation, and was always apologising to his friends for engaging in it—

"Searching auld wives' barrels,
   Och hon! the day!
That clarty barm should stain my laurels;
   But—what'll ye say!
These moving things ca'd wives an' weans
Would move the very hearts o' stanes!"

Despite his antipathy to the office, Burns faithfully discharged his duties. Sometimes, however, he was wilfully deaf, dumb, and blind to petty infringements of the law. Allan Cunningham tells how he and a brother exciseman one day suddenly entered a widow woman's shop in Dunscore, and made a seizure of smuggled tobacco. "Jenny," said the poet, " I expected this would be the upshot. Here Lewers, take note of the number of rolls as I count them. Now, Jock, did you ever hear an auld wife numbering her threads before check reels were invented? Thou's ane, and thou's ane, and thou's ane a' out." As he handed out the rolls he went on with his humorous enumeration, but dropping every other roll into Janet's lap, Lewers took the desired note with much gravity, and saw as if he saw not the merciful consideration of his companion.

A late Professor of St. Andrew's remembered seeing Burns on a fair day in August, 1793, at the village of Thornhill, where, as was not uncommon in those days, a poor woman, named Kate Watson, had for one day taken up the trade of a publican—of course, without a license. "I saw the poet enter her door, and anticipated nothing short of an immediate seizure of a certain greybeard and barrel which, to my personal knowledge, contained the contraband commodities our bard was in quest of. A nod, accompanied by a significant movement of the forefinger, brought Kate to the doorway or entrance; and I was near enough to hear the following words distinctly uttered: 'Kate, are you mad? Don't you know that the supervisor and I will be upon you in the course of forty minutes? Good by t'ye at present.' Burns was in the street and in the midst of the crowd in an instant, and I had access to know that the friendly hint was not neglected. It saved a poor woman from a fine of several pounds for committing a paltry offence by which the revenue was probably subjected to an annual loss of five shillings."*

---

* Edinburgh Literary Journal, 1829.

"I had an adventure with him in the year 1790," says Mr. Ramsay of Ochtertyre, in a letter to Dr. Currie, "when passing through Dumfriesshire on a tour to the south, with Dr. Stuart of Luss. Seeing him pass quickly near Closeburn, I said to my companion—'That is Burns.' On coming to the inn, the hostler told us he would be back in a few hours to grant permits; that where he met with anything seizable he was no better than any other guager; in everything else he was a perfect gentleman. After leaving a note to be delivered to him on his return, I proceeded to his house, being curious to see his Jean, &c. I was much pleased with his *uxor Sabina qualis* and the poet's modest mansion, so unlike the habitations of ordinary rustics. In the evening he suddenly bounded in upon us, and said as he entered—'I come, to use the words of Shakespeare, *stewed in haste.*' In fact, he had ridden incredibly fast after receiving my note. We fell into conversation directly, and soon got into the *mare magnum* of poetry. He told me he had now gotten a story for a drama, which he was to call 'Rob Macquechan's Elchon,' from a popular story of Robert Bruce being defeated on the water of Caern, when the heel of his boot having loosened in his flight he applied to Robert Macquechan to fix it, who to make sure ran his awl nine inches up the king's heel. We were now going on at a great rate, when Mr S—— popped in his head, which put a stop to our discourse, which had become very interesting. Yet in a little while it was resumed; and such was the force and versatility of the bard's genius that he made the tears run down Mr. S——'s cheeks, albeit unused to the poetic strain. From that time we met no more. . . . . . Poor Burns! we shall hardly see his like again. He was in truth a sort of comet in literature, irregular in its motions, which did not do good proportioned to the blaze of light it displayed."

These pleasing anecdotes might be extended.

Burns rose early, and before starting on his long rides busied himself with the work of the farm. Mrs. Burns stated that she has walked with a child in her arms on the banks of the Nith, and seen him sow after breakfast two bags of corn for the folk to harrow through the day.* When

---

* Memoranda by Mrs. Burns—see the Rev. P. H. Waddell's edition of the poet's works.

he returned at night—tired and weary no doubt—he was not inactive, but burned the midnight oil in making up his report for the Excise, in writing letters to friends, or transcribing some lilt he had composed for "Johnston's Musical Museum" when in the saddle. Reader, take down your Chambers from your shelf and glance at the Ellisland period of his existence, and you will feel astonished at the number of songs, poems, and letters he wrote under such circumstances, in the brief space of two and a half years.

There are many glimpses of the poet in his social and domestic sphere to be had during his existence at Ellisland, but suffice it to say that the calls upon his hospitality exceeded the limits of his income; so, owing to this, and his inability to superintend his workpeople throughout the day, the little scheme of having two strings to his bow, or, in other words, of securing an income apart from the profits of the farm, failed, and he was forced to accept an appointment in the Excise in Dumfries, at a salary of £70 per annum. Experiencing little difficulty in getting rid of the lease which bound him to Ellisland, he sold his stock and implements and bade it adieu, "leaving nothing," says Allan Cunninghame, "but a putting stone, with which he had loved to exercise his strength—a memory of his musings that can never die, and £300 of his money sunk beyond redemption in a speculation from which all had augured happiness."

After lingering about the fields and steading of Ellisland for some time, I cast a wistful look at the open door of the dwelling-house and sought the bank of the river. The view up and down is exquisite, and the green swelling slopes of Dalswinton on the opposite bank are very beautiful. The grass and herbage extend close to the water edge, and trees leaning at an angle over the pure pebbly-bottomed channel and the rich drapery of distant woods and dales, go to make up a picture at once charming and delightful.

The lands of Dalswinton belonged to the Comyns, a once powerful family who sternly opposed Robert Bruce. Allan Cunningham, who spent his boyish days in the neighbourhood, remembered seeing the ruins of their castle, and speaks of a tradition which stated that it was burnt by the hero-king after he had given the Comyn "the perilous gash" and

Kilpatrick had "makit siccar" by plunging his dagger into his breast in the church of Dumfries. In 1792 part of the walls were standing, but no portion of them now remains.

"The Nith," says Cunningham, "instead of circling the Scaur of Ellisland, directed its course by Bankfoot, and came close to the castle." He remembered a pool near the old house of Dalswinton called Comyn's Pool, which belonged to the old watercourse, and connected itself with the back water in the Willow Isle, by the way of the Lady's Meadow. Here Comyn is alleged to have sunk his treasure-chest before he went to Dumfries, leaving it in charge of the water sprite. A net, it is said, was fixed in this pool, to which a small bell in the castle was attached, which rang when a salmon was in the snare.

When Burns came to Ellisland, Dalswinton was the property of Mr Patrick Miller, an inventive genius, who not only patronised him immediately after his arrival in Edinburgh, but maintained a kindly disposition towards him while he resided in the district; and, curiously enough, while Burns on one side of the river was composing lays destined to have a lasting influence on the Scottish heart, Miller on the other was trying to elucidate a scheme which has given an impetus to commerce and facilitated navigation to an undreamt of degree. The idea of propelling vessels by machinery originated with him, and it was on a lake in the vicinity of Dalswinton house that he conducted a series of experiments which proved the practicability of his theory. Unfortunately, however, some obstacles occurred which he failed or neglected to surmount, and the fame of perfecting steam navigation was bestowed on others. It is generally admitted that it was from his boat that Fulton and Henry Bell took the plans which they respectively realised on the Hudson and the Clyde.

The path down the furze-clad bank of the river is not only delightful but interesting to the admirers of Burns, on account of it having been a favourite walk of his. While pacing it he composed "Tam o' Shanter" and committed it to paper, making a sod-dyke do duty for a desk. Mrs Burns remembered the circumstances. "He spent most of the day on his favourite walk by the river, where, in the afternoon, she joined him with some of her children. He was busily engaged *crooning to himsel'*, and Mrs Burns perceiving that her presence was an interruption, loitered behind with her little ones among the broom. Her attention was presently attracted by the strange and wild gesticulations of the bard, who, now at some distance, was *agonised* with an ungovernable excess of joy. He was reciting very loud, and with the tears rolling down his cheeks, those animated verses which he had just conceived:

> ' Now Tam, oh Tam! had thae been queans,
> A' plump and strapping, in their teens;
> Their sarks, instead o' creeshie flannen,
> Been snaw-white seventeen-hunder linen!
> Thir breeks o' mine, my only pair,
> That ance were plush, o' guid blue hair,
> I wud hae gi'en them off my hurdies,
> For ae blink o' the bonnie burdies!' "*

While wandering along this footway on one occasion the bard was startled by the report of a gun. Looking round, he observed a poor wounded hare hastening to conceal its mangled form in an adjoining copse. The man who fired the shot related the circumstance to Allan Cunningham. "Burns," he said, "was in the custom when at home of strolling by himself in the twilight every evening along the Nith, and by the march between his land and ours. The hares often came and nibbled our wheat braird; and once in the gloamin'—it was in April—I got a shot at one and wounded her. She ran bleeding by Burns, who was pacing up and down by himself not far from me. He started, and with a bitter curse ordered me out of his sight or he would throw me instantly into the Nith. And had I stayed I'll warrant he would have been as good as his word, although I was both young and strong."

> " Oft as by winding Nith I, musing, wait
> The sober eve or hail the cheerful dawn;
> I'll miss thee sporting o'er the dewy lawn,
> And curse the ruffian's aim and mourn thy hapless fate."

After a walk of something like half a mile along this classic pathway, I came to the tower of Isle, as a square block of ancient masonry, which was at one time the residence of the Fergusons, is termed; and upon rounding it found

---

*Lockhart.

myself in front of an aristocratic looking farm house. Tapping nervously at the door it was opened by a cheerful, motherly-looking woman, who upon learning that I was a pilgrim and a stranger in the land enquiring about Burns, invited me in, and before long I found myself seated in the kitchen with a "whang" of cheese and bread, and a basin of milk before me talking with the household as familiarly as if I had been an old acquaintance. Mr and Mrs Black were assiduous in their attentions, and showed me everything about the place in which they thought I would be interested.

When the house at Ellisland was being built, Burns lodged with the out-going tenant in a hovel which stood under the shadow of the ancient tower of Isle. According to him it was "impervious to every blast that blew and every shower that fell"—indeed, from the glimpse we have of it in a poetic epistle to Hugh Parker, Kilmarnock, its interior appears to have been anything but pleasant:

> "Here, ambush'd by the chimla cheek,
> Hid in an atmosphere of reek,
> I hear a wheel thrum i' the neuk,
> I hear it—for in vain I leuk.
> The red peat gleams, a fiery kernal,
> Enhusked by a fog infernal.
> Here, for my wonted rhyming raptures,
> I sit and count my sins by chapters."

His Jean of a necessity was left in Mauchline for some time after his arrival in Nithsdale, and in his solitary hours his thoughts constantly reverted to Ayrshire; and in one of the numerous flirtations with the muse which he enjoyed during their separation, he declared that "day and night his fancy's flight" was ever with her.

> "Of a' the airts the wind can blaw,
>   I dearly lo'e the west,
> For there the bonnie lassie lives,
>   The lass that I lo'e best:
> There wild woods grow, and rivers row,
>   And mony a hill between;
> By day and nicht my fancy's flight
>   Is ever wi' my Jean.
>
> "I see her in the dewy flowers,
>   I see her fresh and fair;
> I hear her in the tunefu' birds,
>   I hear her charm the air.

> There's no' a bonnie flower that springs
>   By fountain, shaw, or green,
> There's no' a bonnie bird that sings,
>   But minds me o' my Jean."

We have a peep at the bard while living at the Isle in the valuable "Memoranda" already quoted. The name of the out-going tenant was David Cullie. "David," says the writer, "was an antiburgher, and belonged to the congregation of the late Rev. Mr Inglis—a clergyman for whom Burns contracted a great veneration. David by this time was about seventy years old, and had a wife nearly the same age. He was well to live in worldly circumstances. His family were grown up and settled in the world, and therefore he declined the farm. Mrs Burns joined her husband at Martinmas and lived for about five months at the Isle—a place that I know well. David Cullie used to visit at Ellisland farmhouse, and tho' the cheese was Dunlop, Mrs B. used to remark that he never took cheese but he took butter also. Burns used to laugh heartily at this.

"Before this time, Burns had written the 'Holy Fair,' and an impression had gone abroad that he was a scoffer or a free thinker. D. Cullie and his wife were aware of this, and although they treated him civilly as the incoming tenant, during the five months he resided under their roof, still they felt for him as for one who was by no means on the right path. On one occasion, Nance and the bard were sitting in the spence, when the former turned the conversation on her favourite topic—religion. Mr Burns, from whatever motive, sympathised with the matron, and quoted so much Scripture that she was fairly astonished, and staggered in the opinion she formerly entertained. When she went ben [? but] she said to her husband, 'Oh! David Cullie, hoo they have wranged that man; for I think he has mair o' the Bible aff his tongue than Mr Inglis himsel'.' The bard enjoyed the compliment; and almost the first thing he communicated to his wife on her arrival was 'the lift he had got from auld Nance.'"

When the dwelling house of Ellisland was finished Burns and his Jean proposed to take up their residence in it; and to do so in a proper manner, and according to an ancient custom which was meant to insure good luck, they along with a few friends formed a procession, and marched behind a woman bearing a family Bible and a bowl of salt to the new abode. The little cavalcade must have been grotesque in the extreme as it wound along the romantic path on the verge of the river, and doubtless Burns smiled at it as with mock solemnity and measured paces he entered into the spirit of the thing, for, as Chambers remarks, " Like a man of imagination, he delighted in such ancient observances, albeit his understanding on a rigid tasking would have denied their conclusions."

Having taken leave of my new friends at the Isle, I directed my steps to the highway, bade Ellisland and its surroundings " a heart-fond, warm adieu," and walked briskly in the direction of Dumfries. The five miles that lay before me failed to damp my enthusiasm or disturb my equanimity, for the long stretch of road I had to traverse winds through a rich agricultural district ; and as the pedestrian plods onward, his eye roves over a gorgeous panorama of hills, woods, valleys, and cultivated fields, which are interspersed with snug farm-houses and gentlemen's residences.

After a long, pleasant walk, I reached Holywood—an unimportant village whose humble tenements line both sides of the road—and wended my way towards its Kirktown, another hamlet (if it deserves the name) which stands off the highway, a good half mile farther on.

Entering a field a short distance beyond the road leading to the Kirktown, I walked up to and examined a curious row of stones which is said to be the remains of a Druidical Temple. They are huge fragments of rock, and by their systematic arrangement appear to have been planted in position by the hands of man, a task certainly which must have been attended with many difficulties, for one of the blocks is estimated to weigh nearly twelve tons. According to tradition, these stones were surrounded by a grove of oak trees which the Druids deemed sacred, and on that account (or rather, it may be supposed, of a religious enthusiast who took up his abode in its umbrageous recess when Druidism was superseded by a purer faith), was styled the Holy Wood, a term from which the parish derives its name. At an early date a splendid abbey was reared on the site of the hermit's cell, which flourished until the iconoclasts of the Reformation destroyed it, like many another monument of ancient architecture, and left it a prey to wreck and dismemberment.

Passing the manse—a snug old-fashioned building standing off the road in the midst of a nice garden—and a row of homely cottages, I went up to the gate of the churchyard, and to my mortification found it locked. Looking about for the best means of obtaining admission to the spot where

> "Servants, masters, small, and great,
>   Partake the same repose;
> And where in peace the ashes mix
>   Of those who once were foes,"

I observed stone steps jutting from the wall close at hand. Mounting these, I was soon within the enclosure, and,

> "Far from the madding crowd's ignoble strife,"

began to stray among the grassy hillocks. This little place of burial is shaded with some fine old trees, and thickly studded with tombstones, several of which commemorate members of influential local families, but I failed to discover any very old or remarkable memorial. The church is a curiously formed plain building, with a square tower of simple architecture at its front. The abbey which it superseded has wholly disappeared. Indeed, the only remnant of it I could discover was a stone with two rudely executed figures, which are said to represent the Saviour and the disciple whom he loved—some boor having built this memorial into the back wall of a pigstye near the churchyard gate.

After strolling through the tangled grass of this little churchyard, I acted on the advice of a passing wayfarer and forsook the highway, for what appeared a more circuitous route to Dumfries—namely, the old road passing through the Kirktown. Old roads generally wind over heights commanding delightful prospects, and this one is no exception to the rule, for from an elevation at no great distance from the church a wide range of landscape bursts on the view. The spires and tall chimneys of Dumfries are seen peering from a dell in the distance, which, to all appearance, is wholly surrounded by a richly fertile and beautifully wooded country. The bulky Criffel, too, and the range of hills of which it is the termination, loom against the sky, and the lovely valley of the Nith appears more like a paradisiacal scene than a portion of a common-place world.

After passing an interesting group of "toddlin' wee things"

enjoying themselves "wi' flichterin' noise and glee" in front of a row of humble thatched cottages, I turned into a road striking off to the right, and in a short time arrived at the Cairn—a picturesque shallow stream, which is easily forded by vehicles and conveniently crossed by means of a small foot-bridge. Having dallied on the bridge for a short time, watching the rippling water and enjoying the scenery, I resumed the journey, and in due time descried Lincluden's ruined abbey peering from a shady retreat in the distance. Knowing it to have been a favourite resort of Burns when he resided in Dumfries, and that the Muse granted him many favours while straying under the shadow of its dismantled walls, I sought out the approach and found it to be a lane skirting a small farmstead near the highway I was journeying. Having passed through a turnstile, and followed a beaten path running zig-zag through the grass, I reached the elevation on which the ruin stands.

Lincluden Abbey never has been an extensive religious house, but to judge by the crumbling Gothic walls it has not only been chaste in design but elaborately embellished with ornamental sculpture, which, alas! is sadly defaced, for to all appearance wreck and decay have been allowed to run riot and hold high revelry about the pile until a recent date. Oppressed by the solemn stillness which reigned, I approached a splendid Gothic doorway over which there are two lines of faded carving, which are said to have represented the birth and early history of Christ, and upon opening a small iron gate entered a spacious but roofless sculpture-bedecked apartment of great antiquarian interest. In a finely sculptured recess in the left wall of this once splendid hall is the tomb of Margaret Stewart, daughter of Robert III. and wife of an Earl of Douglas. It bears this inscription on the back wall:—
"Hic jacet Dna Margareta regis Scotiae filia quodam comtissa de Douglas Dno Gallovidiae et vallis Annandiae."* When Pennant visited the ruin in 1772 the mutilated recumbent statue of this lady was in the recess, but the bones of the deceased, he states, "were scattered about in an indecent manner by some wretches who broke open the repository in search of treasure."

---

*Translation:—"Here lies Lady Margaret, daughter of the King of Scotland, Countess of Douglas, and Lady of Galloway and Annandale."

This Abbey was founded about 1154, and was at first a convent for Benedictine Nuns, but at the close of the fourteenth century they were expelled by Archibald Earl of Douglas, surnamed THE GRIM, on account, as it is alleged, of the impurity of their lives. Afterwards it was converted into a collegiate church for a provost and twelve bedesmen, and in that condition it remained till the Reformation. Like sister fabrics it underwent the usual vicissitudes of peaceful and troublous times, increased its proportions under mindful custodiers, and suffered neglect, decay, and dismemberment at the hands of the destructive and the indifferent.

While Burns lived in Dumfries a favourite recreation with him was to stroll along the bank of the Nith in the evening to the ruins of Lincluden Abbey and linger there till the moon rose on the scene.

" If you would see Melrose aright,
Go view it in the pale moonlight,"

says Scott, and doubtless when Lincluden is lit up by

" The orb of tranquil light,
Whose soften'd radiance makes the night
Seem fairer than the day,"

the scene will not be readily forgotten.

We have an account of one of his visits in the following verses :—

" As I stood by yon roofless tower,
Where the wa'-flower scents the dewy air,
There the howlet mourns in her ivy bower,
And tells the midnight moon her care.

" The winds were laid, the air was still,
The stars they shot alang the sky ;
The fox was howling on the hill,
And the distant-echoing glens reply.

. . . .

" By heedless chance I turned mine eyes,
And by the moonbeam shook to see
A stern and stalwart ghaist arise,
Attired as minstrels wont to be.

" Had I a statue been o' stane,
His darin' look had daunted me ;
And on his bonnet graved was plain,
The sacred posy, ' Libertie !'

. . . .

> "He sang wi' joy the former day,
>   He weeping wailed his latter times ;
> But what he said it was nae play :
>   I winna venture't in my rhymes."

His caution in this instance is commendable. However, he was not so guarded on all occasions, but uttered his political sentiments fearlessly, and in such an open manner that his superiors in the Excise were doubtful of his loyalty and regarded him with suspicion.

With many a glance at the architectural adornments of the old pile, I strolled to the summit of a small wooded hill in its immediate vicinity and rapturously gazed on the beautiful scene it commands. At my feet lay the Abbey, a little beyond it the birch and alder-fringed banks of the limpid Cluden, and gleaming through the trees were the broad waters of the Nith and a vast track of the lovely scenery through which it winds. Little wonder, thought I, that Burns loved to wander here, for most assuredly the surroundings are eminently calculated to invite the footsteps of a poet. Time, however, did not permit me to linger, so, reluctantly withdrawing my gaze, I descended the slope to the bank of the river, and "with measured steps and slow" began to pace the path which the poet loved to traverse. It winds along the verge of a series of fields, and is within the sight and sound of the rushing stream. A pleasant walk brought me to its termination, which, by the by, is neither romantic nor savoury. Passing along a narrow old-fashioned looking street I crossed the New Bridge and entered Dumfries.

CHAPTER XX.

Dumfries — The Old Bridge — Greyfriars' Monastery — The Castle — A House in which Burns lived — High Street — The Globe Inn and its Associations — The House in which Burns died.

Dumfries is a town of pleasing aspect, its streets being regularly built and its outskirts studded with handsome villas. It possesses a provost, three bailies, and a town council; and its population, including that of Maxweltown —a suburb separated from it by the Nith, but connected by bridges, parliamentary interest, and trade—is 19,500. Formerly it was only notable as a great rural mart and a place of residence for the gentry of the district, but since the Glasgow and South-Western Railway, and the southern section of the Caledonian, have brought it into connection with the entire railway system of the country, its commercial prosperity has been marked, and it is now one of the chief seats of tweed manufacture in Britain. Besides this industry, engineering, ironfounding, basket-making, tanning, and other trades are carried on with great spirit, and afford employment to hundreds of the inhabitants. The river being navigable until within a short distance of the town, an extensive coasting trade is carried on by vessels of a good size, and also a foreign trade, which is chiefly in timber from America. The imports are principally hemp, tallow, coals, iron, tea, and wine; and the exports cattle, sheep, barley, oats, potatoes, wool, woollen goods, and freestone.

Dumfries contains thirteen places of worship, nine banking establishments, and many really handsome buildings. It also forms the scene of many a border story, and not a few interesting historic incidents; but as a minute account of these would be out of place, I will resume the narrative and merely call the reader's attention to notable objects and places met with in the course of a walk to the grave of him

"Who lives upon all memories,
Though with the buried gone."

Entering Dumfries from the Maxweltown side of the river by the New Bridge one cannot fail to be impressed with the magnificent street in front and the beautiful buildings by which it is lined. Being more intent in this instance, however, on viewing the ancient than the modern portion of Dumfries, I turned into an open space on the bank of the river which leads to the Dock Green, a once favourite promenade of our poet. The scene, although commonplace, is pleasing. Spanning the river a little below the new is the old bridge, a ponderous old-fashioned narrow structure resembling the Auld Brig o' Ayr, not only in appearance but from the circumstance that it has withstood the floods and weathered the blasts of six centuries and is now fated to bear no heavier burdens than what may be imposed by occasional pedestrians. Devorgilla, daughter of Allan, Lord of Galloway, and widow of Baliol, Lord of Barnard Castle, has the merit of its erection, and also the founding of a monastery for Grey Friars, which she endowed with the bridge customs.

This institution stood at the top of Friars' Vennel (an antique thoroughfare opposite the bridge), and is historic on account of Bruce having slain Comyn beside its high altar. Near to it was the Castle of Dumfries, a stronghold of great importance which underwent many vicissitudes in the olden time owing to its nearness to the debateable ground between England and Scotland ; but, like its ecclesiastical neighbour, no vestige of it remains, and its site is now occupied by a building dedicated to the worship of God and the brotherhood of man.

After gazing curiously up the vennel, and watching the water of the river as it tumbled over a beautiful weir and churned itself into fleecy foam in its haste, I entered Bank Street, and paused before a humble three-storied tenement near its left corner and read the following on a stone tablet on the front of its second floor :—" ROBERT BURNS, THE NATIONAL POET, LIVED IN THIS HOUSE WITH HIS FAMILY ON COMING TO DUMFRIES, FROM ELLISLAND, IN 1791."

Venturing into the low-roofed, causewayed, narrow passage, leading into its interior, I climbed a badly-lighted ricketty stair, and tapped at the front door on the landing, and while I did so, wondered why Burns and his Jean began life anew in such an abode. Receiving no response, I renewed the tapping, but this time in a more authorative manner. "She's no' in," said a woman whom I passed in the entry. "Is this the house in which Burns lived?" said I. "O aye, an' gin ye come doon you'll see the windows," she replied, as she led the way and pointed them out. "It was at that ane," she went on, pointing to the mid one, "that he wrote a lot o' his sangs an' poetry, an' mony a look folk has at it on that account, but mair especially since the stane wi' the readin' on't was put up." "Do you not think this a very humble dwelling for such a great poet as Burns to have lived in?" I enquired. "There's nae doubt o' that," she replied, "but ye see Burns was never weel aff, an' had but little to come an' gang wi' when he left Ellisland—hoocver, the house is no what it was when he leeved in't, for it's a' gaun tae wrack for want o' repair." Chambers states that "the first eighteen months of Burns' life in Dumfries present him occupying a very small dwelling on the first floor of the house in Wee Vennel (now Bank Street). He has three small apartments, each with a window to the street, besides, perhaps, a small kitchen in the rear. The small central room, about the size of a bed closet, is the only place in which he can seclude himself for study. On the groundfloor, immediately underneath, his friend John Syme has his office for the distribution of stamps. Overhead is an honest blacksmith, called George Haugh, whom Burns treats on a familiar footing as a neighbour; on the opposite side of the street is the poet's landlord, Captain Hamilton, a gentleman of fortune and worth, who admires Burns and often asks him to a family Sunday dinner." While residing in this tenement, Burns composed some of his most popular dities, among which may be enumerated— "The Soldier's Return," "Duncan Gray," "Mickle thinks my love o' my beauty," "What can a young lassie do wi' an auld man?" "Last May a braw wooer cam' doon the lang glen," "My heart is sair, I daurna tell," "Wandering Willie," "My wife's a winsome wee thing," "Flow gently, sweet Afton," "My love is like a red, red rose," "Scots wha ha'e," "Auld Langsyne," "A man's a man for a' that," and a host of others, which in themselves would have been sufficient to stamp him a lyric poet of the first order. John Syme's office is now that of a grain mill in the vicinity, and the house of Captain Hamilton has given place to a handsome modern building.

After lingering by this song-hallowed building, I passed up Bank Street, and entered the main artery of the town. Notwithstanding its irregular construction it is spacious, and contains buildings and places of business equal to any in the principal streets of large cities. One distinctive feature in the scene is a church-like erection termed "The Mid Steeple," which appears to stand most inconveniently in the centre of the street. So far as I could learn, its history is void of interest, and to all appearance, it is of no great antiquity. While viewing this populous thoroughfare my eye caught the signboard of the King's Arms Hotel, a house that Burns occasionally frequented, and in which he scrawled the following verselet on a pane of glass while irritated by some sneering remarks which a company of gentlemen made in his presence about officers of the excise :—

"Ye men of wit and wealth, why all this sneering
'Gainst poor excisemen? Give the cause a hearing.
What are your landlords' rent-rolls? Taxing ledgers.
What premiers, what? even monarchs' mighty gaugers.
Nay, what are priests, those seeming godly wisemen?
What are they, pray, but spiritual excisemen?"

A short walk along High Street brought me to a quaint looking building in which there is a narrow, dark, uninviting passage surmounted by a gilded globe and a portrait of the poet bearing the superscription—"Burns's Howff." It was the celebrated Globe, a tavern fatally familiar to him, whose name is by far too often made use of to stimulate trade. Venturing up the subterranean-like retreat I beheld a long strip of a dimly lighted causewayed path, in which two men might with difficulty walk abreast. On either side rose lofty, black-looking buildings, but one close to the entrance, with a flight of stone steps leading to its open door, rivetted my attention. Mounting the steps—steps often pressed by the poet's feet—I found myself in a gloomy, kitchen-like apartment, partly lighted by the gleam of a fire burning in a cosy corner; but had scarce time to look round when a smart, neatly-dressed lady made her appearance, and ushered me into a room on the left, in which two young men were complacently chatting over their beer. Refreshments being placed before me, I began to look round. The apartment appeared to be some eighteen feet by twelve, and the ceiling and paint-faded panelled walls dingy and dim. In the centre of the floor stood a table, surrounded with common chairs, but the most interesting feature was an old-fashioned armed chair by the fireside, directly beneath an inscription informing visitors that it stands in what was, and still is, "Burns's corner." Often has the wainscoating of this apartment rung with his laughter and echoed the melody of his midnight song when seated in his favourite corner—the life, the soul, the alpha, and the omega of the company. Thousands visit the tavern annually, and few leave the premises without sitting down in the poet's chair. Many do so with levity, but for my part, I did it with reverence and sorrow for him who

"Was quick to learn and wise to know,
And keenly felt the friendly glow
And softer flame"

of love and universal brotherhood.

I have a peculiar habit of making myself at home wherever I go, and some how or other I found my way into the kitchen and the good grace of the worthy landlady—indeed, like Tam o' Shanter and the browster wife in Ayr, we "grew gracious," and the result was that she conducted me up stairs and showed me everything in her possession associated with the poet's name, and for her courtesy I tender thanks. On a pane of glass in the window of a bedroom on the second floor, the following verse is inscribed in the unmistakeable handwriting of the poet :—

"O lovely Polly Stewart,
O charming Polly Stewart,
There's not a flower that blooms in May
That's half so fair as thou art."

And on an adjoining one in the same manner:

"Gin a body meet a body,
Coming through the grain;
Gin a body kiss a body,
The thing's a bodie's ain."

The inscriptions quoted are believed genuine, but one on another pane, as being of a doubtful character, I decline to give. The Globe Tavern has undergone very little change since the days of Burns; indeed, the doors, windows, floors, and panelling are unaltered, and it may be stated that the present hostess—who is in her way an enthusiastic admirer of the poet—has collected several relics of him and his family which she exhibits with pardonable pride; but as an enumeration of them is unnecessary, it will be sufficient to state that they chiefly consist of two jugs and a basin bought at the sale of the poet's household effects, and a punch-bowl recently purchased by her for the sum of ten guineas. Like the before-mentioned vessels, it is common earthenware, but so much shattered that it is held together by ten clasps—a number, as I jocularly remarked, symbolically representing the price paid for it.

When Burns frequented the Globe it was kept by a John Hyslop and his wife Meg. Their frail niece, whom the poet has celebrated in the song "Yestreen I had a pint o' wine," acted as barmaid, and in that capacity became familiar with him. This familiarity, however, it is to be deplored, exceeded the bounds of chastity during a temporary residence of Mrs Burns in Mauchline, and resulted in the birth of a child. No event in the whole course of Mrs Burns' life displayed the noble qualities of her mind to greater advantage than this trying incident, for she not only forgave her repentant husband, but took the helpless babe home and brought it up as one of her own children. In fact, when her father glanced at the cradle and asked in surprise if she had again had twins, she screened her husband by the statement that the second baby was that of a sick friend.*

To redeem this sad association of the Globe, another of a humorous cast may be narrated. "Nicol and Masterton had come to spend a week of their vacations at Dumfries, for the purpose of enjoying the society of their friend Burns. The scene of the *Peck o' Maut* was renewed every evening in the Globe Tavern. Excepting, indeed, that Burns attended to his duty in the forenoon, and that Willie and Allan took a rattling walk before dinner, to give themselves an appetite, it might be said that the week was one entire chrysolite of

---

*This child was named Elizabeth, and resided with Mrs Burns until her marriage. She became a Mrs Thomson, and lived to see the celebration of her father's Centenary.

merry-making. One day, when they were to dine at the Globe, they found on coming in at three that no dinner had been ordered. As Burns had taken on himself this duty, the fault was his, and the other two gentlemen were wroth with him accordingly. 'Just like him,' quoth Mrs Hyslop; 'ye might hae kent that he's ne'er to lippen to.' 'Weel, but can we have anything to eat? You know that we must dine somehow.' Mrs Hyslop, or as Burns called her, Meg, proved propitious. There was a tup's head in the pot for John and herself; and, if they pleased, they might have the first of it. Now a good tup's head with the accompanying trotters—seeing that, in the Scottish *cuisine*, nothing is taken off but the wool—is a dish which will amply satisfy six or even eight persons, so it was no contemptible resource for the hungry trio. When it had been disposed on the board, 'Burns,' said Nicol, 'we fine you for neglect of arrangements: you give us something new as a grace.' Our poet instantly, with appropriate gesture and tone, said:—

> 'O Lord, when hunger pinches sore,
>   Do thou stand us in stead;
> And send us from thy bounteous store,
>   A tup or wether head! Amen.'

They fell to and enjoyed the fare prodigiously, leaving, however, a miraculously ample sufficiency for the host and hostess. 'Now, Burns, we are not done with you. We fine you again. Return thanks.' He as promptly said:—

> 'O Lord, since we have feasted thus,
>   Which we so little merit,
> Let Meg now take away the flesh,
>   And Jock bring in the spirit! Amen.'"*

Upon taking leave of the inmates of the Globe Inn, I held along the gloomy, unsavoury passage, and in a short time emerged into a commonplace thoroughfare named Shakspere Street. Pausing, I accosted a young man and asked in what part of the street Burns was found lying on the fatal morning he quitted the Globe Inn. "There," said he, as he pointed to a portion of the roughly-causewayed footway at the mouth of the passage, "that is said to be the place." He spoke in a careless, matter-of-fact manner; but to me the spot was invested with a very painful interest, and I gazed upon it

*Chambers.

with feelings of the deepest regret for this humiliating incident in the Poet's life.

It appears that early in the month of January, 1796, when barely recovered from a severe illness, Burns ill-advisedly joined a jovial party in the Globe Inn, and tarried till about three in the morning. "Before returning home," says the writer quoted above, "he unluckily remained for some time in the open air, and, overpowered by the effects of the liquor he had drunk, fell asleep. In these circumstances, and in the peculiar condition to which a severe medicine had reduced his constitution, a fatal chill penetrated to his bones. He reached home with the seeds of a rheumatic fever already in possession of his weakened frame. In this little accident, and not to the pressure of poverty or disrepute, or wounded feelings or a broken heart, truly lay the determining cause of the sadly shortened days of our great National Poet."

Nearly opposite the entrance of the Globe Inn passage in Shakespere Street is a crooked, common-looking narrow thoroughfare named Burns's Street. Entering it I rounded an abrupt turn, and having paced a few yards of a steep roadway, stopped in front of a respectable two-storied house on the left, which I at once recognised as that in which Burns died. In the wall of the building next to it there is a bust of the poet and a stone bearing this inscription :—

"IN THE ADJOINING HOUSE, TO THE NORTH,

LIVED AND DIED

THE POET OF HIS COUNTRY AND OF MANKIND,

ROBERT BURNS."

CHAPTER XXI.

The house in which Burns died—his circumstances and last illness—goes to Brow—his anxiety for the welfare of his family—an affecting anecdote—the poet's return to Dumfries—the anxiety of the inhabitants—Jessie Lewars—his death and funeral—the family of Burns—the exemplary life of the poet's widow—sale of household effects.

After a timorous tap and a nervous pause at the door of the house in which Burns died, it was opened by a neatly-dressed lady, who, upon learning the nature of my business, invited me in, and most obligingly conducted me through the various apartments, referring as she did so to numerous little incidents associated with each. "This," said she, "is now the parlour, but it was used by Burns as a sitting room, and in it he wrote many of his songs. That is the kitchen, a place much frequented by him; and up here," she continued, as she led the way up a narrow staircase, "is the room in which he died." It proved a small oblong apartment, some fifteen feet by nine. Its appearance and associations caused very many saddening thoughts to well up in my mind, and as I stood on its threshold, fancy conjured up shadows of the dear ones who surrounded the poet's bed when his spirit forsook its casket of clay. On the same floor there is a room of larger dimensions, as also a closet in which the poet secluded himself during hours of inspiration, or when he had any particular business to perform, and above them a couple of attic bedrooms in which the children slept. This is the accommodation of what constituted the home of Robert Burns, and it will readily be admitted that it is of a superior order to the majority of middle-class people's houses, and that his circumstances at the time of his death were much better than reported. His official income was £50 a year, but extra allowances generally brought it up to £70. "Add to all this," says Chambers, "the solid perquisites which he received from seizures of contraband spirits, tea, and other articles, which it was then the custom to divide among the officers, and we shall see that Burns could scarcely be considered as enjoying less than £90 a year. This, indeed, is but a small income in comparison with the deserts of the bard; yet it is equally certain that many worthy families in the middle ranks of life in Scottish country towns were then supported in a decent manner upon no larger means." The poet's eldest son informed the same writer that this house was one of a good order, such as was used in those days by the better class of citizens, and that his father and mother led a comparatively genteel life. "They always had a maid-servant, and sat in their parlour. That room and the two principal bedrooms were carpeted and otherwise well furnished, and the dining table was of mahogany. There was much rough comfort in the house not to have been found in those of ordinary citizens; for, besides the spoils of smugglers, presents of game and country produce were received from the rural gentlefolks, besides occasional barrels of oysters from Hill, Cunningham, and other friends in town."

Despite this "rough comfort" the associations of the house are saddening. The poet never recovered from the exposure mentioned in last chapter, and in a brief month after it we find him telling his woeful tale to Mrs Dunlop. He says—"I have lately drunk deep of the cup of affliction. The Autumn robbed me of my only daughter and darling child, and that at a distance, too, and so rapidly, as to put it out of my power to pay the last duties to her. I had scarcely begun to recover from that shock when I became myself the victim of a most severe rheumatic fever, and long the die spun doubtful, until, after many weeks of a sick-bed, it seems to have turned up life, and I am beginning to crawl across my room, and once indeed have been before my own door in the street." Some time after this Miss Grace Aiken, a sister of Robert Aiken, Ayr, met him in the street, but he was so much changed that she did not know him, and it was only by his voice that he was recognised. "It was hoped by some of his friends," says Dr. Currie, "that he would live through the months of Spring and that the succeeding season might restore him." But they were disappointed. The genial beams of the sun infused no vigour into his languid frame;

the summer wind blew upon him, but produced no refreshment. As a last resource he determined to try sea bathing, and for that purpose removed to Brow, a watering place on the shores of the Solway, ten miles from Dumfries. Before setting out he told his Jean that he thought himself dying and in a kind of prophetic spirit added: "Don't be afraid; I'll be more respected a hundred years after I am dead than I am at the present day."

On his arrival at Brow, Mrs Walter Riddle, who had been estranged from him for some time, and who was staying in the vicinity, sent her carriage for him. He went to see her, and her account of the interview is of such interest that I may be excused for transcribing it in full. "I was struck," says this lady, "with his appearance on entering the room. The stamp of death was impressed on his features. He seemed already touching the brink of eternity. His first salutation was, 'Well, madam, have you any commands for the other world?' I replied that it seemed a doubtful case which of us should be there soonest, and that I hoped that he would yet live to write my epitaph. He looked in my face with an air of great kindness and expressed his concern at seeing me look so ill, with his accustomed sensibility. At table he ate little or nothing, and he complained of having entirely lost the tone of his stomach. We had a long and serious conversation about his present situation, and the approaching termination of all his earthly prospects. He spoke of his death without any of the ostentation of philosophy, but with the firmness, as well as the feeling, of an event likely to happen very soon, and which gave him concern chiefly from leaving his four children so young and unprotected, and his wife in so interesting a situation—in hourly expectation of lying-in with a fifth. He mentioned with seeming pride and satisfaction the promising genius of his eldest son, and the flattering marks of approbation he had received from his teachers, and dwelt particularly on his hopes of that boy's future conduct and merit. His anxiety for his family seemed to hang heavy upon him, and the more perhaps from the reflection that he had not done them all the justice he was so well qualified to do. Passing from this subject he showed great concern about the care of his literary fame, and particularly the publication of his posthumous works. He said he was aware that his death would occasion some noise, and that every scrap of his writing would be revived against him to the injury of his future reputation; that letters and verses he had written with unguarded and improper freedom, and which he had earnestly wished to have buried in oblivion, would be handed about by idle vanity or malevolence, when no dread of his resentment would restrain them, or prevent the censures of shrill-tongued malice, or the insidious sarcasms of envy, from pouring forth all their venom to blast his fame. He lamented that he had written many epigrams on persons against whom he entertained no enmity, and whose characters he should be sorry to wound; and many indifferent poetical pieces, which he feared would now, with all their imperfections on their head, be thrust upon the world. On this account he deeply regretted having deferred to put his papers into a state of arrangement, as he was now quite incapable of the exertion. The conversation was kept up with great evenness and animation on his side. I had seldom seen his mind greater or more collected. There was frequently a considerable degree of vivacity in his sallies, and they would probably have had a greater share had not the concern and dejection I could not disguise damped the spirit of pleasantry he seemed not unwilling to indulge. We parted about sunset on the evening of that day (the 5th of July, 1796). The next day I saw him again, and we parted to meet no more."

In the midst of these dejecting circumstances the dying bard continued to sing. Witness his last song, the "Fairest maid on Devon's banks," which accompanied the piteous letter to Mr Thomson imploring the loan of five pounds to satisfy the demands of "a cruel scoundrel of a haberdasher" who threatened him with proceedings. After remaining a fortnight in Brow he sent the following to his devoted wife:—" My dearest love,—I delayed writing until I could tell you what effect sea-bathing was likely to produce. It would be injustice to deny that it has eased my pains, and I think has strengthened me; but my appetite is still extremely bad. No flesh nor fish can I swallow; porridge and milk are the only things I can taste. I am very happy to hear by Miss Jessie Lewars that you are all well. My very best and kindest compliments to her and all the children. I will see you on Sunday.—Your affectionate husband, R. B."

Before he left Brow he drank tea with the minister of Ruthwell's widow, and elicited much sympathy by his altered appearance. The evening being beautiful, the sunbeams streamed through the window and illumined the apartment. Fearing that the light would be too strong, her daughter rose to let down the blinds, but the bard observing her intention gave a look of great benignity, and said—"Thank you, my dear, for your kind attention; but oh, let him shine! he will not shine long for me!"

Mr. James Gracie, banker, Dumfries, offered to send his carriage to bring him home, but the poet did not avail himself of the kindness. According to Allan Cunningham, he "returned on the 18th in a small spring cart. The ascent to his house was steep, and the cart stopped at the foot of the Mill-hole brae. When he alighted he shook much, and stood with difficulty; he seemed unable to stand upright. He stooped as if in pain, and walked tottering towards his own door; his looks were hollow and ghastly, and those who saw him then expected never to see him in life again." The writer goes on to say that "Dumfries was like a besieged place. It was known that he was dying, and the anxiety not only of the rich and learned, but of the mechanics and peasants, exceeded all belief. Wherever two or three people stood together, their talk was of Burns, and of him alone. They spoke of his history, of his person, of his works, of his family, of his fame, and of his untimely and approaching fate, with a warmth and an enthusiasm which will ever endear Dumfries to my remembrance. . . . . . His differences with them on some important points were forgotten and forgiven; they thought only of his genius, of the delight his compositions had diffused; and they talked of him with the same awe as of some departing spirit whose voice was to gladden them no more."

The condition his wife was in, and the future of his family, gave him much anxiety, and in an agony of mind he penned the following to his father-in-law:—"My dear sir,—Do, for Heaven's sake, send Mrs. Armour here immediately. My wife is hourly expected to be put to bed. Good God! what a situation for her to be in, poor girl, without a friend! I returned from sea-bathing quarters to-day, but I think and feel that my strength is so gone that the disorder will prove fatal to me.—Your son-in-law, R. B."

Jessie Lewars, the daughter of Mr. John Lewars, supervisor in Dumfries, who resided opposite the poet's dwelling, hovered by his bedside, and attended to his wants like a ministering angel. She was the subject of at least two songs, and even on the bed of death he fancied himself her lover, and wrote the following on the back of a menagerie bill, which his physician handed her upon entering the room :—

> "Talk not to me of savages
>   From Afric's burning sun ;
> No savage e'er could rend my heart
>   As, Jessie, thou hast done.
> But Jessie's lovely hand in mine,
>   A mutual faith to plight,
> Not even to view the Heavenly choir
>   Would be so blest a sight."

Upon another occasion, when she was attending upon him, he took up a crystal goblet containing wine and water, and wrote on it :—

> "Fill me with the rosy wine,
> Call a toast—a toast divine ;
> Give the poet's darling flame,
> Lovely Jessie be the name ;
> Then thou mayest freely boast
> Thou hast given a peerless toast."

When she became slightly indisposed, he proffered to write her epitaph, and on another goblet inscribed :—

> "Say, sages, what's the charm on earth
>   Can turn Death's dart aside ?
> It is not purity and worth,
>   Else Jessie had not died."

When she recovered he said there was "a poetic reason for it," and wrote as follows :—

> "But rarely seen since Nature's birth
>   The natives of the sky ;
> Yet still one seraph's left on earth,
>   For Jessie did not die."

In the "memoranda" already quoted, Mrs. Burns states that before his death he was "scarce himself for an hour together," that is, his mind wandered. He was aware of this, and told her to touch him, and remind him that he was going wrong. The day before he died, he called very quickly, and with a hale voice, "Gilbert, Gilbert!" On the morning of the 21st (July, 1796) the children were brought into the chamber to take a last look of their illustrious parent, "They stood round the bed," says Chambers, "while calmly and gradually he sank into his last repose." The eldest son (he was ten years of age) retained a distinct recollection of the scene, and has reported the sad fact that the last words of the bard were a muttered execration against the legal agent by whose letter, wittingly or unwittingly, the parting days of Burns had been embittered. These words were very probably uttered while unconscious. On the 25th the remains were removed to the Town Hall preparatory to the funeral, which the Volunteers had resolved to make public and conduct with military honours. On the day following the funeral took place. "A party of the Volunteers, selected to perform the military duty in the churchyard," says Dr. Currie, "stationed themselves in front of the procession, with their arms reversed; the main body of the corps surrounded and supported the coffin, on which were placed the hat and sword of their friend and fellow-soldier; the numerous body of attendants ranged themselves in the rear; while the fencible regiments of infantry and cavalry lined the streets from the Town Hall to the burial ground in the southern churchyard—a distance of more than half a mile. The whole procession moved forward to that sublime and affecting strain of music, 'The Dead March in Saul,' and three volleys fired over the grave marked the return of Burns to his parent earth. The spectacle was in a high degree grand and solemn, and accorded with the general sentiments of sympathy and sorrow which the occasion called forth." The same writer adds:—"It was an affecting circumstance that on the morning of the day of her husband's funeral Mrs. Burns was undergoing the pains of labour, and that during the solemn service we have just been describing the posthumous son of our Poet was born."

Burns had nine children by his Jean—five sons and four daughters. Two of the former and the whole of the latter died in childhood. The eldest son (Robert), Chambers tells us, "excited admiration by his general intelligence during his attendance of two sessions at the University of Edinburgh and one at Glasgow." He inherited in no slight degree his father's temperament and poetical taste, and wrote verses, of which the following may serve as a specimen :—

> " Hae ye seen, in the calm, dewy morning,
>   The redbreast wild warbling sae clear,
> Or the low-dwelling, snow-breasted gowan
>   Surcharg'd wi' mild e'ening's soft tear ?
> Oh ! then ye hae seen my dear lassie,
>   The lassie I lo'e best of a' ;
> But far frae the hame of my lassie
>   I'm mony a lang mile awa'.

> " Her hair is the wing of the blackbird,
>   Her eye is the eye of the dove,
> Her lips are the ripe blushing rose-bud,
>   Her bosom's the palace of love.
> Though green be thy banks, O sweet Clutha !
>   Thy beauties ne'er charm me ava ;
> Forgive me, ye maids o' sweet Clutha,
>   My heart is wi' her that's awa'.

> " O love, thou'rt a dear fleeting pleasure !
>   The sweetest we mortals here know ;
> But soon is thy heaven, bright beaming,
>   O'ercast with the darkness of woe ;
> As the moon on the oft-changing ocean
>   Delights the lone mariner's eye,
> Till red rush the storms of the desert,
>   And dark billows tumble on high."

Mrs. Burns continued to reside in the house which had been hallowed by her husband's presence. She used to relate that shortly after his death she thought he came to her bedside, and, upon drawing the curtains, said—" Are you sleeping ? I have been permitted to return and take one look of you and the child, but I have not time to stay." The vision was so vivid that she started up and ever after thought it a reality. Perhaps it was, for there are many similar occurrences on record which cannot be altogether explained away. By the proceeds of a public subscription, and the publication of a posthumous edition of her husband's works, Mrs. Burns was enabled to bring up her sons in a creditable way and maintain herself in comfort. Mr. M'Diarmid of Dumfries states that "hers was one of those well-balanced minds which cling instinctively to propriety and a medium in all things. . . . In her tastes she was frugal, simple, and pure ; and delighted in music, pictures, and flowers. In Spring and

Summer it was impossible to pass her windows without being struck with the beauty of the floral treasures they contained; and if extravagant in anything it was in the article of roots and plants of the finest sorts. Fond of the society of young people, she mingled as long as able in their innocent pleasures, and cheerfully filled up for them the cup 'which cheers but not inebriates.' Although neither a sentimentalist nor a 'blue stocking,' she was a clever woman, possessed great shrewdness, discriminated character admirably, and frequently made very pithy remarks." She survived her husband nearly thirty-eight years, and died of paralysis, in the room in which he breathed his last, on the 26th of March, 1834, in the 70th year of her age.

At her death, the household effects were sold by public auction, and no sale ever created such an excitement in Dumfries. People were so anxious to possess relics of the celebrated family that they paid fabulous prices for mere trifles. According to the *Dumfries Courier*, the auctioneer commenced with small articles, and when he came to a broken copper coffee-pot, there were so many bidders that the price paid exceeded twenty-fold the intrinsic value. A tea kettle of the same metal succeeded and reached £2 sterling. Of the linens, a table-cloth marked 1792, which, speaking commercially, may be worth half-a-crown or five shillings, was knocked down at £5 7s. Many other articles commanded handsome prices, and the older and plainer the furniture the better it sold. The rusty iron top of a shower bath which Mrs Dunlop of Dunlop sent to the Poet when afflicted with rheumatism was bought by a Carlisle gentleman for £1 8s; and a low wooden kitchen chair, on which the late Mrs Burns sat when nursing her children, was run up to £7 3s. The crystal and china were much coveted, and brought, in most cases, splendid prices. Even an old fender reached a figure which would go far to buy half-a-dozen new ones, and everything towards the close attracted notice, down to grey-beards, bottles, and a half-worn pair of bellows. The poet's eight-day clock, made by a Mauchline artist, attracted great attention from the circumstance that it had frequently been wound up by his own hand. In a few seconds it was bid up to £15 or guineas, and was finally disposed of for £35. It was understood that the purchaser would have advanced, if necessary, to £60.

Such, reader, are some of the associations of the house in which Burns died. Sorrowfully I lingered on the threshold of the room where the last sad scene in the drama of his life was enacted, and when I took my leave and descended the steps at the front door, I felt as if they were consecrated by the footsteps of him who will tread them no more.

> "Rear high thy bleak majestic hills,
>   Thy shelter'd valleys proudly spread,
> And, Scotia, pour thy thousand rills,
>   And wave thy heaths with blossoms red.
> But never more shall poet tread
>   Thy airy height, thy woodland reign,
> Since he, the sweetest bard, is dead,
>   That ever breathed the soothing strain."

CHAPTER XXII.

ST. MICHAEL'S CHURCHYARD—THE ERECTION OF THE MAUSOLEUM—
THE DISINTERMENT OF THE POET'S REMAINS—PHRENOLOGICAL
DESCRIPTION OF HIS CRANIUM—THE EXTERNAL AND INTERNAL
APPEARANCE OF THE MAUSOLEUM—INSCRIPTIONS—A GRANDSON
OF THE POET — BURNS' CONNECTION WITH THE DUMFRIES
LIBRARY—CONCLUDING REMARKS.

Strolling along Burns Street, I soon arrived at the gate of St. Michael's churchyard, and finding it open passed along the gravelled walk to view the church, a neat structure with a handsome spire some 130 feet high. The churchyard, although barely three acres in extent, is estimated to contain over 3000 monumental stones of one description and another. Many are beautiful specimens of the sculptor's art, and not a few are interesting on account of their antique appearance and inscriptions. Amongst the latter are three weather-worn slabs to the memory of three stubborn Nithsdale Covenanters, who suffered death rather than submit to the tyranny and injustice so prevalent in their day. All honour to the Dumfries folks for erecting a more enduring memorial to their memory, and also for commemorating the 420 victims of cholera, who perished during its reign in Dumfries in 1832. In meditative mood, I strolled towards the east corner of the churchyard to view the spot that holds the Poet's dust, for

> " Such graves as his are pilgrim shrines—
> Shrines to no code or creed confined—
> The Delphian vales, the Palestines,
> The Meccas of the mind."

At a public meeting held at Dumfries on the 6th of Jany., 1814, it was determined that "a Mausoleum ought to be reared over the grave of Burns." A committee being formed, subscriptions were solicited, and in a brief space sufficient funds were obtained to carry out the proposition. The foundation stone was laid with masonic honours on the 5th of June, 1815, and the building completed the year following. The remains of Burns were originally interred in an out-of-the-way place at the north corner of the churchyard which remained undistinguished until his widow covered the grave with a plain slab bearing an unambitious inscription.

The Mausoleum being erected in a conspicuous part of the churchyard, it was decided to exhume the bodies of the Poet and his two sons, and place them in the vault in its interior. For this purpose a company of gentlemen proceeded to the lowly grave "before the sun had risen, and made so good use of their time that the imposing ceremony was well-nigh completed before the public had time to assemble, or in fact were aware of the important duty in which the others had been engaged. On opening the grave, the coffins of the boys were found in a tolerably entire state, placed in shells, and conveyed to the vault with the greatest care. As a report had been spread that the principal coffin was made of oak, a hope was entertained that it would be possible to transport it from the north to the east corner of St. Michael's without opening it or disturbing the sacred deposit it contained. But this hope proved fallacious. On testing the coffin, it was found to be composed of the ordinary materials, and ready to yield to the slightest pressure ; and the lid removed, a spectacle was unfolded which, considering the fame of the mighty dead, has rarely been witnessed by a human being. There were the remains of the great poet, to all appearance nearly entire, or retaining various traces of vitality, or rather, exhibiting the features of one who had newly sunk into the sleep of death: the lordly forehead, arched and high, the scalp still covered with hair, and the teeth perfectly firm and white. The scene was so imposing that most of the men stood bare and uncovered—as the late Dr. Gregory did at the exhumation of the remains of the illustrious hero of Bannockburn—and at the same time felt their frames thrilling with some undefinable emotion, as they gazed upon the ashes of him whose fame is as wide as the world itself. But the effect was momentary, for when they proceeded to insert a shell or case below the coffin, the head separated from the trunk, and the whole body, with the exception of the bones, crumbled into dust."*
The remains being carefully placed in a new coffin, it was

---

* M'Diarmid.

deposited in the vault and closed in. This took place on the 19th of September, 1815. Nineteen years afterwards it was again opened to receive the remains of the poet's widow, and on the occasion it was resolved to raise the skull of the bard and submit it to a phrenological examination. The consent of the nearest relative being obtained, a company of gentlemen entered the vault at midnight; but the following by Mr. Archibald Blacklock, surgeon, one of the party, will sufficiently describe the proceedings. He says:—" The cranial bones were perfect in every respect, if we except a little erosion of their external table, and firmly held together by their sutures; even the delicate bones of the orbits, with the trifling exception of the *os unguis* in the left, were sound and uninjured by death and the grave. The superior maxillary bones still retained the four most posterior teeth on each side, including the dentes sapientiae, and all without spot or blemish; the incisores, cuspidati, &c., had in all probability recently dropped from the jaw, for the alveoli were but little decayed. The bones of the face and palate were also sound. Some small portions of black hair, with a very few grey hairs intermixed, were observed while detaching some extraneous matter from the occiput. Indeed, nothing could exceed the high state of preservation in which we found the bones of the cranium, or offer a fairer opportunity of supplying what has so long been desiderated by phrenologists—a correct model of our immortal poet's head; and in order to accomplish this in the most accurate and satisfactory manner, every particle of sand, or other foreign body, was carefully washed off, and the plaster of Paris applied with all the tact and accuracy of an experienced artist. The cast is admirably taken, and cannot fail to prove highly interesting to phrenologists and others. Having completed our intention the skull, securely enclosed in a leaden case, was again committed to the earth precisely where we found it."

The cast having been transmitted to the Phrenological Society of Edinburgh, Mr Geo. Combe drew up an elaborate paper on the development of the Poet's brain. It concludes with the following remarks: " No phrenologist can look upon this head and consider the circumstances in which Burns was placed without vivid feelings of regret. Burns must have walked the earth with a consciousness of great superiority over his associates in the station in which he was placed, of powers calculated for a far higher sphere than that which he was able to reach, and of passions which he could with difficulty restrain and which it was fatal to indulge. If he had been placed from infancy in the higher ranks of life, liberally educated, and employed in pursuits corresponding to his powers, the inferior portion of his nature would have lost its energy, while his better qualities would have assumed a decided and permanent superiority." Notwithstanding this criticism,

> " Burns—though brief the race he ran,
> Though rough and dark the path he trod—
> Lived—died—in form and soul a man,
> The image of his God.
>
> " Through care, and pain, and want, and woe,
> With wounds that only death can heal,
> Tortures the poor alone can know,
> The proud alone can feel—
>
> " He kept his honesty and truth,
> His independent tongue and pen,
> And moved, in manhood as in youth,
> Pride of his fellow-men.
>
> " Strong sense, deep feeling, passions strong,
> A hate of tyrant and of knave,
> A love of right, a scorn of wrong,
> Of coward and of slave :
>
> " A kind, true heart, a spirit high,
> That could not fear and would not bow,
> Were written in his manly eye
> And on his manly brow."

The Mausoleum closely resembles a Grecian temple, being formed of pillars supporting a dome-surmounted cornice. On the whole, the building is graceful and worthy of the object to which it is devoted, but its effect is much marred by the sheets of rough glass necessarily inserted between the pillars to protect the interior from the weather.

While mutely surveying the surroundings, an old man, possessed of much official importance and overwhelming politeness, appeared on the scene, key in hand, and, in response to my desire, opened the door and led the way into " the lone —the last abode of Burns." Uncovered, I stood on the threshold, and with feelings which cannot be described surveyed the interior. In front was a piece of sculpture representing Burns at the plough and the genius Coila—an ungainly female figure hanging in a ridiculous manner from a slate slab on the back wall—throwing her mantle of inspiration over him. Although the statuary embodies one of the Poet's conceptions it is not of a high class order, and from it I turned to the plain tombstone which marked his first resting place, for to it and other objects the EXHIBITOR drew my attention with a hilarious volubility which ill-accorded with the sanctity of the place. Beside this relic of domestic affection there are three marble tablets bearing the following inscriptions :—

I.

" IN MEMORY OF ROBERT BURNS, WHO DIED 21ST JULY, 1796, IN THE 37TH YEAR OF HIS AGE, AND MAXWELL BURNS, WHO DIED 25TH NOVEMBER, 1799, AGED TWO YEARS AND NINE MONTHS. FRANCIS WALLACE BURNS, WHO DIED JULY, 1803, AGED 14 YEARS—HIS SONS. THE REMAINS OF BURNS REMOVED INTO THE VAULT BELOW, 19TH SEPTEMBER, 1815, AND HIS SONS ALSO. THE REMAINS OF JEAN ARMOUR, RELICT OF THE POET, BORN, 1765 ; DIED, 26TH MARCH, 1834. AND ROBERT, HIS ELDEST SON, WHO DIED 14TH MAY, 1857, AGED 70 YEARS."

II.

" THIS TABLET IS ERECTED BY LIEUT.-COLONEL NICHOL BURNS, E.I.C.S., TO THE MEMORY OF HIS WIFE, CATHERINE ADELAIDE CRONE, WHO DIED AT CALLUDHEE IN THE EAST INDIES, ON THE 29TH JUNE, 1841. COLONEL WM. NICHOL BURNS, BORN AT ELLISLAND, 9TH APRIL, 1791, DIED AT CHELTENHAM, 21ST FEBRUARY, 1872. HIS REMAINS REST IN THE VAULT BENEATH THIS TABLET."

III.

" THIS TABLET IS ERECTED BY MAJOR JAMES GLENCAIRN BURNS, E.I.C.S., TO THE MEMORY OF SARAH ROBINSON, HIS WIFE, WHO DIED AT NEEMUCH, EAST INDIES, 7TH NOV., 1821, AGED 24. JEAN ISABELLA, HIS DAUGHTER, DIED AT SEA, 5TH OF JUNE, 1823, AGED 4 YEARS AND 5 MONTHS. ROBERT SHAW, HIS SON, DIED IN NEEMUCH, 11TH DEC., 1821, AGED 18 MONTHS. MARY BECKETT, HIS WIFE, DIED AT GRAVESEND, KENT, 13th NOVEMBER, 1844, AGED 52. LIEUT.-COL. JAMES G. BURNS, BORN AT DUMFRIES, 12TH AUGUST, 1794, DIED AT CHELTENHAM, 18TH NOVEMBER, 1865. HIS REMAINS REST IN THE VAULT BENEATH THIS TABLET."

Descending the steps of the Mausoleum, I handed the exhibitor the customary fee, and thoughtfully passed out of the churchyard. Opposite is a curious old building erected and endowed by two brothers named Moorhead for the purpose of providing homes for aged natives of the burgh in reduced circumstances. Amongst the inmates is a son of Robert Burns, the eldest son of our national poet. He was a schoolmaster in Dumfries for thirty-five years, but owing to the infirmities of age and the changes which the new Education Act brought about, his circumstances have become so reduced that he is forced to avail himself of this charity. I had the pleasure of conversing with him, and found him to be not only intelligent but proud that the blood of Burns flows in his veins.

Farther along the street is another old building adjoining the Mechanics' Institute. In it there is a library established by the citizens in 1792, of which Burns was an honorary member. A minute in its records states that on the 5th March, 1793, " the committee, by a great majority, resolved to offer to Mr Burns a share in the library, free of any admission money [10s 6d] and the quarterly contributions [2s 6d] to this date, out of respect and esteem for his abilities as a literary man ; and they directed the secretary to make this known to Mr Burns as soon as possible, that the application which they understood he was about to make in the ordinary way might be anticipated."

This is a pleasing testimony of the esteem in which Burns was held, and says much for his conduct as a member of society.

Reciprocating this kindness, Burns presented four books to the library, namely—" Humphry Clinker," " Julia de Roubigné," " Knox's History of the Reformation," and " Delolme on the British Constitution." On the back of the frontispiece of the last-named volume he wrote—" Mr. Burns presents this book to the Library, and begs they will take it as a creed of British liberty—until they find a better.—R. B." This seems to have been penned on the spur of the moment, but Burns was soon alive to the indiscretion committed, and called at an early hour in the morning after the presentation upon the custodian of the books, and asked to be shown " Delolme," stating as a reason that he feared he had written something upon it "which might bring him into trouble." When handed the volume, he looked at what he had written, and then carefully pasted the fly-leaf to the back of the frontispiece in such a way as completely to conceal the writing. The volume is still to the fore, and anyone holding the frontispiece up to the light can read the seditious passage without difficulty. In this library there is still another book bearing the handwriting of Burns. It is the thirteenth volume of Sinclair's "Statistical Account of Scotland." In a notice of the martyred Covenanters of the parish of Balmaghie, an inscription on a tombstone to the memory of a worthy buried in the churchyard is given. Burns appears to have been impressed with the force of its simple but expressive language, for the following verse appears on the margin of the page, pencilled in his striking handwriting :—

> "The Solemn League and Covenant
> Now brings a smile, now brings a tear;
> But sacred Freedom, too, was theirs—
> If thou'rt a slave indulge thy sneer."

Dumfries and its neighbourhood possess many attractions to the rambler and tourist besides memorials of Robert Burns, but it is these which specially engage the visitor's attention and induce thousands to visit the ancient burgh annually. Few towns are planted in a more lovely situation, and in none can a holiday be spent to greater advantage, there being so many places of interest within easy access. To the south-east is the romantic little village of Glencaple, where the foam-crested billows of the Solway may be seen flowing with race-horse speed; and also at no great distance from it the magnificent ruins of Carlaverock Castle, the supposed Ellangowan of Scott's "Guy Mannering." In Carlaverock Churchyard, too, rests "Old Mortality," the enthusiastic amateur sculptor who wandered the length and breadth of Scotland renewing the lettering on the grave-stones of the Covenanters. Messrs A. & C. Black, of Edinburgh, the publishers of the Waverley Novels, have erected a neat monument to his memory. Then there is Cromlongan Castle, once the residence of the Earls of Mansfield, with Ruthwell Cross near by, which is considered the most important Runic monument in Britain; and also Sweetheart Abbey, a fine ruin, near which one could linger a whole summer day. Everywhere round Dumfries the country is replete with natural beauty and historic interest; but my task is accomplished, I have followed the footsteps of Burns from the place of his birth to the scene of his death and burial, so it only remains to be stated that after visiting the Dock Park, the Observatory, and other places within easy reach, I sought the railway station, and was soon on my way to Kilmarnock.

Reader, adieu! and in taking leave of the subject and of each other, let us exclaim with Thomas Campbell :—

"Farewell, high chief of Scottish song!
That couldst alternately impart
Wisdom and rapture in thy page,
And brand each vice with satire strong;
Whose lines are mottoes of the heart,
Whose truths electrify the sage.

"Farewell! and ne'er may envy dare
To wring one baleful poison-drop
From the crush'd laurels of thy bust;
But while the lark sings sweet in air,
Still may the grateful pilgrim stop
To bless the spot that holds thy dust!"

DUNLOP & DRENNAN, PRINTERS AND PUBLISHERS, KILMARNOCK.

www.ingramcontent.com/pod-product-compliance
Lightning Source LLC
Chambersburg PA
CBHW031341230426
43670CB00006B/408